D1032042

Madder Music, Stronger Wine

for Julie

Madder Music, Stronger Wine

✠ ✠ ✠

The Life of Ernest Dowson, Poet and Decadent

Jad Adams

I.B.Tauris *Publishers*
LONDON ● NEW YORK

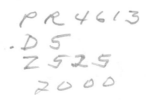

Reprinted in 2000 by I.B. Tauris & Co Ltd
Victoria House, Bloomsbury Square, London WC1B 4DZ
175 Fifth Avenue, New York NY 10010
www.ibtauris.com

In the United States of America and in Canada distributed by
St Martins Press, 175 Fifth Avenue, New York NY 10010

First published in 2000 by I.B. Tauris & Co Ltd

Copyright © Jad Adams, 2000

The right of Jad Adams to be identified as the author of this work has
been asserted by the author in accordance with the Copyright, Designs
and Patents Act 1988.

All rights reserved. Except for brief quotations in a review, this book, or
any part thereof, may not be reproduced, stored in or introduced into a
retrieval system, or transmitted, in any form or by any means, electronic,
mechanical, photocopying, recording or otherwise, without the prior
written permission of the publisher.

ISBN 1 86064 470 8

A full CIP record for this book is available from the British Library
A full CIP record for this book is available from the Library of Congress

Library of Congress catalog card: available

Typeset in Garamond by A. & D. Worthington, Newmarket
Printed and bound in Great Britain by MPG Books, Bodmin, Cornwall

CONTENTS

NOV 1 1 2002

ACKNOWLEDGEMENTS

This book has been very much a labour of love, born out of a passion for Dowson's work and a fascination with his life, which began when I was in school, not so far from the place where Dowson was born, and the site where he lies buried.

As such it has placed more demands on an agent than a more obviously commercial proposition would have done. For their confidence and perspicacity, beyond the call of a literary agent's normal duties, I must thank Diana Tyler and Sophie Gorell Barnes of MBA.

I am very grateful for conversation and correspondence, original material and textual criticism to Desmond Flower and Henry Maas. I am sorry Desmond Flower did not live to see the manuscript in print, but I know it will give comfort to his widow Sophie that his work is still so deeply appreciated.

Professor Kelsey Thornton of Birmingham University had confidence in the manuscript and gave much helpful advice. The late Dr Harold Hewitt gave advice on the text, particularly on medical matters. John Coulter at the Lewisham local history library has given freely of his expertise. Christine Glen advised me on French translations. Steven Halliwell of the 1890s Society has been ever-helpful and encouraging.

It is difficult to express how valuable has been the work of G.A. Cevasco in compiling a bibliography of Dowson in *Three Decadent Poets* (New York 1990).

I am also indebted to those whose example, in their short lives, helped me to understand Dowson: my late friends Peter Blackburn and David Oliver (also a poet).

As always, I am grateful for her consistent practical support and encouragement to Julie Peakman.

Illustrations

INTRODUCTION

Ernest Dowson was the ultimate poet. When he died he had almost literally nothing but the clothes he stood up in and his tattered manuscript book of verse. He was the purest representative of the legendary group of British artists of the 1890s called the decadents, the 'tragic generation'. His dedication to art was nothing short of religious; his life was a human sacrifice, described at the time as being full of the 'swift, disastrous and suicidal impetus of genius'.[1]

He was a friend of Oscar Wilde and W.B. Yeats and his work was illustrated by Aubrey Beardsley. He was at home with Verlaine, Gide and others in artistic circles in bohemian Paris during the romantic fin de siècle period.

Dowson was the writer of some of the most quoted lines in English verse: 'gone with the wind', 'days of wine and roses', 'I have been faithful to thee, Cynara, in my fashion'. His poems delight in the rapture of longing, of unrequited devotion, of blasted hopes in a hesitant man who scarcely dared dream of happiness. His life was tormented by his desperate love for a young girl who never returned his affection. In lyrics like 'You would have understood me, had you waited,' and 'I would not alter thy cold eyes,' his poetry exemplified the suffering of unrequited love: a feeling hymned less frequently than reciprocal love, though experienced more often.

Dowson had a true genius for friendship, with a wide circle of devoted friends including some of the finest writers and painters of his day. He had, as Frank Harris said, the ability to make everyone love him except the one person he really wanted to.[2]

His family history was tragic in the true sense, where foreboding hung over the tiny family from Ernest Dowson's childhood, and in the end it became a contest of which of the evils besetting the Dowsons would finish them first: disease, suicide or bankruptcy.

He was the archetypal decadent poet, combining all the characteristics which made up the decadent temperament: strange delights, sexual promiscuity and wild entertainments co-existing with classical scholarship and devotion to the Catholic Church to which Dowson converted as so many decadents did.

In his short, unhappy life Dowson transformed the sinews of tragic experience into art. He felt the pain of living as pure being; he was so well loved because he confronted people with a realization of how sensitive a human being could be, a poet naked to the cruelties of the world, a man without lies. As Yeats said of Dowson, 'I cannot imagine the world in which he would have succeeded.'[3]

CHAPTER 1

THE PAGAN CHILD

No external facts would indicate that Ernest Dowson was cursed from birth. His father was rich and his mother beautiful. He was the first son of a family which owned a London dock which he would one day inherit. The family was, moreover, not exclusively mercantile but was cultured, with strong literary connections: his father spoke freely of the great poets he knew. No better nascence could be imagined for a poet in the nineteenth century. How others might have envied his prosperity and parental encouragement; yet his life was to become a tangle of thorns.

The Dowsons had been a confident, middle-class family owning property on the Thames for many generations. They also had a long association with literature. Alfred Dowson's father (Ernest's grandfather) Christopher was a close friend of Robert Browning who referred to him as 'dear Chris Dowson'. He was described as being 'of a nervous and mercurial temperament, devoted to the theatre and fond of entertaining his friends.' He and Browning were members of 'The Colloquials', a club of literary friends who would meet at the home of one of them in Limehouse. His brother Joseph was also a member and Browning is recorded as dropping in at his office to find him intent on a contribution to the magazine of the Colloquials rather than more mundane shipping business matters. Alfred Domett, a poet and later Prime Minister of New Zealand, was also a member of the 'set' and Christopher Dowson married his sister Mary in 1836.[1] Their son Alfred (Ernest's father) was born in 1843.

Young Alfred Dowson can have known little of his own father, for Christopher Dowson died of tuberculosis at Blackheath in 1848. Alfred grew into a witty, highly literate man who never achieved his ambition of

1

living by writing. Presumably he found he had neither the talent nor the discipline, so he contented himself with his association with writers. He was something of a literary name-dropper, referring to Meredith, Rossetti and Browning in a familiar manner and using his wealth to cultivate literary friends: he fitted out a boat in some luxury and would invite literary celebrities to cruise down the Thames with him. These included at one time the *Punch* editor Sir Francis Burnand and Algernon Swinburne.[2] Alfred Dowson's uncle Alfred Domett records in his diary that in September 1872 he went to dinner with his nephew at the Arundel and the other guests were the playwright W.G. Wills and W.S. Gilbert.[3]

Alfred Dowson duly inherited 'Dowson's dock', but he had no aptitude for running a business so had it let and lived on the income, continuing to indulge his literary appetites. He tried to write for magazines, but his stories were always 'returned with thanks'.[4] The circumstances of the courtship are not known, but on 19 July 1866 he married Annie Chalmers Swan, the mother of the poet, in St Stephen's Church, Lewisham. She was 17, he was 23. She was of Scottish descent; her father Robert Dalgliesh Swan was an officer in the East India Company. One of Ernest Dowson's friends, Victor Plarr, called her 'accomplished and intellectual' and all remarked on her nervous, delicate temperament, though such remarks may have been made with the benefit of hindsight.

Annie Swan was a hauntingly lovely, fragile woman with deep eyes, dark hair and a pale complexion. The novelist Conal O'Riordan remembered, 'I can distinctly recall his showing a photograph of his mother to me and I was moved to tears ... by something extraordinarily pathetic in her charming face.'[5]

Annie had been living in the village of Lee, south east of London at the time of her marriage, and Alfred Dowson, who gave his profession on the marriage certificate as 'gentleman', was living nearby in Lewisham. They started their life in a villa called Gothic House at The Grove, Lee, which was probably rented. It was a good sized house with a drive for carriages at the front, a conservatory and a reasonable sized garden. There were two live-in servants, a cook and a housemaid. Ernest Christopher Dowson was born there on 2 August 1867 when his mother was 18 years old.

Over the first years of Ernest's life, before he can have been fully conscious of it, the shadow of disease began to fall. Alfred Dowson developed the first signs of tuberculosis, usually known as consumption, a progressively debilitating disease caused by bacteria which occupy the lungs and cause the inflammation and gradual death of tissue by the insidious pressure of their presence, as the victim coughs and coughs to be rid of them.

Illness in the family could be borne, for it had struck before and doubtless would do again, but at the same time as the deterioration in Alfred Dowson's health, the family income began to dwindle rapidly.

Doom inched in on Dowson's dock as the century progressed. The new shipyards of the Clyde and the Tyne, in the north of Britain, were taking over from the docks on the Thames as shipbuilding centres. Ships had become larger and the smaller docks like Dowson's simply could not compete, without total reconstruction, against even the other docks on the Thames.

Lack of investment in the dock, and Alfred Dowson's lack of interest in it, added another burden to the load as the premises became progressively less efficient and thereby even less attractive to shipowners. As Ernest Dowson himself wrote in *A Comedy of Masks*, the character clearly identifiable as Dowson senior was content to 'let the business jog along so much after its own fashion that the popular view hinted at its imminent dissolution.'[6] Alfred Dowson found increasing difficulty in leasing the dock, which stood empty for weeks at a time.

The beneficial legacy of his father's illness was the family's enforced familiarity with the continent of Europe where Alfred was obliged to go for his health. In the 1870s the only treatment for tuberculosis was rest in a warm climate where the lungs might recover to some extent, and at least their condition would not be exacerbated by cold and damp. Good food, rest and a temperate atmosphere would help the body to mount an effective immune resistance to keep *Mycobacterium tuberculosis* at bay. The Dowsons therefore travelled to Mentone on the Riviera where there was already a considerable invalid colony. Alfred Dowson met Robert Louis Stevenson at the Hôtel du Pavillon there in the winter of 1873 and struck up a friendship. They talked about literature and listened to Italian music until Stevenson moved to another, cheaper hotel.

'There's a very nice man here called Dowson, with a pretty wife and son; he talks literature heavily with me,' Stevenson wrote in one of his letters home. Stevenson was excessively fond of children, frequently mentioning in his letters those he met, thus giving us a brief glimpse of the child Dowson: 'I have made myself indispensable to the Dowson's little boy (aet 6), a popularity that brings with it its own fatigues as you may fancy; and I have been fooling about with him all afternoon, playing dominoes, and learning geography with him, and carrying him on my back a little.'[7]

Stevenson clearly did not feel at ease with Annie Dowson, mentioning in another letter that she was very pretty, 'and I should think she was a nice little woman, but she is not very come-at-able. The little boy is also very pretty.' Ernest ran gathering violets for Stevenson which delighted the writer, particularly as he had taken opium that day and was experiencing 'inexpressible bliss'.[8]

An early portrait of Ernest, a pastel of him at the age of five by W.G. Wills, shows him as a light-haired child with large, wide eyes like a faun, and with a frank but somewhat disconsolate expression, as if already in regret. Another extant picture is a photograph of Ernest taken in Turin in 1870. He has long, soft hair, and is dressed in a kilt and the rest of the highland regalia. He has the same melancholy expression, his large eyes staring out of the picture as if imploring the viewer. If Dowson's indecisiveness came from his father, his depression came from his mother: in surviving pictures of Annie Dowson she sits with the same intent, imploring stare as her son.

He was an only child until the age of ten when his brother, Rowland Corbet Dowson was born, but the two were never close. Ernest must frequently have been left on his own, a sad fate for someone who so enjoyed company. As soon as he began to make friends at Oxford, he kept them all his life and in his early manhood he was always in the company of other men, and sometimes of women. He became a reserved man so it is fair to assume he was a shy child: bashful and modest and softly spoken, at home in the company of children younger than himself.

It seems likely that he remembered his childhood as one comparable to that of a character in the first published novel he co-wrote: 'His earliest recollections carried him back to a time when he lived a wandering, desolate life with his father and mother, in an endless series of Continental hotels and pensions.'9 His aunt Ethel Swan remarked in almost the same terms, 'no schooling, just going from place to place, the worst life a boy could have.'10

Doubtless his father taught Ernest a good deal, in his eclectic manner. He may have had some experience as a teacher as there is a reminiscence of Alfred Dowson doing voluntary work teaching slum children in the East End of London.11 There were occasional tutors but educationally, after being taught the basics, Ernest seems to have been left largely to his own devices. Without much difficulty he learned French and once said as an adult that he was fluent in French at the age of 15. The Dowsons also travelled in Italy, where Ernest picked up a little Italian, and once an Italian priest was engaged as a tutor. He stimulated in the boy an enthusiasm for Latin and thus he became acquainted with the literary love of his life, the Roman poets. It is unlikely the priest introduced him to his particular favourites, the love poet Catullus and the excessively melancholic Propertius, though the priest would probably have given Dowson as set texts his other great influences, Horace and Virgil.

Ernest also (though from what source is unknown) learned enough classical Greek to be later enrolled on a degree course in the Classics, and his letters often contained Greek phrases so the language continued to be familiar to him.

His sporadic education left Dowson ignorant of most subjects, except those in which he had exceptional skills. Vast areas of English literature were unknown to him. It was not until literally the last weeks of his life that he became acquainted with the work of Dickens. His ignorance of the facts of geography and history used to amuse and astonish his friends in later years. He was described by his friend Victor Plarr as having 'patches of cultivation and deserts between' and remarks that 'once he averred to me that he supposed the Red Indians in the United States greatly outnumbered the white men, and that he hoped the natives in their war-paint would soon march on New York and destroy it.'[12]

Such an education was not entirely to his detriment. Dowson was not obliged to go to an English public school, which he would certainly have found a beastly experience. What he lacked in breadth, he possessed in depth, in the intimate knowledge of Latin and French literature he gained with the freedom to read as he chose and develop his own thoughts. He became familiar with all things French when French culture was vibrant and liberated, in contrast to the stultifying correctness of English culture. His father's literary interests sometimes gave the boy a practical lesson in literature: he met Maupassant in a country house in France, as he would later recollect. He certainly met enough professional writers to be given the impression that writing could be a career.

As he grew up, Ernest soaked in the work of Dumas, Balzac and Hugo, and luxuriated in Charles Baudelaire's *Les Fleurs du Mal*. The scandalous verses had been published in 1857, ten years before Dowson's birth, the year Baudelaire died. The book was the central text of the French decadent movement and thereby of seminal value to the British decadents.

Young Dowson also became interested in Poe because of the frequent association of his name with that of Baudelaire, and the similarity of outlook and experience between himself and Poe cannot have escaped Ernest. In later life he too, like Poe, loved a young girl who was taken from him. Dowson's young, beautiful mother began showing signs in Ernest's childhood that she too was afflicted with tuberculosis, just as Poe's young mother had been. As Poe wrote, 'the death of a beautiful woman is unquestionably the most poetical topic in the world.'[13] Certainly, Dowson's work would preach that beauty is born to die, but no date can be given as to when he knew his mother was fated. Perhaps an awareness of death was ever with the small family.

The main reason for the paucity of information about Dowson's early years is that he had an aversion to talking about them, which meant few of his friends could give any recollections. He did once write to Plarr that 'my childhood was pagan'.[14] It may well have been that this spiritual person, who wrote some of the best religious verses of a deeply religious century, literally meant that there was little organized Christianity in his childhood.

If it can be said that European culture divides between the Judaeo-Christian and the Graeco-Roman, the Dowson family's cultural life embraced the latter to the virtual exclusion of the former; Alfred Dowson's literary view of life left little room for excessive Victorian religiosity. Dowson once wrote, 'all these fluctuations and agonies of a hypersensitive, morbid childhood with Hebraic traditions are to [me] incomprehensible.'[15] Additionally, 'pagan' as used by Dowson in remarking on his childhood could carry its literal meaning, and be a description of the way in which he spent much of his time in the countryside, a feral creature tutored by little except nature.

There is every reason to assume that the poet's childhood was unhappy. Doubtless his mother and father did not confide their worries to him, but it would be impossible for so sensitive a person not to have been moved by the pall of despair which hung over his parents, with the relentless course of their disease and their financial decline obsessing minds which were far from practical at the best of times. Their frequent moves around England, France, Italy and, briefly, Switzerland, meant the child Dowson never knew a home base to give him security, or simply a stable place with whose environs and neighbours he could become acquainted. Having no habit of homemaking acquired from his parents in childhood, he was never able to settle as an adult. Indeed, Dowson never had a home he could call his own all his life, if we except the rooms above the foreman's home in Dowson's dock.

Ernest Dowson's uncle, Lewis Swan, visited the Dowsons when they were staying at Ilfracombe, England, in December 1880, and remarked, 'Ernest was a good-looking, rather shy boy of fourteen, studious, thoughtful and of a serious disposition. He was a sweet but very odd child – taught himself his letters and would lie in bed reading to himself when only six years old. He was spoiled to death.'[16]

Around 1882 Alfred Dowson began to favour Bordighera for his sojourns as an invalid. He was becoming irritated with expatriate life in Mentone where, he wrote, 'one finds the whole retinue of fashionable life,' while further along the coast 'the visitor meets with nothing but a perfect climate and the loveliest scenery.'[17] It was in this connection that he translated his only book, *Bordighera and the Western Riviera*, a travel guide published in 1883.

Alfred Dowson used to blame himself for his failure to manage his business affairs better, but such fretting uncoupled to any practical intention or ability to do anything about his predicament, simply worsened his health to no avail. His son later referred to such moods as, 'a certain irritation and nerve distress'.[18] The dismal decline in the family's fortunes would tax a stronger man. Alfred Dowson was both weak and, as Ernest wrote of him, 'very litigious', and entered into a dispute with the lessees of the dock who he considered responsible for his decline in income, a move which further debilitated him.[19]

In childhood Ernest Dowson showed one of the indices of a true writer which is to have always written, whether or not there is any hope of publication. He wrote verse from an early age and was highly technically accomplished by the age of 18, if not before. The young man purchased a notebook into which he transcribed his poems in 1886 or 1887 when he was 18 or 19. It was a black leatherette book with marbled endpapers which Dowson had with him throughout his life. He kept fair copies of all his poems in the black notebook until it was filled in 1892. The first pages of this book therefore give a picture of the best poems of his teenage years.

The immediate first impression is of his technical skill. He was already a master of several forms of verse: Petrarchan and Miltonic sonnets, on which he sometimes created his own variations; and of the Rondeau, one of the French 'poetic trifles'. Dowson was to bring this verse form of the troubadours, along with the villanelle, the rondel and the roundel, to a level of perfection unsurpassed by other English writers.

The other immediate shock on first looking at these early poems is the subject matter: the love of small girls, the death of a loved one, the world-weariness of one who knows all life is suffering except the fleeting glimpses of pleasure grabbed from the consuming decay. The complete effect of these teenage poems is that Dowson assumed his poetic mantle fully formed. In the loneliness of his close-pressed thoughts while his family travelled from one hotel to another across Europe, before he was even a man, Dowson had incubated the themes which were to make his verse unforgettable.

Perhaps with the encouragement of his father, he submitted one of his poems to the monthly magazine *London Society* which published fiction and general literature. 'Sonnet of a Little Girl' is dated in his manuscript book 1885 (when he was 17 or 18) and was published in the magazine's November 1886 edition. It describes the poet's contemplation of a child:

... with reverent awe I hold
Thy tender hand, and in those pure grey eyes,
That sweet child face, those tumbled curls of gold,
And in thy smiles and loving, soft replies
I find the whole of love ...[20]

This is one of a series of sonnets called 'Of A Little Girl' which are all supposedly about the innocent love of a child, though they are pervaded with a sense of death and desolation. At the end of the last sonnet he calls on the child to be united with him in death:

Let us go hence, somewhither strange and cold,
To Hollow Lands where just men and unjust
Find end of labour, where's rest for the old,
Freedom to all from love and fear and lust.
Twine our torn hands! O Pray the earth unfold
Our life-sick hearts and turn them into dust.

So many of these adolescent verses refer to a dead child with clearly identifiable characteristics — the grey eyes and curly golden hair, the delight in rustic walks — that it is difficult to escape the conclusion that there was a

prototype perfect child whom Dowson loved and lost. In 'A Mosaic', the
first poem in the black manuscript book (which does not, of course, mean
it was written first, only that it was transcribed first and that it was one of
his earliest poems) Dowson describes the same girl with the 'gleaming gold'
hair and grey eyes, but alone in all the poems, in this one he gives the
location as Italy:

> White horses out on the sea,
> Mist on the hills and a drizzling rain,
> The wind wails loud like a soul in pain:-
> (O Love, my Love and Italy!)
> I called her long yet I call in vain,
> Who came and went as a child from me.

This could have described any two divided lovers, but the imagery has a
distinct sense of death about it. Indeed, in three of the poems Dowson
wrote before he was 20, he specifically conjures up a very physical image of
a dead child lying prepared for burial, on whom the poet bestows, 'one last
long kiss on her beautiful hair' ('Requiem'). In 'After Many Years' he
addresses her, 'thou liest now in Death's mystery'; and in 'It is Finished':
'The pure grey eyes are closèd now'.

Perhaps he was using death as a metaphor for the death of childhood,
when the child would grow up and be his no longer, but the very physicality of the lines,

> The little face is white and cold,
> The parted lips give forth no breath,
> The grape-like curls of sun-bleached gold,
> Are clammy with the dews of death.

suggest this is a real event, whether or not the poet was actually present.

Yet in another five poems over the same period the impression is given
of a sad but necessary parting to 'my sweet child-love' ('Adios!') who shares
the same characteristics, 'Thy pure grey eyes, thy tresses of bright gold,' of
the dead girl. ('Ere I Go Hence'). The others are 'Of A Little Girl VI' and
'VII' and the second 'Rondeau'. It may be that this was a real child Dowson knew, from whom he was parted in his parents' travels and who later
died, or simply grew up and was no longer adorable, but this is pure
conjecture based on the internal evidence of the poems alone.

It may be that the poems relate to a succession of young girls – for
Dowson always made friends with little girls – and he idealized their
features into an archetype. They might have been the daughters of fellow
travellers or hoteliers or tradespeople, and in his verse he romanticized the
parting from each one. Perhaps one or more did die: infant deaths were
hardly a rarity in the late nineteenth century.

There is, however, another reason why it is probable that the poems relate to a personal experience which always gave Dowson pain, for of all the poems quoted here about the grey-eyed, golden-haired child, only two ('Sonnets of a Little Girl IV' and 'VIII') were ever selected for publication by Dowson from his manuscript book, despite the remainder's superiority over some of the poems he did have published. The implication is that these verses related to an experience so deep and painful that he could not expose it to public gaze even ten years later.

What is not in doubt is what the girls gave him: some relief from his consuming melancholy. 'A child's tender love' can calm 'Life's fitful fever with its healing balm' ('Of A Little Girl I'); the very mention of her name will relieve his 'sinking heart' ('III'); her 'trusting smile' is 'the one sweet thing I've known/I' the bitterness of life.' ('VI').

Whatever their factual basis, what we unequivocally have in the early Dowson is a preoccupation with love, with lost love in particular – the parting of lovers by death or distance – and with a deeply melancholic view of the world unrelieved by any hope, where 'tears and prayers are all in vain', ('It Is Finished') and only the brief joys of time spent with little girls can give relief.

It was this young man, lonely and isolated, learned in the Latin and French authors, and already a competent poet, who applied to The Queen's College, Oxford in summer 1886.

CHAPTER 2

THE PESSIMISTIC STUDENT

Dowson's scanty education meant he had little chance of obtaining a scholarship to university. He failed the examination for the Jodrell Scholarship but his facility in Latin, French and Greek (plus his ability to pay the fees) must have convinced the university authorities of his suitability as a student, despite his ignorance of every other field of learning, and he was offered a place. Indeed, he later acted on his tutor's suggestion that he move from a common to an honours degree in Greats (as the Classics are called at Oxford), as being more appropriate to his talents.

He went up to Queen's College in October 1886 at the age of 19. Thirty years later a fellow student, William Thomas, who was the same age as Dowson, wrote a memoir of him in which he described his friend Arthur Moore saying, 'Have you met Dowson?' and taking him up to Dowson's rooms in an attic at the top of staircase Number Five, Back Quad.[1] Dowson was of medium height but light build, with dark, wavy hair, long sensitive hands and distinctive, penetrating blue-grey eyes. His teeth were unattractive but he was otherwise good looking. He was not unwell, but he certainly did not give the impression of robust health. His manner now, as always in the future, was vague and uncertain, and his speech hesitant unless he was talking of a subject he knew well when he became excited and his voice high-pitched.

His dress was that of the average student at the time: striped flannels, a blazer and tie. Thomas also described him as being seen in a brown bowler and spats; and one photograph shows him in the traditional Oxford straw boater with a moustache. There was certainly none of the neglect of personal hygiene which marked his last years; he urged Thomas to join the Union as it was 'the only place in Oxford where you can wash your hands.'

Thomas described him in his late teens as being 'an almost merry boy, with charming manners whose slight peculiarities' were set down to the fact that he had never been to school. He had a disinclination for organized games, and 'a somewhat wider knowledge of such places as the Paris music-halls than most undergraduates possess.'[2] Thomas remembered Dowson running along the tow-path in support of the college boat, which has a ring of truth for Dowson was always more interested in sailing than any other outdoor activity.

An early Dowson biographer, who had the advantage of being able to talk with people who knew Dowson at Oxford, wrote that those who recalled their impressions of him during the months immediately after his arrival reported that he seemed different from his contemporaries, but in no way insensible to their company or interests. He would stand on the outskirts of their circles, listening to what was being discussed, with a strange little smile on his face which some mistook for irony and others interpreted as a sort of envy that he was unable to participate in their talk. His rooms were bare, without the ornament or decoration common to other students, and visitors received the impression that he was just moving in or just moving out.[3] This impermanence was a perennial feature of Dowson's life; it was as if he were not really there, or had come to go.

Dowson was to make friends at the university with men who were to be important to him for the next ten years. A semiformal lunch club was set up between the like-minded friends William Thomas, Arthur Moore, Sam Smith and Dowson. Sam Smith, born the same year as Dowson, and also reading Greats at Queen's, later became a schoolmaster and sometime translator of the *Lysistrata* of Aristophanes. He had a close affinity with Dowson, for the poet maintained an intensely personal correspondence with him, particularly at the most painful time of his life.

Arthur Moore, a year younger than Dowson, was destined to become his best friend at Oxford. He collaborated on three novels with the poet, later writing his own novels and also contributing to *The Yellow Book*. By profession he became a solicitor, though he was the son of a well-known portrait painter and nephew of two other distinguished painters. He met Dowson when the poet was invited to join a group of three playing whist and they required a fourth man. After the game Dowson and Moore went back to Moore's rooms and spent almost the entire night discussing the work of Henry James, with Dowson not leaving until after daybreak.[4]

Through the light lunches these young men had, Thomas gained a rounded picture of Dowson's intellectual abilities, saying his friend,

had certainly done some hard thinking, and the pessimism to which he always remained faithful had been based, in the main, on the writings of Schopenhauer. He never changed the opinion, then formed, that nature and humanity are, in the mass, abhorrent, and that only those writers need be considered who proclaim this truth, whether subtly or defiantly.

Thomas remarks how 'a sincere pessimism' would please the student Dowson.[5] Schopenhauer, 'the philosopher of pessimism', whose work on the will foreshadowed existentialism, was a major influence. Dowson noted in a letter of around the beginning of October 1888 that he has read 'for the 100th time the metaphysic of love according to Schopenhauer' and remarked that, 'It strikes me now – as ever – as about the most – possibly the only – absolutely convincing piece of philosophy that was ever penned.'[6]

An even more important influence on Dowson and similarly minded undergraduates was the Oxford don Walter Pater who by Dowson's time was already the patron saint of the aesthetes. The artistic philosophy of Pater is summed up in his *Studies in the History of the Renaissance*, where he advises, 'Not the fruit of experience, but experience itself is the end. ... To burn always with this hard gemlike flame, to maintain this ecstasy, is success in life ... the desire of beauty, the love of art for its own sake ...'[7]

The year before Dowson went to Oxford, Pater had published his most influential book, *Marius the Epicurean*, and everyone who loved literature and art was talking of its demonstration that beauty can be at the soul of life. In an increasingly secular society, it offered a spiritual goal. Dowson presumably read a library or a friend's copy at Oxford, for after leaving university he purchased his own, despite thereby leaving himself financially embarrassed. His letters frequently report that he is reading *Marius* and he occasionally quotes Pater's remarks such as 'there is a certain grief in things as they are.'[8]

It was at Oxford that Dowson declared he would live as an artist, whatever the cost – and the cost would be great. One of his friends remarked after Dowson's death that if there were an autopsy they would find 'Art for Art's sake' engraved on his heart.[9]

Dowson found a true kindred spirit in his dedication in Lionel Johnson. He was born in 1867, the same year as Dowson, to a military family of High Church Tories in Kent. He rejected his family's Anglicanism in youth and, while at Winchester, began to present himself as a Buddhist. At school he developed the habits of a lifetime – staying up all night talking and reading, and sleeping all day; he also discovered his own homosexuality. He went on to New College where he met Dowson. In terms of scholarship he was, like Dowson, a classicist, being most heavily influenced by Virgil and

Lucretius. As a hard-drinking, classically oriented poet, Johnson was closer in soul to Dowson than his other friends, and they spent long nights discussing art and Latin literature, united in their agreement that to compromise with popular taste would be to betray their art. Johnson's conversion to Catholicism (he was admitted to the Church in 1891) was also to have a profound effect on Dowson.

It had been 20 years since students at Oxford had marched down the High Street arm-in-arm chanting Swinburne's lyrics as later generations would chant revolutionary slogans, but Swinburne still retained the power to shock, and to inspire a poet like Dowson. Swinburne was truly a poet's poet, whose capacity for rhyme and rhythm are unsurpassed by anyone in the century excepting Byron. Dowson considered 'Dolores' one of the greatest poems in the English language. With its riotous music and its passionate physicality, Swinburne proclaimed the glory of the world of flesh which owed nothing to Victorian and everything to classical civilization.

Thomas noted that Dowson's copy of Swinburne's *Poems and Ballads* had the lyrics of 'Hertha' and 'Dolores' heavily scored. Other English influences on Dowson which Thomas lists are De Quincey, Webster and Tourneur. The two Elizabethan playwrights are interesting, particularly as Dowson had no great liking for Shakespeare.

He read English novels widely, and among American authors his main passion was for Poe, Henry James and Hawthorne. Dowson's copy of *Les Fleurs du Mal* was 'pencilled almost from start to finish', according to Thomas. Dowson frequently spoke of French literature, finding Zola's *La Terre* so moving that he considered sending the novelist a fan letter but never did so. Dowson did some last minute translations of Zola for a paper Thomas read to a college essay club, and impressed his friend with his fluency. Thomas listed his French influences as Diderot and Voltaire in the eighteenth century; and in the nineteenth Balzac, Gautier, de Musset and Maupassant.[10]

Dowson took to heart the images for bohemian life from Henri Murger's *Scènes de la Vie de Bohème*. He had no respect for the style of the book but he was inspired by the tale of the impoverished poet Rudolf, living on hack work, who is in love with the consumptive Mimi, and with Murger's description of Parisian café society and the desperate pleasures of 'these brave adventurers who live on the fringes of society and belong to that race of obstinate dreamers for whom art remains a faith ... the called of art [living] a fascinating, yet terrible life, which has its victors and its martyrs.'[11]

There was also the usual student experimentation. Dowson, Thomas and some friends decided to experience hashish after an Indian student, Satis Chandra Mookerjee, later a barrister and civil servant, had spoken to them about it. Dowson was also aware of references to the drug in Gautier and Hugo. He and his friends therefore purchased pills of *Cannabis indica* from a pharmacist and ate them. They walked around the cloisters of the front quad, noticing strange magnifications in their perception of time and space, and later became hungry (characteristically of cannabis users) and ate apples, 'with a general feeling of health and cheerfulness'. Dowson and some of the others repeated the experiment a few nights later but without result and Dowson lost interest in cannabis. Arthur Symons reported that he and Dowson once took the drug in the following decade but the result was merely a fit of the giggles, an experience they were not keen to repeat.[12]

Dowson had 'tasted' absinthe by the time he reached Oxford, according to Thomas, but it was not at this time his drink of choice. This may have been simply because it was difficult to obtain in Oxford at the time. His usual drink was Chablis and soda water and he had rarely or never drank spirits, at least in the first year of his time at Oxford. Dowson always liked card games, and played whist in the afternoons and poker in the evenings. He enjoyed gambling but there is no record of his gambling to excess. Often in later life he was glad of this means to supplement his income.

Another influence at Oxford was the cult of little girls who were considered the most delightful, almost magical creatures. The 'cult' had long predated Dowson: from the 1850s Lewis Carroll was entertaining little girls between the ages of five and eleven in the Oxford rooms he occupied as a mathematics don. Until he ceased the activity in 1880 he used to make nude photographic studies of the girls. Carroll tended to break off his friendships when girls passed the age of 12 and 'Autumn frosts have slain July' as he put it in one of a number of more or less ambiguous lines in the poem at the end of *Through the Looking-Glass*.

Edgar Jepson, whose time at the university overlapped a little with Dowson's, wrote, 'There was at Oxford in the eighties a cult of little girls, the little daughters of dons and residents: men used to have them to tea and take them on the river and write verses to them.'[13]

This was a form of courtly love: a perfect, adoring love with the object of one's affections being unable and not required to reciprocate. The girls were there to be adored. In no contemporary accounts is there the least suggestion of any sexual activity of any kind. Indeed, the artlessness and lack of sexuality of little girls is frequently the subject of comment in Dowson's verse and prose. Of course, one had to be thinking about sex to mention it at all, and there was always a tension between the beauty of the child and the fact that she would soon mature sexually and become undesirable.

Dowson supplied an intellectual justification for what he himself called the 'cult of the child' when he wrote in *The Critic* in 1889 'it is not surprising that an age which is, after all, chiefly pessimist, an age which is so deeply disillusioned, should turn with an immense delight to the constant charm of childhood.' He was writing about the clauses in the Protection of Children Bill which would restrict the employment of children in theatres.

Dowson was against the clause, attesting to the 'delight' child actors aroused and the pleasure the children themselves derived from their work. 'We,' he said (using the first person plural) 'make it our business to "spoil" all our childish acquaintance as much as we are allowed.'[14]

Dowson's excessive love of girls was not considered a matter for scorn or ridicule. It was thought of as a delightful facet of his personality. 'It is as an adorer of childhood that his lovers and friends, who have kept his memory green, will best remember him!' wrote Victor Plarr after his death.[15] Charles Sayle, one of Lionel Johnson's Oxford homosexual coterie, and a friend of Dowson, wrote a volume of verse called *Musa Consolatrix*, published in 1893, in which there is a sonnet to Ernest Dowson:

> Ernest, What holds your heart and care to-night? …
> Is it some talk that you yourself indite,
> Some pleasing fancy newly cradled, or
> Perhaps a child's laugh toddling to your door,
> That makes the autumn evening's glimmer bright?

Another of his Oxford friends who shared his tastes was William Clark Hall, born the year after Dowson, who became a magistrate and was later knighted. He also published several volumes of religious verse. Dowson refers to him as 'properly a worshipper and devout follower of the most excellent cult of la Fillette'.[16]

In a letter of October 1888 to Charles Sayle, Dowson directly connects his love of girls with his melancholy,

> the world is a bankrupt concern and life a play that ought to have been damned the first night. There are, as you say, still books, dogs and little girls of seven years old in it but unhappily, one begins to yawn over the books and the dogs die and, oh Sayle, Sayle – the little girls grow up, and become those very objectionable animals, women.[17]

Over the summer of 1887 Dowson celebrated the golden jubilee of Queen Victoria with his cousins, the Secretans, in Reigate, Surrey. They decorated the lawn together with Japanese lanterns and later went to London to see the ceremonial procession to Westminster Abbey. Though he was glad of any excuse for a celebration, Dowson never had the slightest interest in politics or Britain's place in the world. His later friend, Conal O'Riordan, in talking about the late Victorian period said it was taken up with two ideas: imperialism, meaning Britain's 'prescriptive right to possess the earth', and pessimism, meaning 'we were all better dead'.[18] Dowson was bound up with the latter to the total exclusion of the former.

In October 1887, after the summer holiday, Dowson moved from college to 5 Grove Street and Thomas noted, 'his life assumed a darker shade. Early in the term I noticed his marked depression.' While his reacquaintance with his parents, their illnesses and money worries during the long vacation cannot have been conducive to peace of mind, his depression was almost certainly endogenous, as it existed as an underlying current throughout Dowson's life. It could be alleviated or exacerbated by changes in external circumstances, like the pleasure of being with convivial friends, but it was always present, the nagging pain of a chronic illness.

Dowson talked openly about how he could treat his depression. One evening with Thomas they experimented with drinking whisky. When Thomas left at midnight, Dowson's spirits were considerably lifted and he 'was delighted with the result and thought his troubles were over. The next night the panacea was again applied, but this time he sorrowfully pronounced it a failure, his melancholy intensified as he became more drunk.'[19]

Thomas reported this 'experiment' in strong drink as if it were an isolated event. Thomas may, indeed, have observed the first time Dowson drank spirits to excess as a student, but other contemporaries reported it was far from the last, and his rooms at Grove Street were to be notorious in gossip for the late hours he and his friends kept, the card and drinking parties.[20]

It is to this period that belongs one of the bleakest poems he ever wrote – indeed, one of the bleakest in English verse. The lines about the dead child from 'It Is Finished' have already been quoted. It deals with the grey-eyed, blonde-haired girl mentioned in many early verses, in a cycle of which this is almost the last. The remarkable aspect of this verse is Dowson's specific rejection of any comfort in death. From the description of how the child cannot hear or move or feel, Dowson makes a cry against belief in the 'fantasy' that death is other than it seems or leads to immortality. The last lines are:

She will not speak to thee again,
Tho' thy whole soul in tears be shed,
For tears and prayers are all in vain,
She is but dead, she is but dead!

The problem for a poet is that having touched upon such an absolute certainty so young, there is little more to write. To see such small pleasure in life as Dowson did, and no hope in death, is tantamount to saying life was not worth living and death may as well come as quickly as possible. Sayle and Johnson were able to encourage in Dowson the more spiritual side of his nature, which they doubtless knew might bring him some peace from the pain which racked his soul.

Whatever weight of depression he was suffering, and however he dosed it with alcohol, Dowson still distinguished himself as a true artist by continuing to create. He had a sonnet, 'My Lady April', accepted by *The Temple Bar* though it was not published until April 1889. He wrote only about seven poems while at Oxford (at least, that is the number which he thought worth transcribing into his manuscript book) and he concentrated on his prose. Over that long summer holiday of 1887 Dowson was writing short stories, at least two of which he sent to magazines.

He had written 'Souvenirs of an Egoist' by the end of 1887, for he submitted it then to *Temple Bar*, which was a magazine for the comfortable, literate middle class. It was on its way out in the 1890s but in publishing his prose there Dowson was in the company of Turgenev, Daudet, Gissing, Conan Doyle, Henry James and R.L. Stevenson – a most respectable prose debut for a man of 21, still at university. In it a successful violinist in his forties remembers how when he was a starving waif he was saved from the streets by an organ grinder, an orphan girl called Ninette, whom he abandoned for a rich patron. 'Poor little Ninette ... I wonder what has become of her? Dead, I should hope, poor child,' he thinks, in a very Dowsonian juxtaposition of affection and death.

Dowson was full of plans for the future: he was writing a novel entirely on his own as well as the collaborative novel with Moore, though discussion of *The Passion of Dr Ludovicus* doubtless went into abeyance while Moore prepared for his final exams. Dowson described himself to be 'working like a galley slave at my novel' *Madame de Viole*, in a letter of around 1 October 1888.[21]

From several reports, Dowson cared more for his prose than his verse.[22] This is not so surprising as it might at first seem. His verse is incomparably better than his prose and the prose would be all but forgotten were it not for his fame as a poet, but when Dowson compared them, it was not with what other people got out of them that he was concerned, but with what he put in. The poetry came to him naturally, he was inspired and the lines were there. He polished the work, but he never sweated over it as he did his novels. For a man given to works of jewel-like perfection in a hundred words, who enjoyed drinking and conversation, writing a 100,000-word novel was like undertaking one of the labours of Hercules. Additionally, writing prose might furnish him a living as a novelist, critic or translator; writing poetry would not. He needed to care about his prose.

Moore was soon to join a firm of solicitors in Lincoln's Inn Fields and several other of Dowson's friends were destined for the law which had also been Dowson's intention after coming down from Oxford. A letter to Sayle at Fig Tree Court, Inner Temple, exists from 1887 where Dowson was asking for help, but by October 1888 he was writing, 'I fear I can keep up the legal farce no longer, but I am constantly occupied now that the vac is drawing to an end in breaking the news to my people,'(that he would not become a lawyer) but 'one's people are so sceptical.'[23] Dowson feared disappointing his parents and was hoping to persuade them that, 'a couple of years in Paris with an Oxford allowance would improve my general culture more than any more restricted metier,' but this was not to be.

Thomas records how Dowson left Oxford in March 1888. His tutor had encouraged him to read for Honours, an unusual thing but his enthusiasm for classical learning must have been persuasive. Dowson certainly had the ability, but lacked the personal discipline for sustained study, and Thomas implies he did little or no work. He took the first few papers of 'Honours Moderations', the intermediate examinations, but felt he had done badly and resolved to leave. Thomas went to his bedroom in Grove Street on the morning of the next examination to induce him to change his mind but he said he was not for 'Mods.' nor 'Mods.' for him. Thomas suggested Dowson could have stayed on and taken a pass degree but wisely remarked it would have had no appreciable influence on the rest of his life had he done so.

Gossip in Oxford after he left suggested Dowson was leaving for the Latin Quarter of Paris where the young writer would take up the life of a bohemian. The truth was more prosaic.

CHAPTER 3

DOWSON AND SON

Ernest Dowson, of continental tastes and at home in the night life of big cities, found himself set to work costing the painting, caulking, scraping off of barnacles, mending the pumps and generally supplying ocean going ships for the family dock in Limehouse.

Alfred Dowson, with a superhuman effort raising himself from his torpor of worry and self-pity, determined that only his own resolute action could save Bridge Dock. He instituted proceedings to recover his dock from the now bankrupt Dry Dock Corporation of London, and by a High Court order of 29 October 1888 the dock was surrendered to the liquidator of the Corporation from whom Alfred Dowson recovered it. Now he determined to work it himself, under the title 'Dowson and Son'. Ernest wrote to Arthur Moore 'We neither of us know anything about dry-docking but we have an excellent foreman. "Dowson" has one office – "Son" the other and there is another one for the clerks who have not yet arrived.'[1]

Ernest Dowson was not a lover of England, 'whose climate is unutterably horrible to me, whose cooking ruins my digestion and whose people, ideas, beliefs, prejudices etc are all either ridiculous, unintelligible or irritating to me.' Some parts of England, moreover, he liked even less than others, and the worst of it was that he was 'doomed for the present to live in a suburb – i.e. the most detestable portion of the most detestable, banal, money grubbing, damned, deleterious city in the world.'[2]

The Dowsons had taken up residence at 3 Woodford Villas, High Road, South Woodford, which was the family home from which Ernest Dowson wrote his letters at the weekend. Father and son also had basic rooms at the dock which was situated down a winding, docklands street packed with ships' chandlers, sailors' bars and small restaurants. If Ernest were out too late to get back to Woodford, which was usually the case, he would sleep in his offices at the dock or, if he were too late to get the last train back to Limehouse, would sleep in any friend's rooms in central London and get an early train to work.

His friend Victor Plarr visited Dowson at the dock, and wrote a piece on his impressions in the *Globe* newspaper:

> To gain admittance to the sanctum where our friend the "Dry Docker" trans-
> acts his leisurely affairs you must push strenuously through a heavy yard-gate,
> mount a wooden outside staircase, and knock and ring as though you were at
> the door of a private house. The room within once gained, you are wafted away
> from the nineteenth and into the eighteenth century at once. A quaint hospita-
> ble scent of grog and stale tobacco assaults your nostrils pleasantly. Your eyes
> rest on comfortable ramshackle desks of some dark old wood, placed so that
> the writers at them may sit in arm-chairs and look askance at the vistas of the
> shining grey water outside – at the red sails of the slowly travelling haybarges,
> and the dusky spars of innumerable far-travelled ships.[3]

Plarr noted that above the lit fireplace were faded parchment elevations of the hulls, sterns and prows of antique three-decked ships. There was also a map of the world from early in the century on which Australia was written as New Holland; Greenland was intersected with projected canals which were intended to be built to supply the north-west passage to China and the Indies; and Central Africa was a void. It was all very picturesque for an intellect like Plarr's, but could give shipowners no confidence that they were refitting in a modern dock with up-to-date equipment.

Plarr looked over Ernest Dowson's narrow shoulder when he was writing out a bill and commented on the impressive total of £158. 'He wiggled his shoulders and smiled his inscrutable smile, the smile of a man who ponders,' Plarr remarked.[4]

Indeed he did ponder. For all his whimsical pretence to visitors that he did not even know what the 'front end' and 'back end' of a ship were called, Ernest Dowson knew very well what was happening. As he wrote in *A Comedy of Masks*, a book where many of the physical descriptions are clearly drawn from life, 'No more ships were built there, and fewer ships put in to be overhauled and painted; while even these were for the most part of a class viewed at Lloyd's with scant favour, which seemed, like the yard itself, to have fallen somewhat behind the day.'[5] In industrial terms the dock was finished. In personal terms, Ernest Dowson was spending his best and most productive years nursing a dying business out of filial duty.

As soon as he was able, he would get down from his desk and make his way to the West End. The night was his. As a character in one of his books says, 'Give me the streets and the yellow gas, the roar of the City, smoke, haggard faces, flaming omnibuses, parched London, and the river rolling oilily by the embankment like the Styx at night when the lamps shine.'6

His dark brown hair was curly and wavy, his face agreeable and animated. He wore a wide brimmed black slouch hat, a short 'pea-jacket', dark trousers somewhat the worse for wear, stick-up collars, a black butterfly necktie and French boots. He was the model of the bohemian artist. He walked out with his bright eyes and his determined gaiety – Ernest Dowson would enjoy himself until it hurt.

Despite his reserved, almost shy manner, he made friends easily and was always one of the party, drinking, playing cards and attending music halls. His friends at this time were partly from university, partly other young men out for a good time including a loosely based group called 'The Bingers'. His letters to Arthur Moore at this time are full of the joys of London and the youthful exuberance of a full social life. On 13 November 1888, for example (actually some days before he started work at the dock, but this experience conformed to a familiar pattern), he reported going to the Bedford, a small music hall in Camden Town, with a French friend and a medical student. They took a box and started chatting with a group of other medical students from St Bartholomew's Hospital, who had the other box in the house. They all moved in together and as the programme proceeded invited a member of the management in 'to binge with us' who, in turn, invited them to stay on after the evening's entertainment to meet the performers. Dowson became particularly friendly with a singer called Agnes Hazel before adjourning to the rooms of a medical student who had offered him a sofa for a bed, and with whom Dowson sat up all night.

Two days later Dowson took Agnes Hazel out to dinner at the Cavour in Leicester Square and then by hackney carriage back to the music hall in time for her performance, expecting to go with her to her engagements at the Star in Bermondsey and the Bedford later that week. 'Am I in love?' he wonders, using the French, épris. 'No,' he decides, 'But I shall let the liaison run its course – it will be very amusing and not as costly as an affair with a regular horizontale.' That night he had one or two of the performers in his box all evening – these talented folk obviously knowing where to go to have a good time, and again was up all night, the company this time including an immensely vivacious girl 'who sat up with us imbibing copious café au cognac and smoking cigarettes until 6 am when we adjourned to the St Pancras buffet for breakfast.'7

Dowson remarks that all this gaiety is rather bad for literature and it interferes with *Madame de Viole*, the novel he is writing, but soon his money will run out and he will have go back to literary work. 'Dowson and Son' could not afford to pay him well, and sometimes probably did not pay him at all.

Not all his friends were bingers. Dowson was first introduced to Victor Plarr, four years his senior, in Charles Sayle's room in Gray's Inn in spring

1888. Plarr was to become librarian of King's College and later of the Royal College of Surgeons. Plarr was, like Dowson, a boyish character – he actually uses the term 'childish' of himself – and at their first meeting he confessed to Dowson's question, 'Shall you ever feel old?' that he is 'static – about four years of age.' Dowson remarked that this is what Victor Hugo felt like at 80 and said, 'When I transact serious business – and I do all day – I view myself from the outside as something strange and awful.'[8]

Plarr described Dowson at 21 as 'singularly fresh, young, eager, sympathetic, his charming face unscathed by any serious sorrows or dissipations.' At some time in 1888 or 1889 Dowson visited Plarr to find him and another librarian who shared his lodgings, Frank W. Walton, annotating a volume of *The African Farm* by Olive Schreiner in the German manner – that is, they were making comments on different sections of the book as it stimulated their own thoughts. They did this rather as a literary entertainment, under assumed German names, and were surprised (and not very pleased) when Dowson took the mock pedantic exercise seriously and started writing his own margin notes under the name 'Anatole de Montmartre'. Plarr kept this anthology of Dowson's thoughts and later published some of it. 'Montmartre' introduced himself in part with the remark, 'most decadent friends regard him as somewhat of a heretic,' which is rather opaque but shows that Dowson, even at this early stage, identified with 'decadent' thinking – Dowson wrote of the 'entire inefficiency of all spiritual, supernatural help in one's sorest need,' and he quoted Stendhal, 'La seule chose qui excuse Dieu c'est qu'il n'existe pas' [the only thing which excuses God is that he does not exist]. As he was to convert to Catholicism within three years, it appears he was experiencing swings in his religious sentiments.

'The vital issue is between optimism and pessimism,' he wrote at another point, but he seems to have chosen pessimism, as he remarked later, 'Immortality! Wretched ideal. Infinite ennui – I die at the thought,' and in a response to a character who locked himself in a room with books and a bottle of brandy, which he preferred, Dowson wrote: 'Why not? It is the next best philosophy to suicide or fakir-like asceticism – the latter best of all – only, alas,! the flesh is weak, weak.' He seems already to be a man disappointed by life, and particularly by women, criticizing 'the perverse pleasure ... with which a woman sets herself to degrade and obliterate the feminine ideal if she comes across a man with any faith in it.'[9]

Plarr occupied 'the most uncomfortable rooms in the world in Great Russell Street, and often, late at night, Dowson crept into the house and begged a bed.' He would sleep on a 'horrible horsehair sofa' or on the floor under such blankets as could be found. Plarr kept no drink in the house and would offer him water after midnight, which Dowson drank with grace, saying it reminded him of Milton who always drank a glass of water after supper.

With the distance of time making the experience more palatable, Plarr recorded 25 years later how, 'with other merry revellers, he arrived in the street outside my rooms, and bawled my name, in chorus with his friends, for many minutes,' while Plarr stayed tight lipped in his uncomfortable bed. Later Dowson apologized by letter that he had 'violated the midnight silence of Great Russell Street' adding, 'Forgive me if it was real and not an absinthe dream; as many things seem nowadays.'[10]

Dowson frequently quoted Baudelaire, 'Il faut être toujours un peu ivre' [It is necessary to be always a little drunk] and complained that early nights and mornings and general healthy living made him feel ill. Absinthe, on the other hand, made him feel good. It was the drink of artists in France, earlier in the nineteenth century, with their British counterparts later taking up the habit. The writer Richard Le Gallienne, invited in 1890 to drink absinthe by Lionel Johnson, for it was all he had in the house, remarks:

> I had just heard of it, as a drink mysteriously sophisticated and even Satanic. To me it had the sound of hellebore or mandragora. I had never tasted it then, nor has it ever been a favourite drink of mine. But in the '90s it was spoken of with a self-conscious sense of one's being desperately wicked, suggesting diabolism and nameless iniquity.[11]

The bright green liquid, which turned a turbid dull green with the addition of water, was said to evoke new views, different experiences and unique feelings. Strongly alcoholic, it was produced from a variety of leaves and flowers with a predominance of the bitter wormwood, which bestowed its flavour, and the extract of the thuja tree, thujone, which affected the central nervous system. Binge drinkers suffered hallucinations from acute intoxication, chronic drinkers from brain damage.

Dowson knew from personal experience that he was overdoing his consumption as early as 1889. 'On the whole it is a mistake to get binged on the verdant fluid,' he wrote to Moore, 'I understand that absinthe makes the tart grow fonder. It is also extremely detrimental to the complexion. I believe that even in the full swing of the campaign of my last term [at Oxford] I never presented a more deboshed appearance than I do this morning.'[12]

Plarr was 'ordinarily' a teetotaller and so not a drinking companion of Dowson, and claims to have known him drunk only once, though he does qualify that where he grew up in St Andrews, Scotland, 'only those were called drunk who lay in the gutter on their backs.' He recalls Dowson leaning,

> smiling meditatively, against a lamp-post, exactly where the Irving statue now stands [outside the National Portrait Gallery]. He manifestly required support. A lady, who had been mercifully blind to his condition, was being shown into a cab, and I shall never forget – I see the scene now vividly – how he leapt from his dream – he had been standing stork-like, one leg crossed over the other –

and presented the lady, or the cabby, with her fare. It was done in a flash of lightning, with a dreamy delicacy quite incomparable. ... He took out a florin [10p] and I wondered at the time that he had so much money in his pocket.

Plarr writes of being 'startled' by Dowson's poetic brilliance. 'We had not, so to speak, expected it of the pleasant youth, who played billiards punctually at six o'clock every evening and smoked rather vile Vevey cigars!'[13]

It was Dowson's habit when he was happy with a new poem to make copies and send them to his friends, and when he finished 'Amor Umbratilis' he sent it to Moore and Plarr, the latter's copy written in pencil on the back of 'a fierce letter' dated 7 October 1890 referring to Dowson's Oxford bills which he had agreed to pay by degrees but had clearly not kept up the payments. The poem was to be published in the *Century Guild Hobby Horse*. Dowson also had a sonnet, 'April', published by *Temple Bar* in 1889, and a roundel ('To Hélène', later called 'Beyond') accepted by them the same year but not published until 1893.

Before the end of 1888 Dowson had written a popular novel probably of not very great length, which he referred to only as 'a shocker', and submitted it to at least one magazine but was not accepted. Dowson and Moore, who had left Queen's in 1888, had already got some way with *The Passion of Dr Ludovicus* by the end of 1888, as Dowson wrote to Moore at the beginning of January 1889 that he wished to resume work but, 'I have got the idea of at least three novels germinating in my head – and shall start off on one of them immediately *Madame de Viole* is finished.'[14] He received some advice from Moore on the continuation of his solo novel after Moore had read the first two volumes, but Dowson had trouble in finishing it and it was not completed until after the joint novel. In the meantime they went back to *Ludovicus* which featured a doctor in love with a young woman betrothed to someone else. Dr Ludovicus attempts to undermine the credibility of his rival, who has a guilty secret, and who mysteriously dies on the wedding day. It is a story full of Gothic mystery and suspense in a popular style and (though only the plans for the novel are extant) appears to be of little literary merit.

They worked from a manuscript book in which they both wrote, along the lines of a plot which had already been worked out by them together, each sending the book to his co-author when the chapter was finished, 'via the penny post'. As Moore later said, 'We did very little by way of revision of each other's work, alterations being rarely more than a few words in a chapter.'[15] To submit a single manuscript to the mail shows a touching faith in the postal service but it seems to have been vindicated as there is no record of the four novels they worked on in this way having been lost. When proposing this method, Dowson remarks, 'of course we must get at least one chapter done a week', which shows what extraordinary energy he had when he put his mind to a project.[16] This is the more remarkable because he was still working on *Madame de Viole* during the times Moore had control of the *Ludovicus* manuscript.

In April 1889 Victor Plarr was offered an unpaid post on a weekly review, *The Critic*. He passed it on to Dowson who accepted it, giving him an entry into journalism, the usual way for artists to earn a living while attempting to get on in the world of letters; and free review tickets for every theatre in London. Though it massively increased his workload to be busy at the dock till four, then at his desk on *The Critic* at five every day, the discipline was good for him. It is unlikely he would have spent the time more constructively left entirely to his own devices, though of course he did not see it that way and complained of criticizing, 'silly plays and reviewing in the interim novels even more fatuous than the plays.' He was relieved by seeing Ibsen's *A Doll's House*, which opened at the Novelty Theatre on 7 June 1889, about which he was enthusiastic.[17] The Dowson scholars Flower and Maas analysed the edition of *The Critic* of 1 June 1889 and found Dowson had reviewed four Covent Garden operas, four plays and a novel. Dowson remarked that though the periodical's life might be destined to be short, it would survive its staff.[18]

This was a highly productive period of Dowson's life and a record of his industry at this time confounds those who would write him off as a drunk who produced some good poems, as if by chance. He was putting in a day's work on his ledgers, working at *The Critic* office or on reviews until late, writing two novels, leading an active social life, as well as writing occasional poetry and stories.

Dr Ludovicus was finished in April 1889 and the writers began submitting it to publishers, hoping to make ten pounds apiece from it, but Dowson wrote to Moore in one of his self-abnegating moods which were much more commonly expressed in person than by letter:

> The evil which is done in perverting and warping one's intellectual vision by vicious and trashy novels, such as "Dr Ludovicus" is simply incalculable. For heaven's sake let us assert our reason and soothe our consciences by writing an antidote – a novel without any love-making in at all – or with only love-making à la Zola.[19]

However, by 11 February the following year he was describing the book, which he had re-read after it was returned by yet another publisher, as 'an extremely good work'.[20]

The fact is that, sadly, Dowson was unable to translate the extraordinarily painful veracity of his poems, or even the quiet intensity of his stories, into the novel form. This was partly because the work was collaborative, and could therefore only deal with things the two friends might discuss together out loud, which diminished the range of feeling which could be involved. Partly it was because the tremendous labour of constructing a work of fiction, even when co-authored, sapped most of Dowson's creative strength and left little for genuine artistry. Partly it was because Moore and Dowson referred back to other novels and plays for their inspiration rather than to life: the best passages in the published novels, *A Comedy of Masks* and *Adrian Rome*, are clearly those where the characters or locations are drawn from life.

The absence of the impression of real experience in the early novels is presumably because these men were young and had insufficient personal experience to fictionalize, but this could hardly be said to be the case as they grew older – Dowson in particular went through the most harrowing experiences, most of which were simply not translated into literature. The simplest answer is a combination of deficiencies: Dowson lacked the stamina, the physical tenacity, and ultimately the moral courage to write a great novel.

Madame de Viole was finally finished (after having needed an ending for over a year) in spring 1890 and it was doubtless sent to at least one publisher but without the spur of Moore's interest, which he of course had for the joint novels, Dowson's enthusiasm for having his own work published appears to have flagged. He had long been criticizing his own book as being too slow and wordy.

Dr Ludovicus was completed by April 1889 and Dowson and Moore sent it to one publisher after another, suffering a painful round of rejections with 'the usual formula of regrets and thanks, and the only evidence of its being read, the dirty editorial thumb mark.'[21] This lasted at least until September 1891 when the last rejection is recorded.

While *Dr Ludovicus* was doing the rounds, Dowson and Moore started work on *Felix Martyr*, another work which was not to find a publisher, and they may have abandoned it uncompleted because of difficulties in its construction which it was not thought possible, or perhaps desirable, to remedy. The notes which remain of it suggest a commonplace romance involving the Oxford fellow Felix Martyr, Lord Hildreth, the Comtesse Diana de Lussac and the obligatory seven-year-old girl, which character Dowson begged Moore not to 'blackball', so clearly there had been some disagreement about his interpolating little girls into their narratives inappropriately.[22]

Dowson's story, 'The Diary of a Successful Man', was accepted by *Macmillan's Magazine*, to appear in February 1890. It had probably been written in autumn 1889. In it a successful barrister returns from India to the town where, 20 years before, he had loved a woman who was also loved by his best friend. She chose between them, sending each a letter, but in the anguish of the moment mixed the letters up and sent the wrong envelopes, so all three lovers spent the rest of their lives in bitter disappointment and regret. It is Dowson's cleverest piece, and is also of interest because of the Catholic imagery. For the wretched central character the

Church, 'seems in some of its more sombre aspects to exercise an extraordinary fascination over him,' as it did to Dowson. Some of the story is set in a church and the disappointed woman joins a strict religious order which forbids her ever to be seen, but the men who love her can stand in the church and hear her beautiful voice singing from behind a screen. The work also indicates Dowson's awareness that decisions taken in young manhood would stay and affect the whole of the rest of life, sometimes disastrously.

At 22 Dowson was, unsurprisingly, on the lookout for new experiences, in particular those he could use in his fiction. He wanted to be in love as an experiment, to have an object of devotion like Mimi, the consumptive heroine beloved by the impoverished poet in *Scènes de la Vie de Bohème*. He urged Arthur Moore to do the same, 'I wish you would start an "experiment" of your own, though. i.e. a spiritual mistress taken from one of the classes outside Society: we might compare notes with mutual advantage and work our result when the disillusionment comes into an agreeable étude – in collaboration.'[23]

To this end he took up with a 16-year-old barmaid called Lena, sometimes referred to as Mimi, whom he met in the Horseshoe public house in Charlotte Street. She seems an interesting young woman who, as Dowson recorded, read the modern novelists, quoted Tennyson and wrote him long letters to which he responded, though with something of a lack of candour. 'The only defect in it was,' he wrote to Moore of his letter,

> the vital defect, that it was perfectly factitious, and that unless the girl is exceptionally naive she must see that I didn't believe in it myself. ... She is very young and I suppose innocent as innocence goes after the earliest teens – and therefore if the experiment is to be made, isn't she about as good a specimen as I could find? ... I contemplate nothing gross, mind you.[24]

which last remark presumably means Dowson would not seduce her sexually for the sake of art.

Much of this attitude was a pose, as he wrote five days later, 'The girl is an admirable creature. I grovel for having so blasphemed her and her adorable age in the last – this, mind you, without prejudice, and reserving my full right to assume the old attitude when the glamour is gone.'[25]

The relationship progressed with Dowson taking Lena out to the zoo or the park on the occasional free afternoon she was given from work, and ultimately to the theatre, though she forbade him to visit her at work. He found her, 'in spite of her audacity in public ... really shy – blushful – full of charming reticences'[26] and within a month of their first meeting she had dropped the formal 'Mr' in her letters to him. Soon she left her job after some disagreement with the patron and moved in with a waitress friend, then spent her time walking about and looking at the shops. Dowson clearly feared that she was going to become a burden to him, or a prosti-

tute, but was quite distraught when she bolted, without telling him she was
going. In an ambiguous letter he wrote:

> It's finished after the fashion which I foresaw. ... She must be a most accom-
> plished little liar – after all it's one of the qualities of her sex – to have
> hoodwinked me for so long. I grasp her attitude now which hitherto I confess
> puzzled me. There are depths of cynicism which one doesn't easily realise.[27]

This probably means she was more sexually experienced than she made out
to be, and perhaps was already working as a prostitute, or simply had
another man friend which was why she was so keen to keep Dowson away
from the Horseshoe. Whatever the exact reason, it is obvious that this
bright girl had her own experiment in hand and was more than a match for
Dowson.

He continued to adore children and while working as a critic he was
corresponding with theatre girls like 'Little Flossie', a nine-year-old music
hall performer. He also loved the seven-year-old Minnie Terry, the star of a
play called *Bootle's Baby*, and had a built up a collection of photographs and
souvenirs of her.

The poet quickly recovered from being crossed in his affections by Lena
and continued to enjoy the pubs, theatres, music halls and eating houses of
the West End. He had started to go to the Café Royal, a favourite haunt of
the literary, and was soon to become acquainted with literary friends to
supplement his current circle who were (usually student) librarians, lawyers
and doctors, some of whom dabbled in literature.

Dowson and his friends were young men about town and they liked the
company of women who enjoyed a good time. This certainly included sex.
Dowson refers to Moore as 'gai Lothario' and once asks after a sexually
transmitted disease which may be an infestation of crabs – which Dowson
refers to with mock delicacy as 'crustaceans'.[28] It is unlikely Dowson ever
formed a relationship with a woman of his own age, intellect, or station in
life. His letters give frequent references to his abhorrence of society
women. 'I keep well away from them,' he remarks, comparing them
unfavourably with the women of the music halls and prostitutes whom he
prefers.[29]

There are few clues as to why or how Ernest Dowson came to have
such attitudes towards women, though Stevenson noticed that his father
had an attitude towards women which was contemptuous, or lecherous or
both. In an isolated passage he wrote, '[Alfred] Dowson and I nearly came
to disagreement last night about women; it really is his only crying sin,' but
there are no further details.[30]

Some part of Ernest Dowson's rejection of society women was the
disgust which anyone of advanced views felt for the restraints and formali-
ties of English society. Dowson was an advocate of sexual freedom, and
argued against 'the monstrous division drawn between licensed and

unlicensed lust.'[31] This is only part of the story, however, for Dowson writes of being bewildered by women. 'What a charming world it would be if they did not exist – or rather if they never grew into their teens,' he wrote.[32]

Dowson favoured women younger than himself, and endeared himself to barmaids, show girls and others in professions considered dubious in contemporary terms, by treating them with the exaggerated courtesy of the Victorian drawing room, to which they were not accustomed. There are numerous accounts that he reacted towards prostitutes with the same gallantry, and he certainly found their company agreeable.

In late 1889 he struck up a relationship with a tobacconist's daughter called Bertha Van Raalte whom he described thus: 'The tart is aged fifteen and three-quarters and belongeth to a tobacconist of Piccadilly who apparently views his parental responsibilities lightly. ... She hath the torso of seventeen at least, and wonderfully fine eyes.'[33] They would write to each other, go to the music hall together and on at least two occasions Bertha and a girlfriend of her own age sat with Dowson and a friend – a law pupil in one case and a medical student in another – in more or less chaste embraces on a sofa.

While Dowson's girlfriends were sexually mature, they were as young as propriety would allow them to be. It is at this point that Dowson's love of girl children, and his need for sex simultaneously begin to approach each other and are instantly repelled. The adult passion combined with the unnatural yearning for innocence is a central contradiction in his nature, and one which lay like an offshore rock in a stormy sea, waiting for him to smash his life against it.

Dowson's meeting with the person with whom he was to form the most important relationship in his life occurred during one of his habitual nocturnal rambles in search of a cheap place to eat after he had arrived in Piccadilly from the dock. He chanced upon a small restaurant in Sherwood Street with red blinds, squeezed between a bootmaker and a greengrocer. It became the model for the dim little Soho restaurant in *A Comedy of Masks* with its 'perennial smell of garlic, its discoloured knifehandles, its frequentation of picturesque poverty.' Dowson was to call it 'Poland', as it was run by a Polish tailor, Foltinowicz, who found running a restaurant a better way of making a living than tailoring in his adoptive country. He was assisted by his wife Adelaide and their daughter of the same name, aged 11 on the night at the beginning of November 1889 when Dowson first set eyes on her.

The cuisine was fair and the food cheap. Dowson wrote to Moore, 'I am the whole clientele, and there is a little Polish damoiselle therein whom it is a pleasure to sit and look at.'[34] He described Adelaide Helen Foltinowicz as looking like Minnie Terry which would have given her thick dark hair, large eyes which tended toward the sensual, for a child, and a frank open face still retaining the plumpness of childhood.

He was not instantly in love with the girl, and his relationship with Bertha continued over the first few weeks he knew Adelaide, but by 24 December 1889 he was writing, 'I dine there every night now and little Mademoiselle de Poland is beginning to greet me with a smile.'[35] Quite what she made of him is uncertain; probably she regarded this admirer as a charming young gentleman whose custom was highly prized by her parents, particularly as he so often brought his friends to dine with him. It was hard to obtain evening trade in their business – the restaurant mainly catered for lunches. Dowson was, moreover, the son of the owner of a dock who went to the theatre or music hall every night. In the Foltinowiczes' eyes, they were poor and he was rich, and his friendship was to be encouraged.

CHAPTER 4

THE SERIOUS RHYMERS

Considering the large part the Hobby Horse House was to play in Dowson's life, he was very dismissive of it when he first heard of the idea of an artistic community. In March 1889, he had written of those who, 'contemplate a colony à la Thoreau of "Hobby Horse" people and a few elect outsiders each with a "beloved" … where there will be leisure only for art and unrestrained sexual intercourse.'[1] Dowson enjoyed wild exaggeration like this, which his correspondent would recognize for what it was. If the Hobby Horse people were not always models of Victorian propriety, they were in the main the most respectable of men.

The artistic settlement which was properly called the Century Guild of Artists was the link between the ideas of the artists of the 1890s and those of the Pre-Raphaelite movement. It had been founded by the eminent architect Arthur Mackmurdo who in 1882 gathered round him a group of artists who could undertake the design and construction of a building. One of his chief collaborators was Selwyn Image, an artist in stained glass and a poet. He was an Anglo-Catholic classicist, who had been curate of St Anne's, Soho, but who gave up the church to devote himself to art.

Herbert Horne, three years older than Dowson, was a talented architect and architectural writer, also a poet, who had worked with Mackmurdo on the design of the Savoy Hotel. Horne edited the Guild's periodical, *The Century Guild Hobby Horse*, founded in 1884 to propagate the ideas of the Guild. Promoting the ideas of William Morris, Matthew Arnold and John Ruskin, it anticipated the designs of art nouveau and gained an influence far beyond its small circulation.

Towards his aim of reuniting the arts and crafts as he believed had happened in the Middle Ages, Mackmurdo founded a house at 20 Fitzroy

Street, Bloomsbury, which was equipped with living rooms, studios, offices and a concert hall. Painters, sculptors, poets and critics lived there or met each other in its rooms, and it was inevitable that Dowson would be drawn into the circle. By autumn 1889 Dowson had met Mackmurdo, probably by the introduction of Plarr who was to live in the 'Hobby Horse House', and was soon to meet Horne whom he described as 'very erect and slim and aesthetic', while he described Image as 'the most dignified man in London'.[2] Dowson was soon attending 'swarries' at what he came to call 'the sacred house in Fitzroy Street', and his links with the house were increased by the publication of his verse in the *Hobby Horse* and his Oxford friend Lionel Johnson's taking up residence in June 1890.

Dowson was keen to be a member of artistic circles, not only for professional reasons; he recognized also that the pleasure of like-minded company gave him some respite from his consuming depression. He joined the Arts and Letters Club, and later (in 1893) the Sette of Odd Volumes, an antiquarian and bibliographical society founded in 1883 for 'conviviality and mutual admiration', and occasionally writes of dining at these clubs and meeting other writers.

By November 1890 Dowson was thinking of forming his own group, and was writing about a 'symposium' meeting at Poland, mentioning to his Oxford friend Charles Sayle that he should have been there one recent evening to enjoy the company of Johnson, Plarr, Moore and Dowson's French friend Jean Bouthors.[3] Later Dowson suggested to Moore that Poland should host a 'decameron' in a private room which was being planned by the restaurateur though it seems never to have been put in hand. In listing possible members Dowson notes people who have dined with him at Poland and the name of their college which shows that, even two years after leaving university, most of his friends were still Oxford men. 'Yourself, Swanton, Smith, Tweedie, Berridge, Lefroy (Queen's). Sayle, Johnson, Money (New). Plarr, Hillier (Worcester). Walton (Keeble). W. Hall, Ghose (Christ Church). Bouthors, Noblet (Paris).'[4] This also shows the number of people Dowson was able to attract to the restaurant, many of them dining there several times – hardly a matter of indifference to the Foltinowicz family.

This project was never set in hand, Dowson had no organizational ability, and the impetus for the most important literary club of the period, the Rhymers, came from that great literary organizer, the Irish patriot W.B. Yeats.

Yeats, a frequent visitor to Fitzroy Street, was just two years older than Dowson. He had been born into an artistic, Protestant family in Dublin but had been educated in London and lived there from 1887. Steeped in Irish folklore, he was a mystical and visionary thinker who was at this time engaged in an analysis of the prophetic books of William Blake with Edwin Ellis, another poet who became a 'Rhymer'. Like Dowson, he was hopelessly in love with a woman, Maud Gonne, who was an inspiration to his verse but the curse of his emotional life. While he is justifiably regarded as one of the greatest poets of the twentieth century, it is as well to remember that at the time of the Rhymers he was a minor poet among others, though one who had already experienced some success, his first volume of verse being *The Wanderings of Oisin and Other Poems* published in 1889.

The first three members of the Rhymers were Yeats; Thomas Rolleston, a significant figure in the Irish literary renaissance; and Ernest Rhys, a Welshman who was the editor of Everyman's Library of classics in uniform volumes. The first written reference to the Rhymers is in a letter Ernest Rhys wrote to the American poet E.C. Steadman on 21 May 1890 where he mentioned that the 'Rhymsters Club' had been 'lately formed'.[5] The first meetings of the Rhymers (the alternative appellation was quickly dropped) were held at 20 Fitzroy Street and it was here that Dowson was introduced to the company. He wrote on 12 January 1891 that he was going there to see 'Oscar and a select assembly' at what was probably the first meeting of the Rhymers' Club proper. Oscar Wilde, another Irishman, was the lion of the decadent stage, having just published his novel, *The Picture of Dorian Gray* in *Lippincott's Magazine*. He was also a poet and a journalist who had been building a solid reputation for outrage in literary London. In meeting with the Rhymers he was a poet among others, his first success as a playwright was more than a year away.

Dowson excitedly described the next meeting as

> a most queer assembly of "Rhymers"; and a quaint collection of Rhymes. Crane [Walter, an illustrator] read a ballad: dull! one Ernest Radford some triolets and rondels of merit: "Dorian" Gray [John Gray, a protégé of Wilde] some very beautiful and obscure versicles in the latest manner of French Symbolism; and the tedious [John] Todhunter was tedious after his kind. Plarr and Johnson also read verses of great excellence; and the latter, also, read for me my "Amor Umbratilis": And Oscar arrived late.[6]

The reading of Dowson's verse by Johnson in his stead was common: Dowson was usually too shy to read his work out loud, though he must have overcome this sometimes as several Rhymers had memories of his reading particular verses.

It may well have been this meeting that Victor Plarr remembered when he wrote:

> Mr Walter Crane stood, with his back to the mantelpiece, deciding, very kindly, on the merits of our effusions. And round Oscar Wilde, not then under a cloud, hovered reverently Lionel Johnson and Ernest Dowson, with others. ... I marvelled at the time to notice the fascination which poor Wilde exercised over the otherwise rational. He sat as it were enthroned and surrounded by a deferential circle.

Johnson's diminutive size and Dowson's slight build must have increased the comic effect of the two young poets paying literary homage to Wilde who was a big, fleshy man.

The aesthetes, whose creed was underpinned by Walter Pater and exemplified by Wilde, were now transforming themselves into the decadents, of whom Dowson was a leading example. Plarr contemptuously describes how, 'A telegram came one day from the Oscar Wilde entourage, peremptorily ordering [Dowson] to appear at the Café Royal to lunch with the then great man. His excitement was marked: he was flattered and flustered.'[7] Dowson knew that his debt to Wilde was considerable, in that he was setting a tone in literary society in which Dowson's work could flourish. This was something writers such as Dowson, Johnson, Symons and Gray did not have the stature to do for themselves. In a direct reference to the decadent period of the Roman Empire, a critic of Wilde, Arthur Lynch, calls him, 'The new Petronius of a "squalid village"' by which he meant London.

Lynch describes how Wilde perches on a velvet throne:

But mark how, near the throne, a bevy sits
Of strange young men, and sickly to the view,
Who chirp in minim key, like fledgling wits,
Whene'er their Sultan utters something "new."

He lambasts another 'Rhymer', Richard Le Gallienne, in saying there is in him,

A certain taste, from Wilde, for things exotic,
The symptom of this dear "decadent" age.[8]

There has never been an adequate definition of English decadence, despite its being easily identifiable at the time, because the word itself took on different meanings. Principally it was a French literary movement which had its antecedents early in the nineteenth century, but is best dated from Baudelaire's *Les Fleurs du Mal* in 1857. The most characteristic prose work, ushering in the brief period in which decadence was fashionable in France, was Joris-Karl Huysmans' *A Rebours* (Against the Grain) of 1884, about a sybaritic aristocrat, both apathetic and devoted to elaborate pleasures. In his essay 'The Decadent Movement in Literature' in *Harper's New Monthly Magazine* in November 1893, Arthur Symons, another Rhymer, defined the movement as almost entirely French, citing Verlaine, the De Goncourt brothers, Mallarmé, Maeterlinck and Joris-Karl Huysmans.[9]

Symons acknowledged that many decadents preferred not to use the term, and said the decadent movement was also referred to as Symbolism and Impressionism. It

has all the qualities which mark the end of great periods, the qualities that we find in the Greek, the Latin, decadence: an intense self-consciousness, a restless curiosity in research, an over subtilizing [sic] refinement upon refinement, a spiritual and moral perversity ... really a new and beautiful and interesting disease ... typical of a civilisation grown over-luxurious, overinquiring, too languid for the relief of action, too uncertain for any emphasis in opinion or in conduct.[10]

There was a certain amount of pencil-sucking on Symons' part when he tried to describe the English decadent movement, and he came up eventually with Walter Pater and W.E. Henley, which latter name was dropped when Symons reprinted the essay in book form at the end of the century as *The Symbolist Movement in Literature*. To be fair to Symons, these terms were often interchangeable; Dowson wrote in March 1891 that he had been 'writing verses in the manner of the French "symbolists": verses making for mere sound and music, with just a suggestion of sense, or hardly that; a vague Verlainesque emotion.'[11]

The most common English definition of decadence was of moral laxity and personal lassitude, and the literature of such conditions. It is also descriptive of decline and finality, a use Dowson adopted in his 'Transition':

Short summer-time and then, my heart's desire,
  The winter and the darkness: one by one
The roses fall, the pale roses expire
  Beneath the slow decadence of the sun.

The chief French use, gradually adopted in Britain, was that decadence described the end of empire, when the riches built up in more stoical times are enjoyed for their luxury, which is why references to declining classical civilizations are so frequent in descriptions of nineteenth-century decadence.

The French origin of decadence meant the movement was regarded with suspicion by the general public and their periodicals, and the word was often spelled with the acute accent on the first 'e' to emphasize its foreign provenance. France was not only a nation whose literature was thought to be corrupting virtually by definition, but war with France was believed to be inevitable, and an association with things French to be approaching treason.

A reasonable definition of English decadent writers is that they had a number of characteristics in common: a love of the artificial for its own sake, an obsession with death, decay and blighted love, a dedication to art, a predilection for exotic religion, a love of classical literature, a French perspective on artistic matters, greater sexual licence than was commonplace (if not actual perversion, in contemporary terms), a search for inspiration in the life of cities, particularly London, a passion for drugs, including alcohol, and a tendency to self-neglect. It is fair to say that any artist who displayed more than half of these characteristics, as Dowson did,

could be described as a decadent. No one displayed them all, though
Arthur Symons came close, but he was always suspected of playing at
decadence in retreat from a religiously restrictive childhood, rather than as
a sincere artistic expression.

Not all Rhymers were decadents by any means. Only a full volume
could do justice to the Rhymers Club whose great virtue was that it
encompassed everyone: Irish nationalists, the religious, the mystical,
classicists, decadents, aesthetes, political activists and simple bookmen who
wrote a little lyric verse. Here only those Rhymers who had a close relationship with Dowson can be considered.

The first three Rhymers aimed at a 'comfortable number' of ten
members but ended up with a core of fourteen and a number of frequent
guests like Oscar Wilde, John Gray, Herbert Horne, Arthur Moore and
Edgar Jepson who never contributed to Rhymers' publications or 'joined',
in as much as there was a membership in a club without rules. The core
members were Edwin John Ellis, George Arthur Greene, Arthur Cecil
Hillier, Lionel Johnson, Richard Le Gallienne, Victor Plarr, Ernest Radford, Ernest Rhys, Thomas William Rolleston, Arthur Symons, John
Todhunter, William Butler Yeats, John Davidson and Dowson himself.

The immediate question is: where are the women? But if it were asked
at the time, there is no record of the reply. It was not because of a shortage
of women poets: Dollie Radford, for example, was quite as good a poet as
her husband Ernest who was a member. Kathleen Tynan was not invited
though Yeats was in contact with her and she was as good a poet as all but
the best three Rhymers; nor was Alice Meynell ever a guest despite her
friend and fellow Catholic poet Francis Thompson being invited to attend,
which he did once. Nor were Katherine Bradley and Edith Cooper who
were well known to Arthur Symons; Althea Gyles and Alice Milligan, who
were known to Yeats; Leila MacDonald and doubtless any number of other
able women poets. The Irish Literary Society, which had a close relationship with the Rhymers, had no such restrictions. Lady Wilde, the Irish
nationalist poet who wrote under the name 'Speranza' was a member, and a
meeting was once held for a visit by Maud Gonne, the love of Yeats's life
who was a leading nationalist.[12]

It may be that women would not have felt at home after the club
decided to meet in an upstairs room of the Cheshire Cheese in Fleet Street,
as public houses were not considered places for respectable women.
Dowson's letters show, however, that some bohemian women did join him
and his friends on licensed premises. The club chose to meet in a public
house, moreover, after having met at the Hobby Horse House and in
private homes where women might have been invited, and if need be they
could have chosen another permanent venue. It may have been that either
implicitly or explicitly they wished to keep themselves pure for their art and
introducing a sexual element would be a distraction – though many of the

poems, of course, dealt with amorous subjects. Dowson would certainly have felt uncomfortable had there been any women present, he was diffident enough about his verse even when only fellow Rhymers were listening. Whatever the reason, it was a single-sex club.

It was also a club with a distinctly Irish flavour – the Fenian John O'Leary visited in early 1890 because of its combination of Irishness and lyricism. There were in fact two strands of society coming together in the 'core group' of Rhymers: Dowson's Oxford men, comprising himself, Plarr, Johnson, and Hillier; and Yeats's Irish men: Todhunter, Ellis, Rolleston, Greene and Hillier. Arthur Hillier, who fitted in both groups, nine years older than Dowson and a good friend, was working as the London correspondent for the *New York Herald.* Johnson felt himself to be in both camps too, being an Oxford man who eagerly embraced Celtic literature and claimed Irish descent.

'Celtic' was sometimes felt to be a more inclusive designation for the Rhymers: Rhys was Welsh, Symons Cornish, Davidson Scottish, and Dowson's mother was of Scottish descent, though he made little of it and did not support Davidson when he tried to introduce another four 'Scotchmen' (as Dowson called them) into the club. Precise nationality aside, it could be said that Plarr's boyhood in Alsace (his father was Alsatian) and Dowson's upbringing in France and Italy bonded them more closely with Catholic, rural Ireland than with urban England. In the summer of 1890 Dowson was to go on a walking tour of Brittany with Arthur Hillier, during which he fell in love with the land which supplied him with some of the inspiration for a number of poems, notably 'Yvonne of Brittany', 'In a Breton Cemetery' and 'Breton Afternoon'.

The members would gather at the Cheshire Cheese once a month. They would dine simply downstairs in the old coffee-house boxes which were like high, double-seated pews with a table between. After supper they went upstairs to a gloomy, ill-lit, panelled room. There they drank beer and smoked long, disposable clay churchwarden pipes, and pulled fresh poems from their pockets which they read and discussed.

Yeats said that but for the Irish members 'who said whatever came into their heads', the club would not have survived its first difficult months. He commented, 'The meetings were always decorous and often dull: someone would read out a poem and we would comment, too politely for the criticism to have any value.'[13]

Arthur Lynch describes a visit to the Rhymers' Club as, 'a small assemblage of poetically pious young men.' He felt that only he and the waiter were outcasts, and he may well have been right.[14] An occasional visitor, Edgar Jepson, described the Rhymers as 'all seething with the stern sense of their poetic mission', and described meetings as gatherings 'of a profound solemnity. I never heard a Rhymer laugh, their smiles were rare and constrained.'[15]

Morley Roberts, a journalist and not a serious poet, was invited to the gathering by John Davidson and, knowing the obligation on attendees of reading some of their own work, sought among his writings, 'some gloomy verse which might possibly appeal to a set of semi-moribund geniuses who probably felt life to be a failure,' and he finally came up with a verse about worms being cut by the gravedigger's spade, which went down tolerably well, given that enthusiasm was not the Rhymers' strong point.[16]

They did take themselves rather seriously, frequently referring back to the literary pedigree of the Cheshire Cheese. 'The Toast at the Rhymers' Club' by Ernest Rhys proclaimed that they would drink defiance to science in the old tradition:

As once Rare Ben and Herrick
  Set older Fleet Street mad.

In 'The Ballad of the Cheshire Cheese' Thomas Rolleston recounts:

Beneath this board Burke's, Goldsmith's knees
  Were often thrust – so runs the tale –
'Twas here the doctor [Johnson] took his ease,

Despite the fact that there were some genuine poets among them, the Rhymers' admiration for the 'wine and blood and reckless harlotry' of Marlowe was mere posing.[17] Only Dowson really lived the life of whoring and drunken brawls which the others professed to believe romantic – nor was this only a feature of his later life. As early as 1889 he was writing to Moore of a cauliflower ear and other injuries received in a brawl the previous Saturday night.[18] The similarities between himself and 'Kit' Marlowe were frequently remarked upon: John Gray in dedicating a copy of his volume of verse, *Silverpoints*, to Dowson in 1893 signed it 'To Kit Dowson – The Master Singer.'[19] Gray had a high regard for Dowson. Samuel Smith, one of Dowson's Oxford friends many years later remembered a fragment of conversation in Poland when Gray said, 'Kit, there are only three men in England who can write English: you, I, and Pater.'[20]

Most of the other Rhymers, with their bourgeois tastes, found him rather odd. Rhys asked Dowson where his dock was, 'hoping to go some afternoon and inspect him in his strange surroundings.' Dowson agreed but cannot have been too welcoming as the promised adventure never came off. Still, Rhys acknowledged,

the one Rhymer we believed to be most potential in the group was Ernest Dowson. Not that he was able to make the rhythm tell, when he read his poems; but they had an individual savour unlike that of any other poet, which seemed to point to the rarer imaginative work he might yet do. But he was frail physically, had no idea at all of taking care of himself.[21]

The critic Le Gallienne said Dowson was, 'a frail appealing figure, with an almost painfully sensitive face, delicate as a silverpoint, recalling at once

Shelley and Keats, too worn for one so young, haggard, one could not but surmise, with excessive ardours of too eager living.'[22]

Yeats described Dowson as 'gentle, affectionate, drifting', and said he thought Dowson's best verse 'immortal, bound that is, to outlive famous novels and plays and learned histories and other discursive things, but he was too vague and gentle for my affections. I understood him too well, for I had been like him.'[23] In another recollection he said,

> Dowson, vague and drifting, gave me always [a] sense of that weakness that seems to go with certain high virtues of sweetness and courtesy. I cannot imagine the world where he would have succeeded. ... As it was he was burning to the socket, in exquisite songs celebrating in words full of subtle refinement all those whom he named with himself "us the bitter and gay".[24]

The quotation is a line from Dowson's 'Villanelle of the Poet's Road', which opens,

> Wine and woman and song,
>   Three things garnish our way:
> Yet is day over long.

The best reader among the Rhymers was Yeats, who intoned his verse in his musical voice with a haunting cadence while Johnson had a demure, gentle voice. Dowson not only read rarely – he rarely said anything. He diffidently called his work verses rather than poems. 'I have never done any more than play with verse,' he wrote.[25] Yeats said, however, that among a few other Rhymers, Dowson 'had what I lacked, conscious deliberate craft, and what I must lack always, scholarship.'[26] He put his respect in verse in 'The Grey Rock':

> You had to face your ends when young –
> 'twas wine or women or some curse –
> but never made a poorer song
> that you might have a heavier purse,
> nor gave loud service to a cause
> that you might have a troop of friends
> You kept the Muses' sterner laws,
> and unrepenting faced your ends,
> and therefore earned the right – and yet
> Dowson and Johnson most I praise –
> to troop with those the world forgot,
> and copy their proud steady gaze.

The Rhymer to whom Dowson was closest was Johnson. He had taken up residence at 20 Fitzroy Street in rooms which were described as monkish and scholarly, with a monstrance on the mantlepiece and a silver crucifix on the wall, a portrait of Cardinal Newman, a religious picture by Simeon Solomon, and works on theology in Greek and Latin. The walls were papered in brown wrapping paper and there were grey corduroy curtains over the door, windows and book-case. Yeats remarks that in talking there with Johnson in the candlelight there was 'a general air of neatness and severity', as if he had omitted the accidental and vulgar from his life. Dowson and Johnson would regularly sit up all night drinking and talking, often with Yeats, though he had no head for all-night literary vigils and would leave comparatively early.

Johnson had a private income from his family and could afford to turn night into day, for he simply slept during the day, a luxury denied to Dowson who had to go to work after a long night. Yeats called on Johnson one afternoon at five and found the servant Johnson shared with Horne and Image saying, 'He is always up for dinner at seven.'[27] Rhys once went on a Rhymers night to collect Johnson at 9 pm and the servant boy who opened the door said, 'I don't think he's up yet, sir.' Rhys went to find him in his darkened room and Johnson said in a small voice he was 'too busy' to go to the club.[28]

Johnson was five foot three inches tall, and was said to have developed not at all since the age of 16. Stories abounded of his being mistaken for a boy who had wandered into a literary gathering by mistake. Edmund Gosse actually asked him if he would like to go into the garden, thinking he was one of his son's friends. Le Gallienne wrote of his 'almost diaphanous frame'.[29]

Johnson's attraction to Catholicism – he was received into the faith on St Alban's Day, 22 June 1891 – had a deep influence on Dowson. It was natural for Johnson to write about the Church and his own struggles with religiosity, best exemplified in 'The Dark Angel', one of his finest poems, beginning,

> Dark Angel, with thine aching lust
> To rid the world of penitence:

He had something of a struggle with his homosexuality, and his conversion may have been partly to assist in the repression of his natural urges, as conversion certainly was for Lord Alfred Douglas and may have been for John Gray. Johnson took the path which Gray did and sublimated his homosexuality into a cult of friendship with males. He often dedicated his poems to friends, as Gray and Dowson did. Some poems are implicitly homosexual, like his Latin poem to Oscar Wilde written after the publication of *The Picture of Dorian Gray* which translates as,

> Avidly he loves strange loves, Savage with beauty
> Plucks strange flowers …
> Here are the apples of Sodom;
> Here are the hearts of vices;
> And sweet sins.[30]

Johnson had first introduced Wilde to Lord Alfred Douglas and later broke with Wilde over what he considered to be his ill-treatment of the younger man, which gives an interesting slant on the oft-told tale of Wilde's relationship with Douglas. Johnson wrote a sonnet castigating Wilde which started, 'I hate you with a necessary hate.'

Johnson fancied he was a good influence on Dowson, which Symons joked was limited to those times when Dowson had heard enough about the Fathers of the Church and declared his intention to go and look for a 'ten-penny whore', and Johnson would encourage him to stay to have another drink instead.[31]

Plarr writes of himself, Dowson and Johnson discussing literature for hours over a bottle after which Johnson came out with them to light them on their way, and for no reason Plarr could see, Johnson and Dowson lost their footing and rolled over one another down the first flight of the wooden stairs, illuminated by the flare of the lamp which rolled with them, though there were no injuries.[32]

Membership of the Rhymers gave Dowson an appreciative audience and his relationship with Herbert Horne meant he had a periodical which would accept almost anything he offered. The importance of publication cannot be over-stressed for one with a more than usual sense of the futility of life: it was always hard for Dowson to stir himself to work. The anticipation of a series of rejections from one magazine after another would be yet another disincentive edging him towards lethargy.

Dowson had his own publishing scheme in mind, intending to have privately published a volume of verses by himself and Plarr titled *Vine Leaf and Violet*. The project came to nothing but the proposed title is interesting in view of Symons, remark that Dowson believed 'v' was the most beautiful letter, and it could never be brought into poetry too often. He quotes Dowson as saying that his ideal of a line of verse was Poe's 'The viol, the violet and the vine'.[33] Such conversations suggest that Dowson rather lacked the practical skills to become a successful publisher.

The Critic survived until June 1890 when it was merged with a magazine called *Society* – presumably a merger in which only the title was bought up, as there was no job offered to Dowson.

Dowson tried to work in the British Museum Reading Room, attempting to obtain sixteenth and seventeeth-century French memoirs for an essay he was writing on the Pléiade, a sixteenth-century group of French writers who wished to elevate French to the level of classical languages and who therefore borrowed from classical writers and revived such forms as the Alexandrine, in which Dowson was to write. His letters often mentioned how he would rather be in the British Museum Reading Room than at Bridge Dock, but soon after he arrived at the museum he would usually meet some friends, and be off for a drink. Ernest Rhys used to refer to the

Reading Room as a great club where everyone he knew or had heard of could be encountered.

Dowson's literary collaboration with Arthur Moore continued with his sending Moore on 8 June 1890 the idea for the next book which was worked on for the following two years under the name *Masquerade* but for which Lionel Johnson suggested the name *A Comedy of Masks*. Dowson supplied the plot, principal characters and locations and, given that he had written a fair amount of prose on his own, it is perhaps surprising that he wanted to share it with Moore at all. However, Dowson had the self-knowledge to appreciate that he could realize a great project only if he had the support, encouragement and constant pressure of a collaborator.

The action takes place in an East End dock, a Soho café, the invalid colony at Bordighera, a gallery and a painter's home and studio. The locations were deliberately chosen as ones which either Dowson or Moore could draw from life. The chief character is the owner of the dock, Philip Rainham, who is tubercular, 40 years old, and likes to associate with artists. In his tastes, his illness and his inability to take control of his life Rainham is a portrait of Alfred Dowson, and an affectionate portrait at that.

One of Rainham's friends is an up-and-coming artist called Richard Lightmark; he marries Eve Sylvester, a young woman whom Rainham remembers 'in so many phases of a childhood and little girlhood', and he is still devoted to her now she is a young woman. Rainham does not wish her to marry Lightmark, whom he considers to be too frivolous, and he has suspicions about the man's decency, but he keeps them to himself, part of the consistent failure to take action which makes Rainham so psychologically interesting.

Lightmark is stealing ideas for compositions from more inspired artists and, worse, Rainham becomes acquainted with a destitute model whom Lightmark has seduced and abandoned with a child. Through a misunderstanding she is thought to have been seduced by Rainham, who is in fact simply helping the young woman out of natural generosity. When it seems inevitable that Eve will find out that the seducer is her own husband, Rainham takes the blame himself, in order to spare her pain. The model dies of consumption, leaving the inevitable adorable girlchild to be looked after by Rainham.

Lightmark's nemesis is a mercurial, absinthe-drinking artist called Oswyn who has a tendency as the evening wears on to, 'lapse from the eloquence to the incoherency of drunkenness.' He is in terms of conviction and artistic dedication the closest Dowson came in prose to a self-portrait. Many apologists for Ernest Dowson have tried to minimize his dissolute behaviour in the belief that such a life is incompatible with producing fine work – or, perhaps, should be. It is interesting therefore that Oswyn's drunkenness and almost frightening intensity are not intended to diminish his moral stature as an artist. 'I may fail or I may succeed, as the world-counts those things. It is all the same: I believe in myself,'[34] he says and he pours scorn on an artist of talent like Lightmark who paints to please popular taste and become rich, and will not be remembered 50 years hence.

Rainham dies of consumption in a deeply felt scene, showing an accent on death which is very Dowsonian: for a quarter of the book the central character is dead but action still revolves around him. Oswyn sets out to avenge his friend, and Eve finally is told that Rainham had sacrificed his reputation for her happiness, and 'death had sealed their estrangement ironically for all time.'[35] Now she knows the fact that he was trying to conceal from her. Moreover, she is now doubly cursed, both by the knowledge of her husband's infamy and the love which Rainham had borne her. To add to the irony, Rainham's sacrifice was in vain. She returns to the party she has just left, to her dishonest husband, prepared to live the rest of her life as a lie.

The story told in this way makes it seem rather stronger than it does in the novel. There are long passages of mediocre writing and some characters – significantly Eve – who never come to life. This is hardly a great work, but it does give a flavour of the times and is of enough merit to justify its re-publication 80 years later as one of 42 titles published as *The Decadent Consciousness*.

It is also a mine of biographically interesting information. Dowson is clearly writing from life when he remarks on how the dock had, 'altered the tenor of his existence, destroyed his youth and his ambitions, and represented for many years, more completely than anything else, the element of failure which had run through his life.' Rainham felt there was within him, 'that curious flaw which had made life seem to him at last ... a long disease of the spirit ... his long habit of spectatorship had made the personal effort ... impossible.'[36]

This is the point where Rainham as a portrait of Alfred Dowson kaleidoscopes into a portrait of Ernest Dowson, for they had similar weaknesses, as Ernest must have realized, though he cursed and chased his demons with drink and sex and hard living while his father had learned to live in a sort of quiet despair.

In a moving passage which could be his own epitaph Dowson wrote:

Certainly, the world was full of persons who had been broken on the wheel for their proper audacity, because they had sought so much more than was to be found; but might it not be equally true that one could err on the other side, expect, desire too little, less even than was there, and so reap finally, as he had done, in an immense lassitude and disgust of all things, born neither of satiety nor of disappointment, the full measure of one's reward?[37]

At least Philip Rainham's life was nearly finished when he came to think these thoughts. For his creator, life's worst was yet to come.

CHAPTER 5

DOWN AMONG THE DAYCADONGS

In the early 1890s Dowson settled into a nightly routine which satisfied his needs for order and entertainment, and allowed his many friends to know exactly where he was likely to be at any time. He would arrive in the West End around six o' clock, take an absinthe and perhaps play billiards in the Cock in Shaftesbury Avenue, where he would meet whatever friends happened to come along – now generally other writers, actors or lawyers – and they would walk the short distance through Piccadilly to Poland where they would dine. The plat du jour cost eightpence but with the addition of cheese, beer, coffee and a tip the meal cost one and threepence (6½p).

If they were not all to go to the theatre, Dowson's friends would then adjourn to the Café Royal while Dowson would stay behind to play cards with Adelaide. Then he would walk down Shaftesbury Avenue, past the noisy pubs and the music halls and theatres with crowds already spilling out, to round off the evening at the Crown in Charing Cross Road.

Edgar Jepson, who often accompanied Dowson at dinner, described Adelaide as 'not quite pretty: her nose was a little crooked. But she had the beauté du diable, the beauty of freshness and youth, and was slim of figure and of a warm colouring, with a rather long face and dark eyes and hair.'[1] She had no trace of cockney, but spoke a slightly accented English. Those games of cards with her gentleman admirer must have been a delight to her after a long day of school and then waiting at table.

'The dear child becomes daily more kind and gracious,' Dowson noted, and learned more about her as she overcame her initial shyness. He was charmed to find she could play the violin 'very prettily' and spoke at least some French.[2] He received such pleasure from the mere friendliness of children, he remarked, that nothing was more important than multiplying those moments and trying to make them last. At another time he wrote, 'The value of contact with children is chiefly, I think, that it enables you at least for a time to consider with a sort of mellow melancholy what you would otherwise do with extreme bitterness and acrimony.'[3]

In a more buoyant mood he wrote,

My dinners there now remind me more than anything else of certain hospitable "nursery teas" at which some years ago I was a frequent visitor before my cousins who partook of them [the Secretans] had grown up into formidable young ladies. La Petite comes and sits by me and paints or talks as a matter of course whenever I have not "company" – and her adoring mama from time to time favours me with anecdotes in most unintelligible English of her amazing qualities and her extreme gentillesse.[4]

Her family were more than tolerant of his interest. Once when Adelaide was indoors with a cold, Dowson was allowed up to see her in the family's rooms. Her father then shared a bottle of port with Dowson and the poet was shown pictures of Adelaide as a young child which delighted him.[5]

By early 1890 he was taking Adelaide, whom he generally called 'Missie' out to popular amusements like the Egyptian Hall of magic tricks and 'Niagara', a panorama of the Falls with other American views. He also took her to theatre matinees like that of 'Nixie' at the Globe Theatre where Dowson was able to watch the eponymous child star with his own child girlfriend beside him, indeed a rare treat. He gave her a copy of the works of Lewis Carroll and was pining for her pitifully when she was away hop-picking in Kent (the usual holiday for working-class Londoners) in August 1890.

He was writing verses like 'Ad Domnulam Suam' (To His Little Mistress) with its last verse:

Little lady of my heart!
   Just a little longer,
Be a child: then, we will part,
   Ere this love grow stronger.

At the same time as his relationship with Adelaide was developing, he was writing stories with themes which related to art and the love of young girls. 'The Story of a Violin', published in *Macmillan's Magazine* in August 1891, found Dowson again writing of arts other than his own – in this case music, as he had done in 'Souvenirs of an Egoist'. In this story, later republished as 'An Orchestral Violin', the narrator becomes acquainted with a violinist in a Soho restaurant he frequents, and after the opera one night the old man tells the story of the diva whom he trained as an orphan child and who now fails to recognize him. He developed her great talent as he realized he would never himself be a great artist, and would forever be a second violin or a music tutor. After his death the narrator of the story confronts the diva with her neglect of her old tutor, and he remarks on 'the tradition which has always ascribed something fatal and inevitable to the possession of great gifts.'

'A Case of Conscience', published in the *Century Guild Hobby Horse* in April 1891, was worked on in October 1890, when Dowson was well and truly under Adelaide's spell. It is set in Brittany where a man of over 40 falls in love with a teenage Breton girl and intends to marry her but he is divorced, a state not recognized by the Catholic Church. His friend, with whom he has been touring Brittany, intends to tell the girl's uncle (she is an orphan like so many of Dowson's fictional girls) but his conscience is tormented by doubts over his own motives, for he too is in love with the girl.

Dowson's finest poem also comes from this period, written on 6 February 1891. Normally called (including by himself) 'Cynara', or 'the Cynara poem', its title is a line from Horace's odes: 'Non sum qualis eram bonae sub regno Cynarae', where the poet protests that he is not the man he was when his gracious lover Cynara ruled his heart. It is not only the literal meaning of the Latin (Odes IV, 1, line 3) which Dowson wishes to convey, however, but also the sense of the verse. The speaker in the Ode feels love welling up in him and begs Venus to desist, for he knows what pain it will bring: 'After a long cessation, O Venus, again are you stirring up tumults? Spare me, I beseech you, I beseech you. I am not the man I was under the dominion of good-natured Cynara. Forbear, O cruel mother of soft desires.'[6] Dowson had more than most to fear from the dangers of love.

Dowson wrote it in the Cock tavern, sitting at one of the little marble-topped tables as he habitually did, with an absinthe in front of him and a cigarette hanging out of his mouth, writing with the stub of a pencil on scraps of paper torn from business letters.

If the image of a poet sitting in a bar scribbling deathless verse on the back of an envelope seems impossibly clichéd, the stuff of legend, it is because Dowson lived the legend and thereby invented it. There is an anecdote that he would sometimes run out of paper and write on the white marble tabletop itself, but the barman would rub it off with his damp cloth.

Dowson wrote verse fast – one poem he wrote in a single sitting – but this is not to say he did not perfect his verse. The many variations in different versions of 'Cynara' which he sent to his friends, show that he worked the verse over and again, changing individual words and punctuation. 'When the feast is finished', for example, was written after the alternatives 'when the cups are empty' and 'when the viols are silent' had been rejected.[7] Nor was it a matter only of inspiration springing to the page: Dowson used the Alexandrine, a verse form which he admired and knew well from his study of the poets of La Pléiade who had revived the form of twelve syllable lines to make it the dominant poetic form of the French Renaissance. It is particularly ill-suited to the English language, usually tending to the monotonous, which makes it the more remarkable that Dowson should have been able to vary the caesura and the stress to arrive at such a light, inspired lyricism. He has been described in this as adding a new melody to English poetry and certainly the verse scans in a remarkably light yet definite fashion which makes it impossible to imitate.

> Last night, ah, yesternight, betwixt her lips and mine
> There fell thy shadow, Cynara! thy breath was shed
> Upon my soul between the kisses and the wine;
> And I was desolate and sick of an old passion,
>   Yea, I was desolate and bowed my head:
> I have been faithful to thee, Cynara! in my fashion.
>
> All night upon mine heart I felt her warm heart beat,
> Night-long within mine arms in love and sleep she lay;
> Surely the kisses of her bought red mouth were sweet;
> But I was desolate and sick of an old passion,
>   When I awoke and found the dawn was gray:
> I have been faithful to thee, Cynara! in my fashion.
>
> I have forgot much, Cynara! gone with the wind,
> Flung roses, roses riotously with the throng,
> Dancing, to put thy pale, lost lilies out of mind;
> But I was desolate and sick of an old passion,
>   Yea, all the time, because the dance was long:
> I have been faithful to thee, Cynara! in my fashion.
>
> I cried for madder music and for stronger wine,
> But when the feast is finished and the lamps expire,
> Then falls thy shadow, Cynara! the night is thine;
> And I am desolate and sick of an old passion,
>   Yea hungry for the lips of my desire:
> I have been faithful to thee, Cynara! in my fashion.

'Cynara' was to become the defining masterpiece of the period and it is easy to see why. It is full of the iconography of decadence with the writer trading, like Swinburne, the 'lilies and languors of virtue/For the raptures and roses of vice'. It is full of the scent of love and wine and innocence and sin. It is the archetypal decadent poem because it is so obviously written from an age which took its pleasures with guilt: eighteenth or twentieth-century writers would have sex with prostitutes and drink to excess and think nothing of it. It was specifically at the turn of the Victorian period when public morality was still stern but sensuality was rife that such small vices were luxuriously sinful.

The archaisms which irritate in so much late nineteenth-century verse (including some of Dowson's own) here seem appropriate to the subject. The weariness and longing for inaccessible innocence have the air about them of true emotion, genuinely felt. Dowson's perfect touch is demonstrated by comparison with a leaden poem on the same subject which was written by Arthur Symons more than a year after 'Cynara' had appeared. To 'One in Alienation' starts,

> As I lay on the stranger's bed,
> And clasped the stranger woman I had hired ...

and ends

> ... when I kissed her, for your sake,
> My lips were sobbing on your name.

The question 'who is Cynara?' has perplexed writers who reason that she is a real, lost love. They feel she is certain to be a past love as she is described as 'lost', an 'old passion'. For this reason it could not be Adelaide who was very much a present, innocent love when Dowson wrote the verse.

In fact Adelaide represented for him the distillation of every girlchild he had ever loved. His present and developing fear was that she would soon grow up and no longer be his. As he wrote in 'Growth',

> I watched the glory of her childhood change,
> Half-sorrowful to find the child I knew,
>   (Loved long ago in lily-time)
> Become a maid, mysterious and strange,

Dowson was suffering prospective pain for the event he knew would take place, not an unknown occurrence in verse. To take another famous poem: Laurence Binyon (born two years after Dowson) wrote his lines in 'For the Fallen', 'At the going down of the sun and in the morning/We will remember them' in September 1914 virtually before anyone had died in the First World War; the poet was enjoying in prospect the melancholy of remembrance. Binyon was, incidentally, also using Alexandrines.

So Cynara can be associated with Adelaide, to the extent that Adelaide symbolized an ideal of love which must ultimately be lost. The identification with Adelaide is increased by a verse Dowson wrote in pencil on the front end-paper of his poetry notebook. Titled 'To Cynara', it is unequivocally addressed to Adelaide with the lines, 'Take these songs my love. ... Songs thou shalt never see,' and a description of part of their relationship.

Dowson recognized the quality of his Cynara poem immediately, sending copies to several friends and having it read by Johnson at the next

Rhymers' meeting. Not all were fully appreciative. John Davidson later said to Arthur Symons, 'I say that this is not a great lyrical poem; that it is the reverse of intoxicating, and I say, further, that it calls for a libation of carbolic.'[8]

Dowson feared a similar reaction from the public. He submitted it to the *Century Guild Hobby Horse* but wrote to Sam Smith, 'I have seen the proofs of my Cynara poem for the April *Hobby*. It looks less indecent in print, but I am still nervous! though I admire Horne's audacity.'[9] He advised Arthur Moore to confiscate his copy of the April *Hobby Horse* before his family had a chance to see it.[10]

In fact, the world was slow to notice genius, as is so often the case. Even Dowson's fellow Rhymer Richard Le Gallienne, in his 'Log-Roller' column in *The Star* of 14 May 1891 only remarked upon, 'a very fine love poem by Mr Ernest Dowson, whose work I should be glad to see again.'

Decadents were always treated with derision by the mainstream press, as in the parody of Lewis Carroll which began:

Twas rollog, and the minim potes
Did mime and mimble in the cafe;
All footly were the Philorotes,
And the Daycadongs outstrafe [11]

Dowson's slowly growing reputation as a writer made him a welcome participant among the 'daycadongs' whose chief meeting place was the Crown, just north of Cranbourne Street and the Hippodrome, and conveniently placed for the stage doors of the Empire and the Alhambra. It was full from eleven to half past twelve, which was closing time, with poets, painters, dramatists, ballet girls, critics, patrons, novelists and hangers-on of the arts. The journalist and publisher Grant Richards described it:

One entered, and the narrow space opened out and disclosed a bar-parlour. The bar itself flanked one of its sides. Prosperous cab-proprietors and book-makers' runners and the male assistants at the neighbouring music-hall and theatres stood at the bar and drank. The patrons of whom I treat had nothing to do with them. My friends were of the intelligentzia [sic]; they talked learnedly about the ballet and Walter Sickert and the latest art movement in France and Edmund Gosse's last insincerity. There were settees round the wall and we sat on them and drank hot gin and water. Certain celebrities you were quite sure of finding. Selwyn Image was one of them and Herbert Horne another, and with Herbert Horne would be Arthur Symons. These last you could depend upon to turn up within a few minutes of the closing of the Empire and the Alhambra. … Ernest Dowson would, as likely as not, be the first to arrive. These were the regulars. They were the men to whom late hours were natural. Night birds, most of them.[12]

Dowson had many other friends and acquaintances who would call in at the Crown in the early years of the 1890s. Lionel Johnson would perch on a stool; Oscar Wilde would occasionally drop by with his acolytes Robert Ross and John Gray – the latter to become a close friend of Dowson. Others were the novelist Conal O'Riordan then known as Norreys Connell, who was later to tour Belgium with Dowson; the artist Charles Conder, to become known for his exquisite painting on silk fans; fellow Rhymers John Davidson with his short beard, silk hat and morning coat, and Victor Plarr, taking everything very seriously; the publisher John Lane, soon to publish *The Yellow Book*; and Hubert Crackanthorpe, the writer of a celebrated volume of short stories, *Wreckage*, which Dowson much admired.

Dowson was also acquainted with the Fabian socialist, the Rev Stewart Headlam, a member of the London County Council who founded the Church and Stage Guild in 1879 to break down the prejudice against theatres, actors and music hall artists. He was normally accompanied by young women from these professions, as were Horne, Symons and Image.

Among Dowson's actor friends were Lennox Pawle and Marmaduke Langdale, of Sir Frank Benson's company which took Shakespeare to the provinces. Langdale was 'an ardent Swinburnian' which of course endeared him to Dowson.

Grant Richards continued with his reminiscence:

> This visit to the Crown was not a dissipation; it was the end of the day's work, a chance of meeting and talking with congenial friends, of exchanging ideas. ... Looking back, it seems to me that one of the oddest things about the Crown was that in spite of the cheapness of the liquor there dispensed no one in the gathering – except, perhaps, poor Ernest Dowson – ever became drunk.[13]

Unconventional behaviour was more than tolerated in Dowson's circles, and though he was often drunk, he was far from being the most extreme character on the scene. He himself wrote, 'The latest Rhymer is one Barlas, a charming poet and anarchist, who was lately run in for shooting the House of Commons.'[14] Dowson sponsored John Barlas at the Cheshire Cheese. He had impeccable revolutionary credentials, having served as an organizer for the Social Democratic Federation, contributed to Morris's *Commonweal* and had suffered for the cause: at the riot in Trafalgar Square in November 1887 he was struck by a policeman's baton and was said to have fallen bleeding at the feet of Eleanor Marx. The incident Dowson referred to was when he was arrested on 31 December 1891 for shooting a pistol near the residence of the Speaker of the House of Commons to show his contempt for authority. Oscar Wilde stood bail for him. Dowson had no detailed interest in the politics of the man, but opposition to authority alone was inspiring to him. In French politics Dowson declared himself a Boulangist, not because he knew anything of the radical right-wing movement, but because he wished to be against the government.[15] To consider the government is always wrong is, of course, no more unsophisticated a view of politics than that of those who think authority is always right. Dowson's only other recorded political view is that he was a Neo-Jacobite, one of those who considered descendants of the Stuart king to be the only legitimate heirs to the throne of Britain, truly the most lost of lost causes.[16]

John Barlas attended several Rhymers' meetings. Seven books of his verse were published, but he did not contribute to the Rhymers' anthology then being considered. It was hearing Dowson's verses which compelled Yeats to suggest the Rhymers publish a volume of their own. He was specifically referring to 'O Mors!' ('Exceeding sorrow/Consumeth my sad heart!') and 'Villanelle of Sunset' ('Come hither, Child! and rest') and remarked on 'the desire to hold them in my hand. ... They were not speech, but perfect song, though song for the speaking voice.'[17]

Early in 1891 Dowson wrote to Plarr to say the club had decided to issue its first anthology. Johnson, Greene and Yeats organized its publication with Elkin Mathews in November 1891. Dowson was on the selection panel which allowed Rhymers up to six poems each. *The Book of the Rhymers' Club* was published in an edition of 350 copies in February 1892 and they were sold out within a month. Reviews were positive, if lukewarm in most cases, except that of Richard Le Gallienne who described it as a 'gracious coronal of song', notable for its 'modest, commonsense note ... English character ... absence of affectation,' without emphasizing his own contributions.[18]

By far the best works were those of Dowson and Johnson, the latter contributing what became his most anthologized poem, 'By the Statue of King Charles at Charing Cross'. Dowson's best poem was 'Nuns of the Perpetual Adoration', which had previously been published in the *Century Guild Hobby Horse* with two other verses, 'Flos Lunae' and 'Amor Umbratilis', under the title 'In Praise of Solitude'. It is Dowson's first explicitly religious poem and demonstrates the way his mind had been playing on spiritual matters. It is a simple description of the timeless life in a convent while,

> Outside, the world is wild and passionate;
> Man's weary laughter and his sick despair
> Entreat at their impenetrable gate:

Dowson was attracted by the mystery and dedication of monastic life. He visited a Carthusian monastery at Cowfold in Sussex in spring 1891 and wrote his verse *Carthusians* about them. He was impressed with their separate cells where the monks would read, eat and meditate, having only one hour a week for conversation together, would see each other only at the various offices, 'and pass each other in the cloisters with a formal bow and a "memento mortis frater!"'[19] His poem compares the monks, 'despising the world's wisdom and the world's desire', to his life and that of his friends:

> We fling up flowers and laugh, we laugh across the wine;
>> With wine we dull our souls and careful strains of art;
> Our cups are polished skulls round which the roses twine:
>> None dares to look at Death who leers and lurks apart.

Yeats said, 'His poetry shows how sincerely he felt the fascination of religion, but his religion had certainly no dogmatic outline, being but a desire for a condition of virginal ecstasy.'[20]

When Dowson tried to give shape to his religious feelings, only the Catholic Church attracted him. On 10 March 1890 he wrote to Sayle, who was to visit the city of Rome, 'Happy man to be going to Rome. ... If you go there – to Rome – in another sense as well – I envy you still more.'[21] Sayle did not in fact convert to Rome, remaining an Anglo-Catholic, though he did receive an audience with the Pope. There were a large number of converts among Dowson's acquaintances: Arthur Galton, sometime inhabitant of the Hobby Horse House and the editor of Matthew Arnold's letters, became a Catholic priest. Dowson reported in October 1890 that R.B.S. Blakelock, another Oxford friend 'with flashing and excited spectacles is careering Romewards'. Two of Dowson's own cousins, D.L. Secretan and Gerald Hoole, converted about the same time. He also thought Sam Smith would convert 'any day. ... But I am sure that none of these good people adore Catholicism more than Johnson and myself.'[22]

As early as summer 1890 Dowson was taking definite steps towards Catholicism when he was seeing a good deal of Johnson who he considered a 'wonderful, quite beautiful person. He took me to the Servite Church last Sunday,' he confided in Sayle, who was more open to Dowson's religious impulses than some of his other friends. He continued:

> The fact is that Our Lady of the Seven Hills s'impose on me more and more – and in short I am afraid there is no help for it. I practically succumbed in Brittany [whence he had just returned] – it's so utterly impossible to continue as an outsider. I shall try and put it off a little longer – if possible until next summer when I can take a month out of England and get the disagreeable part of the business over by myself. Besides I should very much prefer on all grounds to be received abroad.[23]

There may have been something of a deep childhood memory in his wish to convert: churches would have been beautifully awesome places for the young Dowson as he trekked across Catholic Europe with his parents. There is more than a little in the jib that many artists converted not because they found Catholicism more spiritually true than other forms of faith, but just more beautiful. They would answer that beauty is a form of spiritual truth, and if religion is not beautiful it cannot be true. As Frank Harris said

Dowson told him, 'I am for the old faith. I've become a Catholic, as every artist must.'[24]

The decadent life was said to be destined to lead to suicide or the foot of the cross. Religion, but specifically Catholicism, was always part of the decadent make-up: the decadent role model, Oscar Wilde's Dorian Gray, was rumoured to be 'about to join the Roman Catholic communion; and certainly the Roman ritual had always a great attraction for him.' It had too for Wilde himself who did not in fact convert until his death-bed, but certainly had the inclination to become a Catholic while at Trinity College, Dublin. It would have been a rather more cataclysmic event for an Irish Protestant to convert in his youth than it was for Dowson's English friends, however.

The exemplar of converts was John Gray, Wilde's principal protégé before Lord Alfred Douglas and some (including Dowson) would say the original for Dorian Gray though he successfully sued the *Star* newspaper for libel for daring to say so in a gossip column. Dowson addressed Gray as 'Poeta Optime'.[25] With less reverence, the *Pall Mall Gazette* called him 'Le Plus Décadent des Décadents' in 1893 when his book of verse, *Silverpoints*, was published.[26]

Gray, a year older than Dowson, was the son of a carpenter who passed the civil service examinations and was working as a librarian in the Foreign Office for most of the time Dowson knew him. He converted to Catholicism in 1890 and later went on to become ordained as a priest. A close friend, André Raffalovich, with whom he lived for most of his life, also converted, in 1896. Lionel Johnson finally took the step he had much discussed with Dowson on 25 September 1891. Other notable decadent converts were Aubrey Beardsley who converted in 1897, Robert Ross who converted in 1894, and Lord Alfred Douglas who did so in 1911. Catholicism was not the only outlet: the flamboyantly decadent Count Eric Stenbock set up his own exotic theology – as did Yeats and Davidson though these latter two would have claimed to be contemporary with, rather than part of, the decadent movement. Likewise Pearl Craigie ('John Oliver Hobbes'), the only playwright to be significantly influenced by Wilde, converted in 1892.

Decadence was not a special requirement for Catholic conversion; many others, like the poet Alice Meynell, who could hardly be called decadent, also converted in their youth. She formed an interesting link between the decadents and the mainstream versifiers of the late Victorian age, her home being open to both the lifelong Catholic Francis Thompson, a poet and an opium addict, and the Catholic convert Coventry Patmore. The older poet's immensely popular 'The Angel in the House' also shows that the idealization to an ethereal level of a loved woman was hardly a decadent monopoly. The fact that he too was a Catholic who made his beloved into a saint, purified of any earthly attributes, as Dowson and a number of his poetic co-religionists did, is hardly coincidence. A religion which focuses on a woman, on a fecund virgin, a young wife who is also the mother of God, who is both approachable and celestial, gives a range of symbols of unattainable love.

Dowson merged religious devotion and earthly love, particularly in his prose. In 'Diary of a Successful Man' the object of the men's devotion joins a closed order, as the beloved girl does in 'Apple Blossom in Brittany'. This story, worked on in summer 1892 though not printed until October 1894 in *The Yellow Book,* is set in the fictional Breton village of Ploumariel where Dowson also set 'A Case of Conscience' and to which he frequently referred when saying he wanted to be back in Brittany. In the story Benedict Campion, an English Catholic of around 40, is visiting his ward, a girl of 16. Marie-Ursule is an orphan, being educated at a convent under the supervision of the local Curé who, recognizing Campion's love for the girl, urges that he marry her. Campion delays, returns to London, and when he next sees Marie-Ursule she is turning to him for advice on whether or not she should enter the Ursuline convent. He feels he cannot deflect her from this higher path, 'that any other ending to his love had been an impossible grossness, and that to lose her in just that fashion was the only way in which he could keep her always.'[27] So he acquiesces, and she never knows of his love for her, thus combining religious vocation with the sacrifice of love for a higher purpose.

This is similar to the way in which Philip Rainham's death in *A Comedy of Masks* begins the process by which his reputation is redeemed and his beloved comes to a realization of true love. His sacrifice leads to a higher understanding. As Oswyn tells Evelyn, 'you had absorbed his whole life ... his devotion to you was a kind of religion.'[28]

This introduces the other incentive for Dowson to convert. Adelaide was a Catholic, she attended the Notre Dame de France just off Leicester Square. Dowson went to see her after Vespers in a procession of white robed little girls of the Enfants de Marie, a long line of them walking gracefully through the swirling incense. He wrote, 'I just managed to discern my special Enfant in spite of her veil, carrying a very big banner and looking as usual extremely self-possessed and mistress of the situation.'[29] If he converted it would be, he hardly dared hope, one more barrier removed from his eventually marrying her.

CHAPTER 6

MORAL TORTURE

Not everyone was sympathetic to the adoration of the girlchild. *Punch*, scourge of aesthetes, decadents and all unconventionality, printed a spoof child-poem called 'To Dorothy, My Four-Year-Old Sweetheart' on 1 September 1894. While the satire cannot emphatically be said to refer to Dowson, it is characteristic of Dowson in its subject matter, its emotional simplicity and its form as a poetic trifle (it is a roundel). *The Book of the Rhymers' Club* had included such poems as 'Ad Domnulam Suam' ('Little lady of my heart') and 'Villanelle of Sunset' ('Come hither, Child! and rest') and other of Dowson's verses clearly identified children as the object of his affections. The beginning and end of the *Punch* skit runs:

> To make sweet hay I was amazed to find
> You absolutely did not know the way. ...
> I kissed your pretty face with hay entwined
> We made sweet hay. But what will Mother say
> If in a dozen years we're still inclined
> To make sweet hay?

These were true words spoken in jest. Dowson had only a very limited period to enjoy Adelaide's company as a child. While his relations with her had been free of sexual content or explicit future intentions, it was clear this could not continue for long. She was 13 in April 1891. It is worth considering what a 'girl' was in urban Britain in the 1890s. It was only in 1886 that the previous year's Criminal Law Amendment Act raised the age of consent from 13 to 16, a decision which was taken directly in response to the *Pall Mall Gazette*'s series of articles, 'The Maiden Tribute of Modern

Babylon', which detailed the successful efforts of their reporter W.T. Stead to purchase a 13-year-old virgin in 1885.

Dowson was well aware of the law, and needed to be, as he was having amorous relationships with girls as young as possible. He wrote of his girlfriend Lena, 'Her greatest charm is her youth.'[1] When he was in a position to have sex with 15-year-old Bertha, in the company of his friend Lefroy with his girl of presumably the same age, Dowson specifically referred to the Criminal Law Amendment Act as the reason they did not proceed. He recounted, 'we agreed that in view of the new Act le jeu ne valait [the game wasn't worth it].'[2]

The experiences of 'Walter', the otherwise anonymous writer of *My Secret Life*, covering sexual exploits through the whole of the second half of the nineteenth century, show that it was far from uncommon for girls under 16 to be sexually experienced. Indeed, he invariably remarks on having sex with a girl who is a virgin (or who is made out to be one by her procuress), that if he does not have her, some costermonger's boy will and she will receive no payment for the working class lad's attentions, so having sex with Walter is in her best interests.[3]

Of more direct relevance to the story of Dowson, and particularly, perhaps, in the manipulative nature of the girl involved, is the case of Philip Wilson Steer. He was seven years older than Dowson, a painter and contributor to *The Yellow Book* who delighted in the painting of pubescent girls, often naked or with their clothes disarranged while they dressed or played. Steer met the girl with whom he was to fall in love, Rose Pettigrew, in 1888 when he was 28 and she 11. She and her three sisters were earning a living as artists' models and had posed for many of the great Victorian artists. In a memoir she describes, after a first introduction, deliberately going to his house to flirt with him, and lying about her age.[4] She soon began to pose for him gratis and he was painting no model but her. They kissed, drank wine and went to dances together and she accepted a ring from him, as they intended to marry. They quarrelled over a trifling difference one day at a dance hall when she was 18, and she returned his ring. Thereafter she refused to see him again, despite the artist's pathetically returning with the ring day after day for months. She married a musician, Steer remained a bachelor. 'We pitied his suffering when the lady married,' wrote George Moore.[5]

Dowson's consideration of what his relationship with Adelaide was, and where it was proceeding, was thrown into sharp focus by events which occurred when he was not even in the country. In August 1891 he went to his beloved Brittany with Arthur Moore. On his return he chanced to read in *The Star*, in ordinary accounts of Police Court business, committal proceedings against a man called Newton, accused of abducting a 15-year-old girl called Lucy Pearman and having sex with her.

Edward Arthur Maurice Callender Newton was a 39-year-old journalist with a small private income. He had first encountered Lucy, the daughter of a tobacconist living in the Strand, when she was 11 and had watched her playing in Fountain Court (where, coincidentally, Arthur Symons lived). He chatted with Lucy and her siblings and took to visiting her father's shop to buy cigars, and became friendly with her mother. He became a frequent visitor to their home, bringing gifts and having meals with them. He had been very attentive to Lucy, and about a year before the trial when she was 14 or 15, she had taken to missing school in order to be with him. He had rented rooms in Gower Place where he received visits from Lucy, sometimes with her brother. In recent months she had been visiting as often as four times a week, Newton's landlady recalled, and staying during the day.

When Lucy's mother discovered that her daughter had been 'walking out' with Newton she forbade her to see him again, and accused him of 'ruining' her. He said he had never disguised from Mrs Pearman that he loved the girl and would marry her when he was able to divorce his wife from whom he was estranged. Lucy told her mother she was in love with Newton 'and would have him'.

Lucy and Newton had been in the habit of writing to each other. He addressed her as 'My dear sweet little girl-wife' and she called him, 'My dear Hubbie'. Her letters testified to their passionate relationship, 'To one I dearly love, and never mind what else,' she wrote, 'My long desire is at last fulfilled, I know you will be pleased to know what this long-looked-for desire is (sacred to you and I). It is your love which I have now and your thought.'

Lucy argued with her mother and begged Newton to take her away. He consented and she slipped out of school, had her hair cut, dressed in clothes he bought for her, and they went to Hastings together where they posed as father and daughter. He rented an apartment with two bedrooms, though they used only one. It was here that they were apprehended. Interestingly, the police found a copy of the Criminal Law Amendment Act 1885 when they searched the rooms for evidence.[6]

To give the ending to the case (though Dowson does not remark on it): at trial at the Old Bailey some two weeks later Newton pleaded guilty to two counts of 'unlawfully taking' Lucy Pearman and being improperly intimate with her. Both Newton and Lucy said they had been having sex only since she was 15 and the prosecution could offer no decisive evidence to the contrary, though it seems likely they did start earlier than this. The judge accepted in mitigation that the offence had only recently been made a crime, and remarked that had the girl been a few months older there could have been no proceedings. Newton received a six-month sentence.[7]

Dowson was shocked to the core, far beyond what might be considered a natural reaction to a story from the law courts. He declared it was 'a most disgusting story of a disgusting person, which I suppose is a notorious scandal.' In fact it was one court report among many, and there is no reason to assume it was particularly widely discussed. He wrote to Moore:

> The worse of it was that it read like a sort of foul and abominable travesty of – pah, what is the good of hunting for phrases. You must know what I mean, and how I am writhing. I imagine all the comments and analogies which one's kind friends will draw, and unfortunately I can't help feeling that even her people – and mine, as far as that goes – might take alarm and suspect my motives. And yet I swear there never was a man more fanatically opposed to the corruption of innocence – even where women are concerned – than I am. Unfortunately the excellence of my conscience doesn't make a difference. This beastly thing has left a sort of slimy trail over my holy places.

Poor Dowson seems to be protesting too much, so as to raise suspicions rather than quell them.

He continued the letter to note what was his real torment: the imposition of sex on his relationship with Adelaide: 'I am simply stupid with disgust and anger at everything and everybody in this very gross world; and sick to death at the notion of things changing, and my one consolation being done away with.'[8] The same day he wrote to John Gray, 'the gods have been tormenting me with a grievous neuralgia in France; and since I came back they have devised a peculiarly refined and indefinable form of moral torture, which on the whole is worse than the neuralgia.'[9]

Really, there was no reason for him to have felt that anyone would change in their attitude towards him. If he were guilty of nothing before the Newton case, why should another man's guilt make people treat him differently? He tried to act as if he felt nothing and Adelaide's parents acted as if nothing had happened – indeed, it had not. Dowson's disgust and anger were self-generating but they were gnawing at him nevertheless, and he was neglecting his share of the work on *A Comedy of Masks*. He apologized to Moore, but excused himself by saying that, 'This thing is killing me. ... Her people are as kind and cordial as ever, there are no obvious differences made: only I can feel there is a difference and that it will become more apparent daily.'[10] This is as obvious a case of pathological guilt as could be found. Clearly at Poland there was no problem, it was all a matter of Dowson's morbid sensitivity.

It was the intolerable pressure of this guilt, wedded to the religious devotion which he already felt, which finally impelled him into the Catholic Church. Charles Sayle had offered to introduce him to a sympathetic priest who would place him under instruction but Dowson refused and found a priest himself, presumably with assistance from John Gray or Lionel Johnson. Somehow he dealt with 'the disagreeable part of the business' – the first general confession – and he was received into the Catholic faith in the spectacularly beautiful surroundings of the Brompton Oratory on 25 September 1891.

On the day of his conversion he came across Victor Plarr and shook his hand, as Plarr remembered:

> His hesitating handshake, alas! always betrayed a sorrowful fatigue. "I have been admitted," he said, but he seemed disappointed, for the heavens had not fallen, nor had a sign been vouchsafed. The priest who had admitted him had done so quite casually and had seemed bored. Afterwards, it seemed to me, he forgot all about his religion with surprising alacrity.[11]

It should be remembered that Plarr had no general sympathy with conversion nor, it seemed, with Catholicism, and he compared converts to people who declared a belief in socialism – thus neatly marrying the bête noire of nineteenth with that of twentieth-century conservatives.

A more sympathetic response came from Richard Le Gallienne, who described Dowson's 'charming, affectionate, high-strung nature, capable at times of strange frenzies of excitement, deeply spiritual, and sensuous, too, as such natures usually are, he was of those who passed untimely from the scene, finding peace at last like others of his generation "too avid of earth's bliss" in the bosom of the Catholic Church.' Lionel Johnson was understandably delighted and referred to, 'my dearest friend Dowson who is now, Laus Deo, a Catholic.'[12]

Dowson did not forget 'all about his religion'; he attended church for the rest of his life, frequently if not regularly. His family moved to 15 Bristol Gardens, Maida Hill (Maida Vale) in September 1891 and he was soon writing that his 'usual church' was Our Lady in Grove Road, St John's Wood.[13]

Doubtless fortified by spiritual sustenance, he decided he must take decisive action and declare his intention to marry Adelaide. He wrote to Moore in January 1892:

> I have not any longer a shadow of doubt that my condition is transparently obvious to everybody concerned, and that the Damozel perfectly understands the situation, and since it is merely an English tradition which assumes Heaven knows why? that a girl is not Amabilis [loveable] when she is at her most amiable age – why should I delay in putting a rather untenable situation easily right?

With some self-knowledge he wrote, 'my scrupulousness is only accounted to my indecision and lack of courage.'

It was not, he hastened to assure Moore, that he had changed his views on marriage:

> I do not believe in marriage in the abstract in the least. Only it is the price, perhaps a heavy one, which one is ordered to pay if one has an immense desire for a particular feminine society. In the present case, I would pay it ten times over, sooner than risk the possibility of some time or other regretting that I had let go irrevocably something which promised a good deal, which I have never had, and which is perhaps after all the best thing obtainable in this stupid world – simply out of lâcheté [cowardice].[14]

It was easier to make the decision, however, than to put it into practice. As Dowson correctly assessed, the difficulties were not legal. A girl could legally be married at 12, and a boy at 14; the ages were not raised to 16 until the Age of Marriage Act of 1929. Though convention dictated that such early marriages did not take place, betrothal was possible. Late marriage, at least for men, was a Victorian convention with a good justification: to allow the man to establish himself in business before having a family.

Having made the decision to marry, there were a series of problems to overcome. Dowson had to convince Adelaide herself, her family, and his family. He must also demonstrate to all that he could keep himself and a wife and children by his own efforts – something which was by no means obvious.

He does not seem to have troubled at all on the question of whether Adelaide would have him, so perhaps they had some kind of an understanding. Her voice is lamentably absent from the record which includes comments from his friends, both gallant and otherwise, and Dowson's own soul-searching about her. Yet no single word of hers has been recorded. It is as if, as the least charitable of Dowson's friends said, she was not real but a symbol for him.[15]

Adelaide in her early teens was pretty, 'an attractive child of gipsy type' as John Gray remarked,[16] with blue eyes, thick dark hair hanging on either side of her face and a nose which was said (though not by Dowson) to be slightly crooked. Edgar Jepson called her 'a cheerful, healthy spirit'. She was somewhat shy, but usually willing, with encouragement, to go to the tables and talk with the men, mainly Poles, dining there. She spoke to the clients in French or Polish. Her mother watched the people in the restaurant over a partition and if she saw any she did not like the look of, she would shout to Adelaide to come away.

Dowson would keep a long vigil at the restaurant, gradually coaxing Adelaide to come and talk to him. She enjoyed cards and games like halma, a board game involving pegs, which she frequently played with Dowson. As a girl she would paint at the back of the restaurant, presumably with a child's watercolours, and would sometimes play the violin. When Dowson was away she would write letters to him.

As she grew older she became coquettish. John Gray remarked that she would sit down at Dowson's table and behave like a wayward child – teasing Dowson and deliberately driving him into paroxysms of jealousy.[17] This is all that is known, save the occasional glimpses of her by Dowson's friends.

Dowson confessed his love-sickness to the journalist Frank Harris (if we are to believe Harris's account, and Gray said it was accurate) and took him round to see her, but his friend remembered 'I could find little attraction in her except the beauty of youth and the fact that she evidently didn't care much for Dowson – a girlish, matter-of-fact, pleasant creature. I could not believe that the fever would be lasting or profound. I was mistaken.'[18]

As she became older Adelaide must have realized, even if her mother did not impress it upon her, that Dowson was behaving more like a boyfriend than an uncle. Dowson wrote that Adelaide, 'makes the blood dance in my veins whenever She speaks or smiles or moves.'[19] When he was struggling with the question of whether he should marry her he remarked that, 'she has never been more intimately charming.'[20]

No one, not even those of Dowson's friends who liked Poland the least, has ever suggested that Adelaide was a fool. Even given that Victorian girls matured later than their counterparts a hundred years in the future (mainly because of different nutritional standards) she would still, at 14, have had a young women's interest in matters of the heart. There is no evidence to say whether or not she was as manipulative as Lucy Pearman or Rose Pettigrew, whose stories have been mentioned, but time would show her to be a confident and self-willed young woman who knew her own mind very well. The suspicion must be strong that she knew the power of Dowson's attachment to her, knew she was the centre of attention, and enjoyed the part she was playing a great deal.

It would be extremely difficult for him to tell his family that he intended to marry beneath him. The Dowsons were outwardly prosperous property owners, after all, and Adelaide was the daughter of a man of the small shopkeeping class. Dowson tried to persuade his friends – and perhaps himself – that the family had been in better circumstances before coming to London, and they were certainly a respectable family, but in the class-ridden society of England, marriages so far across caste lines were forbidden.

Quite how Dowson dealt with his parents, if he ever did, is not known. He took his mother to Poland at least once when they went to the theatre together, so she knew of his delight in Adelaide's company. Alfred and Annie Dowson cannot have been in complete ignorance, as his maternal uncle Stanley Hoole knew of Dowson's problem. His situation was talked of at the table in spring 1892 by Lionel Johnson who was dining with the Hooles. Dowson was very upset that 'this infatuation of mine was openly discussed the whole of dinner-time par tous les gens [by everyone].' He therefore did not see how it could continue for long 'without an understanding or a fracas – the latter I suppose will be inevitable first – with my people.'[21]

Dowson spent a night arguing with Johnson about the affair, and this may have been the start of the cooling of their friendship. Dowson found Johnson a 'hostile critic' but told Plarr:

> I have long passed the point at which one is seriously moved by hostile criticism of anybody in these questions or can feel any more than a tolerant

contempt for the point of view from which it is uttered. … God or the Flesh or the Devil – an artist may be in bondage to any one or other or all of these powers and retain his self-respect – but the world mustn't, positively must not exist for him – or so much the worse for his art.[22]

The terms of Dowson's denunciation – that he does not care what the 'world' may think – and Johnson's appeal directly to Dowson's family on the matter, imply that Johnson's objection to the union was on snobbish grounds: the difference in social station between Dowson and Adelaide.

He may have delayed telling his parents in the hope that the whole business would be better dealt with when they were in better health. His mother, who must by now have been clearly recognized as being consumptive, had been ill for the whole of the winter of 1891–2 with influenza, which left her so weak she could not cross the room. His father too was in steadily declining spirits and they were now not wealthy enough to travel abroad for their health. His letters show that Ernest Dowson himself was always prey to colds, catarrhs and bronchial infections, indicating a weak resistance to disease.

In order that Adelaide's age should be less of a problem, it was sensible for him to wait until she was 14, in April 1892. But spring 1892 came and went with no action taken by Dowson. 'I go on in precisely the same situation,' he confided to Sam Smith, 'I can't somehow screw myself up to making a declaration of myself to Madame, although I am convinced it is the most reasonable course. Any day however with favourable omens it may arrive.'[23]

At this time, *A Comedy of Masks* was under consideration by Bentley, the first publisher to look at it. Like many people given to procrastination, Dowson linked two unconnected events. 'If the result is favourable,' he wrote, 'I really think I shall be inspired to make the disagreeable necessary overtures in Poland.'[24]

He was aware that the Foltinowicz family had different views on betrothal from those of an English family. He wrote:

one remembers how very much earlier abroad these matters are arranged – and especially in Germany [whence the family had come]. … An English mother would be scandalised at your proposing for the hand of her daughter before she were sixteen; a foreign mother might reasonably be equally scandalised if you were attentive to her daughter, without making your mind clear to her, at a much earlier age. But there are objections either way.[25]

Once he felt that 'things are coming to a crisis'. He described the teas he had alone with Mrs Foltinowicz where they would talk of Adelaide. He wrote excitedly:

We are constantly on the verge of an understanding. Yesterday it was the nearest shave of all. She gave me an admirable occasion. I am sure she expected it. I was just coming out with a protestation, to the effect that my one object and desire in life was to be of service to her admirable daughter – when we were interrupted. We were both curiously moved!

Dowson went out and bought himself a gin and bitters which he spilled all over his shirt in his agitation, and stayed awake all night fretting over the interruption.[26]

Perhaps, matters having come to such a head, he felt he had achieved what was necessary for an understanding and need do no more. Certainly, no direct request for Adelaide's hand took place in 1892. 'I think a sort of tacit understanding establishes itself better and more securely every day,'[27] he wrote to Victor Plarr. Such a tacit understanding might be sufficient for a poet's fine sensibilities; for a Polish restaurateur whose command of English was not good, a more explicit arrangement was required.

The lassitude which tugged at his whole being weighed him down in this, the most difficult decision of his life. He was happy or melancholy about the situation with Adelaide, but what he never could be was the one thing he must be: decisive. His state of mind is aptly demonstrated by his remark, 'I become almost sanguine, although, of course there are all the other difficulties still to be surmounted. It is useless to make plans however, it will arrange itself some way or other.'[28]

The frustrations Dowson's friends and family felt in their dealings with him scream out across the years when one reads such a sentence. Of course he must make plans. Yet his friends were either indifferent or actively against his marriage to Adelaide; they would not encourage him and neither would his parents, if they actually knew the situation in any detail. At his time of most need, he had no help.

To be fair to Dowson, he did set about trying to find paid employment. It was more than apparent that the income from the dock could not support the Dowson family plus the foreman, who was now taking an even more leading role in the business. There were the already grave difficulties that the dock was too small and ill-equipped to deal with the large ships coming up the river, but to add to Dowson and Son's problems, a relaxation of the Port of London regulations now meant ships no longer had to come into a dock but could be refitted mid-stream.

Over the period when Dowson tried to find work his friends helped him as much as they could, though none of them were yet very senior in their own professions. Plarr passed on to him a commission to translate some Heinrich Heine but Dowson felt his German was not up to the task. He was interviewed for a job by someone wanting a person to read German and play the violin to an invalid, but Dowson was no musician. He applied to be secretary of a theatre company. He applied for a job as librarian at Newington Public Library, asking Plarr to recommend him as 'a competent person to hand out dime novels to transpontine shop boys' and requesting Plarr to mention he had a knowledge of French and Italian (but not German, interestingly, though Dowson certainly had more knowledge of the language than he had of Italian). The position carried a salary of £160 and an unfurnished apartment.[29]

To the same end he obtained another reference from Charles Sayle, also a professional librarian, but to no avail. In a later letter he noted pitifully that he could not attach too much importance to the application as 'I am afraid it [the post] is too substantial to be attainable.'[30] These are simply the rejections which have been mentioned in extant letters. Doubtless there were more. For a shy man in a physically weak condition it must have been a torment to face a series of applications, interviews and rejections for jobs he did not want in the first place.

There was, however, still the precarious profession of letters. Dowson retained hopes that he could make a living from writing and in early summer 1892 he received encouragement when Heinemann, the second publisher to whom it was sent, accepted *A Comedy of Masks*. It must have made the young authors very happy. Unfortunately there is no record of this joyous time as Dowson was now living so close to Arthur Moore that the regular interchange of letters ceased. It would be a year before the book was on sale, but their success in having this novel published gave them the impetus to start another.

This time Moore wrote the first chapter of what was to become *Adrian Rome*, and Dowson the second. It is possible to see, therefore, from the first few chapters, how Dowson has a psychological depth and under-standing of his characters far in excess of that of his collaborator. Still, the novel is not a success: there is rather too much in it about the very wealthy, like Adrian Rome himself, and the society of dukes and earls about which Dowson and Moore knew next to nothing from personal experience.

It is, however, of considerable interest biographically. Adrian Rome is a young man who both writes verses and paints. Rome's philosophy is, 'To be concerned with high passions, to live as fully and intensely as one could, rather than as long and as peacefully as one might, – it seemed to him that it was only under such conditions that the born artist could properly work out his salvation.'[31] Rome's life is full, as Dowson's was, of people ques-tioning: what is the artistic life? Rather as in earlier centuries the young had agonized over the question of what was the truly devout life. 'His successes are brilliant, but his failures more frequent,' another character says of Rome, and this is not his only similarity to Dowson. He has 'a habit of abstraction' and 'a nervous horror of making up his mind; he expected the future to arrange itself for him without the necessity for cogitation on his part.'[32]

This indecision is central to the plot. Adrian has never been to school, he is an orphan who has been brought up with a tutor in the countryside, the responsibility of his guardian, Lord Hildebrand. It is in the country that he comes into contact with Sylvia Drew, a beautiful and innocent girl five years his junior, so she is 14 when he is 19. There is a charged scene between the two of them written when Dowson was beset by personal confusion and conflicting advice about his relationship with Adelaide, which clearly was the source for much of the emotional material. When he is due to leave for Oxford, Adrian tells Sylvia he will come back for her. She protests that there are barriers to their relationship; they cannot continue to be intimate friends as they were when they were children; they are grown-up now. Adrian Rome protests that they can stay close, virtually asking her to marry him but not quite doing so, as he thinks,

> Life without her seemed impossible and cruel. But there was none the less a note of unreality in his words, of which he could not but be dimly conscious, and of which the consciousness irritated him, against society, against circumstances, against himself. Lightly as he glossed over them, there were difficulties in the way of this relation, differences which grew larger as one looked at them close.

She tells him not to treat her like a little girl, remarking, 'I am thinking of your position, your place in the world. I can see things now, the difference between us. We are altogether different: even your way of talking is different to mine, and mother's ... we must go our different ways, with our own folk.' His friends, she says, will never accept her. But even as she says this he realizes, 'that she was a grand creature, far too precious to lose, that it was impossible to let her go.'[33]

His friend Lord Henry emphasizes the view of what Dowson called 'the world': 'You must see, she is not your equal. It isn't even a kindness to marry her; it's damnation for both of you.' Rome tells him, as Dowson must have told his friends, 'You must leave me to settle this matter with my conscience, or consciences – I have several which you know nothing about, and wouldn't understand.'[34]

Eventually his own scruples and Sylvia's common sense prevail and he foolishly marries a society woman, in order to do what is expected of him, which is also the symbolic sacrifice of his art to the things of the world. In time he meets Sylvia again, who has since become an actress and he a playwright. His loveless marriage has completely broken down and he asks Sylvia to come away with him on his yacht. She writes to him that she will not, but cannot withhold herself. She goes down to Southampton where he had said he would meet her but she is too late: he has died saving a drunken sailor from drowning.

There were long lacunae in the writing of Adrian Rome, and by the time the book was finished Dowson had long since lost interest in it so Moore had to complete it himself. This may be the cause of some of its deficiencies, not least the pusillanimous ending. For Dowson, the death would have had to be suicide or at least equivocal – leaving an uncertainty as to whether it had been suicide or an accident.

There are some interesting portraits of men in Dowson's circle in *Adrian Rome.* Lionel Johnson was the original for Gerald Brooke whom Rome meets at Oxford; the actor Marmaduke Langdale was the model for Archie Longdale and it is possible that the journalist in the novel, Dalrymple Green, is based on Frank Harris. None of these portraits, however, have any depth or development. Yet it is more than tempting to see in the paradoxical descriptions of Sylvia a reflection of Dowson's confusion over Adelaide.

Adrian Rome ponders, as Dowson must have done in the months when he was working on these scenes, how

> there was to be no more of the old, frank love-making, when there was no need to count the kisses, to think of the morrow. Sylvia had of a sudden become desperately practical, surprisingly worldly. ... A Sylvia with whom one had to pick and choose one's words; to be on one's guard: he found the development somewhat disconcerting. She had never looked so charming, she had never treated him so unkindly. He was desperately in love with the creature ... but he was bewildered, tired, uncomfortable.[35]

Dauntingly, as Adelaide grew up she became more adept than Dowson at dealing with the world, as anyone would be but a child.

CHAPTER 7

THE ADVENTURE OF LITERATURE

The two years between summer 1892 and summer 1894 were the happiest of his life, though Ernest Dowson would not have recognized this at the time. It was a period of rewarding friendships and a success which, if not glamorous, was at least well grounded in hard work. He was writing verse and stories which had ready publication, had one novel accepted and was starting on another, and was asked by the American actor and poet William Theodore Peters to write what became his only play, *The Pierrot of the Minute*.

Peters, a 'permanent guest' at the Rhymers' Club, lived in London and later in Paris in the 1890s. Dowson and Peters used to go to the theatre together and Dowson wrote warmly to him from the middle of summer 1892. He asked Dowson to write him a Pierrot play: a short, very mannered production featuring the traditional French character Pierrot who is tall and thin and wears a white costume with his face whitened. Peters, it seemed, had consented to perform a piece for a Mrs Hartshorn who was producing an evening's entertainment in aid of the Primrose League, a Conservative Party organization dedicated to the memory of Disraeli.

The pay was slight, but Dowson had always admired drama and he went with some enthusiasm to the task of composing a verse play in the three weeks Peters gave him for it. He was soon saying his agreement had been 'rash', that it was 'mightily oppressing me. And I am horribly afraid that when it is written I may be worried with rehearsals and enforced company with terrible South Kensington young ladies and fashionable Chelsea Mesdames.'[1]

Dowson worked frantically in his longest ever period of sustained labour and managed to produce the play in time. He had to copy out the parts for Peters and the other actor, Ida North, but very late in the day Peters told Dowson he must make another copy and obtain a licence from the censor, the Lord Chamberlain, without whose permission no play could be performed. Dowson had days of fretting about this, wishing he had never been foolish enough to write a play, and asking around his friends to find out how to go about obtaining a licence. He was unwell after his exertions in writing the piece, and also felt very put upon, complaining that 'Peters is very indignant with me because I refuse to complete the catastrophe by running off to rehearsals at all hours of the day and night.'[2]

The Pierrot of the Minute was licensed, with a few days to spare, and the first performance took place at Chelsea Town Hall on 22 November 1892. Dowson's guests included his parents, John Gray, Teixeira de Mattos (with whom Dowson was to collaborate in translations), Herbert Horne and Arthur Symons. In the play the lights come up to reveal a glade in the Parc du Petit Trianon at Versailles. In the centre is a Doric temple, with steps coming down to the stage, on the left a little cupid on a pedestal. It is twilight. Enter Pierrot with his hands full of lilies and a little basket from which he soon produces a flask of wine. He is joined by the Moon Maiden, a personified moonbeam who is pursued by Pierrot, eludes him and finally teaches him how to love her, but before their love can be consummated, it is daybreak and she must depart. She says,

> Go forth and seek in each fair face in vain,
> To find the image of thy love again.
> All maids are kind to thee, yet never one
> Shall hold thy truant heart till day be done.

She then sings a song – popularized as 'The Moon Maiden's Song', to lull him to sleep.

The writer of Amateur Dramatic Notes in the *Lady's Pictorial* on 3 December 1892 said that the play suffered from an 'awkward plunge into bathos' but Cecile in *Woman* of 30 November 1892 was more positive, calling it 'a delicate little drama in porcelain'. The play, which is in heroic couplets (iambic pentameters rhyming AA BB) has more generously been described as a symphony in white, with the two characters plus the stage in white, and white light playing a dramatic part.

'Symphony' is an interesting description, considering that *The Pierrot of the Minute* has given itself more easily than Dowson's other work to musical presentation. 'The Moon Maiden's Song' was later set to music by Noel Johnson, but there is no record of Dowson's opinion of the resulting effect. Still later, after Dowson's death, Grenville Bantock scored the entire play and it became a pièce de résistance at classical concerts.

It was also performed at the Officers' Club, Aldershot with the stringed band of the Royal Horse Artillery playing *The Moonlight Sonata* softly at intervals throughout it. The following year it was played at a studio before an invited audience in Clareville Grove, Kensington. Dowson had trouble filling his eight complimentary seats but John Gray and Teixeira de Mattos came again, joining Arthur Moore, Dowson's cousin the actor Gerald Hoole, and another actor friend called Charles Goodhart who lived in the Temple with de Mattos and Calvert Swanton. There were other performances: Plarr remembered at least one in which Mabel Beardsley, sister of Aubrey, took the role of the Moon Maiden.

The brilliant illustrator Aubrey Beardsley, who was 21 in 1893 when he first started going to the Crown, was one of a number of new people Dowson met in the period when literary London was sparking with excitement. It was a time of hope and enthusiasm, when artists came from all over the world to meet their contemporaries in the bars and music halls of the West End.

One such was the novelist Edgar Jepson whom Dowson had perhaps met briefly at Oxford. Jepson had returned from four years in Barbados in 1893, to try his hand at the 'Adventure of Literature' in London. He was invited by Selwyn Image and Victor Plarr to go to the saloon bar of the Crown where he met Dowson and quickly recognized a fellow classicist and lover of Swinburne. Jepson wrote of Dowson's conversation that he, 'was always the dreamer; his eyes were always a little bemused; always he seemed to awake, to withdraw himself from some aloof world of the imagination to come into our talk. Awakened he talked well, but he only took the trouble to talk much on his own subjects, literature and beauty.'[3]

> He had the air of being submerged in a dream, and plainly enough he rose out of that dream only when you called him into the world in which he was actually moving. But he was not really concerned with it, and I think that a great deal of his uncommon charm came from that attitude to life: he never cared enough for this world to pose before it. It was the charm of an uncommon simplicity and sincerity, and the charm of an extraordinary gentleness. He was always just Ernest Dowson. It was a delightful person to be.[4]

Two days after meeting Dowson in the Crown, Jepson visited him at his detested dock. The guest remembered, 'We lunched in an office that was half office and half sitting room and gritty to the eye and cold, with a dreary December view through the ill-fitting eighteenth-century window on to the water of the dock. We munched on cold boiled beef, from a Stepney cook-shop, and bread and cheese and beer.' More convivial were the card parties where Dowson, Jepson, Teixeira de Mattos, Arthur Moore and some of the actors they knew would gamble in Teixeira's rooms, or at the

Author's Club of which Jepson was a member; or they would go to Moore's house in St John's Wood which they attained by 'the choking Underground Railway' newly built to take travellers to this place which was, Jepson remarked, 'out of civilisation'.[5]

Dowson's drinking was rarely out of control at this time. Jepson said:

> As long as I could keep Dowson to wine or beer, he was sober enough. When his nervous irritation with life drove him to the poisonous juice of the potato, there was little to be done. Sometimes when we left the Crown I would get him to my lodgings, sobering him up by the long walk; sometimes I gave it up and left him to that Providence which makes drunken men its special care.[6]

Jepson's lodgings up to the beginning of 1895 were in Harleyford Road, Vauxhall. Dowson would accompany him there to sleep in an armchair. Jepson remarked that his friend, 'had the cat's happy aptitude for sleeping where night found him.'[7] Neither were very talkative in the mornings and the two breakfasted in a sombre silence: '... we must have looked like two mortal enemies forced to feed together, and the silence lasted until he went away to that chilly dock.'[8]

Jepson once asked his friend to write in his birthday book, and Dowson contributed, 'The small things of life are odious to me, and the habit of them enslaves me; the great things of life are eternally attractive to me, but indolence and fear put them by.' Dowson was fond of this remark, he believed it to be a quotation but could not recall whence it came.

Another cosmopolitan attracted to London was the journalist Frank Harris, who was born in Ireland but was brought up in the USA. He met Dowson intermittently through the 1890s but got to know him well in this period of Dowson's life, when Harris was editing the *Fortnightly Review*. He said Dowson

> was very like Keats without Keats's strength or joy in life; a fragile, scholarly Keats. On first acquaintance shy; yet impulsive and frank with a singular charm of manner; he appealed to the heart as some girls do with a child's confidence and a child's hesitancy and a sort of awkward unexpected grace, quite indescribable. He was gentle too and gay with quaint quirks of verse, unprintable often, amusing always – a delightful companion, quick-changing as an April day ... he was sensitive to all courtesies, vibrant with enthusiasms, yet instinctively considerate. ... Under his shyness he was intensely affectionate; when moved, he liked to touch and caress one as a woman does and loving kindness and mental companionship were what he most desired on earth and most prized.

One day they had lunch together. Harris said:

> I was astonished by his range of reading and his intimacy with the Latins, especially Propertius; he was saturated too in French and Italian poetry and had modern English verse at his tongue's tip ... he loved Horace and any curious, arresting epithet pleased him beyond measure. I said something about "eventful

originality" and he jumped up and clapped his hands and crowed with delight, repeating again and again "eventful ... eventful originality".[9]

They went for a stroll in Hyde Park and Dowson quoted his poem 'Sapientia Lunae' (The Wisdom of the Moon). He was evidently prepared to recite his verse to an individual, however unhappy he was to do so for an audience like that of the Rhymers. The two spent the afternoon and evening together, dining at the Café Royal. This was an occasion when Dowson was all day in the West End, something which must have happened increasingly often as work at the dock dried up. The ease with which he took time off from the dock to write *The Pierrot of the Minute*, too, testifies to the limited use Bridge Dock was making of his talents.

Another of Dowson's friends from the Crown was Alexander Louis Teixeira de Mattos San Payo y Mendes, normally called Teixeira de Mattos. He was a multilingual Dutchman who had been brought up in England and who was to become the most sought-after translator in the country, at a time when there was a great appetite for foreign literary work, which was morally more adventurous than English fare.

In autumn 1893 Dowson was asked by Teixeira to translate Zola's *La Terre* (The Earth) for a fee of £50. He was eager to do so. He had long admired Zola and had spent hours sitting up into the night discussing the great novelist with his biographer, Robert Harborough Sherard, in Teixeira's rooms. Sherard normally lived in Paris at this time, but had come over with Zola on the novelist's successful visit to London at the head of a delegation of French writers.

Teixeira and a small group of his acquaintances had formed the Lutetian Society to translate and publish works which appealed to the educated elite who generally had a supercilious attitude to what passed for morality in the Victorian period. The intended limited circulation was partly from what would later be termed intellectual elitism, but mainly for very practical reasons.

Many of Zola's novels – and the work of other French writers – had been translated and circulated in the 1880s by the publisher Henry Vizetelly. He was attacked in the *Pall Mall Gazette* by the puritans' terrier W.T. Stead, who also gave assistance to the National Vigilance Association which issued a summons for obscenity against Henry Vizetelly in respect of three of Zola's novels: *La Terre*, *Pot-Bouille* (Piping Hot), and *Nana*. At the trial in October 1888 at the Old Bailey the Solicitor General, Sir Edward Clarke, gave his literary judgement of *La Terre*: 'This book is filth from beginning to end. I do not believe there was ever collected together between the pages of a bound volume so much bestial obscenity as is to be found in almost every page of this work ... there is not a single scene described which is free from vicious suggestion and obscene expressions.'[10] He demonstrated by reading from a scene about a bull mating, at which the shocked jury told him to stop as it was too offensive to them even to hear it read out. Vizetelly's counsel almost immediately threw in the towel and advised his client to plead guilty. Vizetelly was admonished, fined £100, entered into a good behaviour bond for 12 months, and ordered not to circulate any of Zola's books as obscene as the ones which had been prosecuted.

Vizetelly therefore continued selling other Zola novels, which were mild in content or could be rendered so with editing. W.T. Stead and the National Vigilance Association had scented blood, however, and they issued another summons. In May 1889 Vizetelly stood trial again, this time for circulating another five Zola novels, and Maupassant's *Bel Ami*. He was sentenced to four months in prison. He had been seriously ill during his trials, and died four years after his release from Holloway.

To undertake the translation of Zola within four years of the last translator's imprisonment was a high risk endeavour, therefore, and it is a test of the character of this weak and indecisive man that when an issue which really mattered was involved, one of artistic integrity, Dowson was undaunted by the dangers. Nor was he alone: Teixeira was translating *Pot-Bouille*, Arthur Symons *L'Assommoir* (The Drunkard), and Victor Plarr *Nana*. The Lutetian Society argued that if their translations were sold at two guineas (£2.10) each, they could not be accused of corrupting public morals as the books would not be available to the public, only to the upper class. They were in a quite different situation, it was reasoned, from Vizetelly who issued his books at six shillings (30p) with illustrations and five (25p) without, making them widely available to people who were considered to be morally at risk, as the educated and wealthy were not.

Dowson was soon enjoying Zola less, writing that he was 'working tooth and nail to get a translation done of that wearisome work *La Terre* at the stipulated time.'[11] He eventually borrowed fellow Rhymer Arthur Hillier's country cottage at Easter in order to spend his time getting a solid 20 pages a day written. Teixeira had to prompt Dowson repeatedly to finish the translation at a time near to the deadline he had set. Plarr writes that he discussed the finer points of the translation with Dowson from time to time, 'finally deciding to render certain Rabelaisian phrases into something less offensive in English – into common cleanly blasphemies at least.'[12]

There is a tale that Teixeira promised the task of translating *La Terre* to Dowson then tried to have George Moore undertake it. Moore refused rudely, and Dowson berated him for being so impolite to his friend Teixeira. Unfortunately the story is so obscured by the fastidiousness of its reporters, unwilling to quote exact words, that it is impossible to establish who said what, or even if it has any basis in fact.

It is said that Teixeira de Mattos distanced himself from Dowson because of his unkempt appearance. Dowson was always careless of his wardrobe, and even when well-dressed he looked as if he had slept in his clothes, as he often had. Teixeira's rooms were Dowson's most frequent resting place after the Crown had closed though there is a report that Teixeira de Mattos was sometimes eager for Dowson to leave at night.

Teixeira was certainly a dandy and may well have taken exception to Dowson's appearance on a number of occasions, but he frequently played cards with him, dined with him at Poland, and went twice to performances of *The Pierrot of the Minute*; so they were not arm's-length acquaintances in the 1893–4 period when Dowson was translating for him. Still, Robert Sherard noticed something of a coldness about Teixeira's relations with Dowson, remarking that Teixeira possessed that 'flair which scents dissolution and reveals to those who possess it which men amongst their acquaintances are not going to be prosperous in life.'[13]

While the rationale for the Lutetian Society's high cover charge for its books was enough to forestall legal action, it also impeded profitability. The translations were under-subscribed and the 300 copies of Dowson's *La Terre* were not all sold. It was a personal success for Dowson, however, in that he now had a solid translation of a major work to his credit and could seek other work as a translator – which became his principal means of income for the rest of his life.

Teixeira de Mattos later asked Dowson to complete a translation of the novel *Majesty* by Louis Couperus for him. In 1894 he was asked to join with two other Rhymers' Club members, George Greene and Arthur Hillier, in the translation of a three-volume history of art from the German, Richard Muther's *Geschichte der Malerei im Neunzehnten Jahrhundert* (History of Modern Painting). Where Dowson learned enough German to translate a work like this is unknown – he never even visited a German-speaking country – but he successfully completed his share of the more than 2000 pages.

Dowson has been given little credit for his skill as a linguist or the determination with which a naturally lethargic man put in long hours on translating work with which he had little sympathy. He translated far more than the works listed in his bibliography would suggest. Edgar Jepson recalls going to Bridge Dock to work on an eight-hour shift of translation with Dowson in what must have been 1893 or 1894. They translated a volume of French memoirs 'as fast as we could in turn drive the pen to the other's dictation.'[14]

He had to learn to work fast, as translation paid so poorly. In a bar off Leicester Square, Dowson recited some of his translation of Verlaine to Frank Harris who said that while it caught the sadness of Verlaine's verse, the translation was really rather poor. "'So was the price paid for it," he laughed, "a measly ten shillings.'"[15]

Still, Dowson's admiration for Paul Verlaine was uncurtailed. He was the most lyrical of the French poets, a link between the Romantic poets and the decadents, guiding French verse away from the rhetoric of his predecessors and towards a poetry of nuance and music. Arthur Symons wrote, 'Verlaine's poetry has varied with his life; always in excess – now furiously sensual, now feverishly devout – he has been constant only to himself, to his own self-contradictions.'[16] He was an older counterpart of Dowson in many ways: in his sensuality and religious devotion, his heavy drinking, and in his unusual loves. When he was 26 he fell in love with 16-year-old Mathilde Maute and they married the following year, though they later parted because of Verlaine's love for the younger poet Arthur Rimbaud.

Dowson was introduced to Verlaine when Arthur Symons and the historian York Powell invited the French poet to lecture in Britain in November 1893. On the day after his arrival Dowson was invited to Arthur Symons' Fountain Court rooms to meet Verlaine in the company of Symons, John Lane, Herbert Horne, Hubert Crackanthorpe, the musician Arnold Dolmetsch, Symons sometime girlfriend Muriel Broadbent and a young woman identified only as Miss Belloc who called to interview Verlaine.[17]

Dowson looked forward to meeting him, and on a later day dined with Verlaine, Herbert Horne and Horne's father at the Constitutional. He wrote to Plarr, 'If I have the courage I will even suggest to the master that he should honour his disciples with a visit to the Cheese.'[18] While it is questionable how many of the Rhymers actually considered themselves to be disciples of Verlaine the way Dowson did, it is said that all the Rhymers attended Verlaine's lecture at Barnard's Inn in High Holborn. Verlaine did not visit the Cheshire Cheese, perhaps because Dowson could not summon the courage to invite him.

Verlaine later went to see the sites of bohemian London, like the Alhambra, a place of some wistful nostalgia for Verlaine: he was now lame as a result of syphilis he believed he contracted from a prostitute he met on leaving there 20 years before. He had been in exile in England following the fall of the Paris Commune in 1871, to whose council he had been press officer. The London decadents also took him to the Crown where one of the company taught a ballet girl just enough French to proposition the ageing poet, to everyone's amusement. Verlaine went on to lecture at Oxford and Salford, then returned to Paris.

Dowson's place in these major literary events shows he was never less than highly regarded by his friends and those of the public who had access to his work. While he was never paid enough for his work to live easily, he certainly did not suffer the pain of literary obscurity and incessant rejection. The time for the publication of *A Comedy of Masks* approached in autumn 1893, and Dowson viewed it with some trepidation. He wrote to Plarr, 'I tremble at the prospect of being reviewed – I am painfully conscious of the innumerable blemishes and alas! the weakest points are in the first volume so that I fear sleep will overcome the reviewer before he reaches any of our less banal passages. What fools we are to write – or rather to publish!'[19]

The novelists' first good notice came from *The Bookman*, which reviewed both the book, 'an interesting novel of artistic life', and the authors. It briefly mentioned the facts of Dowson's life, including that he was a Catholic, so Dowson must have stressed this in whatever biographical material he gave to Heinemann. The article continued, 'Since leaving Oxford he has lived chiefly in London, and has been steadily making his way in literature.' It mentioned his contributions to *Temple Bar, Macmillan's*, the *Hobby Horse, The Book of the Rhymers' Club* and his forthcoming contribution to the new Rhymers' book. It said a volume of his own verse would soon be published by Mathews and Lane, and that the collaborative authors were now at work on their new novel.[20] Dowson thought *The Bookman* had made 'quite a creditable article of our meagre biographies, although it is news to me that I have been "steadily making my way in literature".'[21]

The review of the book said, 'While showing some marks of immaturity, some looseness of construction, perhaps the consequence of collaboration, some over profuseness of description which makes the story needlessly long, this novel of artistic life in London is a book of promise and power. When these defects have been mentioned, and one's conscience thus relieved, one can praise without stint.' It asked for more work from the authors.

Less positively, the *Athenaeum* said it was 'subtle and interesting rather than convincing'.[22] The *Spectator* said, 'the authors have it in them to do a work that, if not stronger, shall be less faulty,'[23] and *The Critic* said it was the 'same old thing told in the same old way'[24] which implies the reviewer had not read it, hardly a unique occurrence. 500 copies of the book were printed in 1893 and they sold sufficiently well for another edition of a thousand to be published in 1894. *A Comedy of Masks* was also published in America.

Now Dowson was a name in the world of the arts, he began to be invited to the salons of the fashionable in Kensington and Chelsea. It was not his natural milieu, and he was not a frequent attender, but he went at least once with Lionel Johnson to the salon of Sir John and Lady Simon in Kensington Square. Simon was a former friend of Ruskin, Thackeray, Rossetti, Ellen Terry and William Morris. Dowson later talked of meeting an old lady there, a survivor of the time of Waterloo.[25] Dowson also attended the salon of Sir Joseph and Lady Prestwich, and went to gatherings at the home of Professor and Mrs Warr, but such social engagements were occasional – Dowson's friendships were made in the bars and music halls.

Dowson may have attended Father Stewart Headlam's Church and Stage parties where ballet girls mixed with men in supposedly respectable professions, and which Plarr describes as 'a brilliant and picturesque episode in the crowded artistic life of the early nineties.'[26] Only Dowson's apologies for non-attendance are extant, as in his writing in January 1893, 'I was too sick and sorry to come. I fear my affairs will not bear talking over, or writing about. They are like a Chinese puzzle; and grow more confused and inextricable the closer one considers them. ... It is a vile and stupid world; and it will be good to have done with it.'[27]

He appended the poem 'Terre Promise' (Promised Land) whose last two verses show how he still held back form declaring himself at Poland:

Always I know, how little severs me
From mine heart's country, that is yet so far;
And must I lean and long across a bar,
That half a word would shatter utterly?

Ah might it be, that just by touch of hand,
Or speaking silence, shall the barrier fall;
And she shall pass, with no vain words at all,
But droop into mine arms, and understand!

The chance that Adelaide herself would make the first move, and swoon into his arms, was remote indeed. Not that she did not fully appreciate his position. Dowson wrote, 'I am no longer in the least doubtful that to Her I am perfectly obvious.' She could be very cruel to him, such that he remarks upon it when she has been pleasant for a length of time. 'She has been extraordinarily sweet for the last four weeks,' he wrote to Victor Plarr, 'so that in spite of my invincible pessimism I begin to think that there is, really, behind her double perversity of enfant gâteé [spoiled child] and jeune fille coquette [flirtatious young girl] a solid foundation of affection.'[28] It was hardly a glowing testimonial to her.

Another crisis approached at Poland in spring 1893 as Adelaide's fifteenth birthday neared. Her father Joseph Foltinowicz had long been unwell. Dowson wrote the previous year that his 'days are obviously numbered' and hinted at the cause when he remarked, 'I have hardly the right to reproach him with an undue love of alcohol.'[29] Still, Dowson had found him 'genial and harmless enough' and had always been treated with a great deal of consideration by the older man. It is clear from these dismissive descriptions of Adelaide's father that hers was a house in which women made all the decisions, which explains why Dowson was so eager to declare himself to Mrs Foltinowicz, not her husband.

By April 1893 Dowson reported that her father had been 'given up by the doctors and sinks from day to day'.[30] He did what he could as a friend of the family, and asked a solicitor he knew, W.B. Campbell, to help Foltinowicz draw up a will. Campbell, a Catholic, also called in a priest for the dying man. It is tempting to think that 'Extreme Unction', one of Dowson's finest poems which was finished later this year, was to some extent inspired by this visit. The poem begins,

Upon the eyes, the lips, the feet,

On all the passages of sense,
The atoning oil is spread with sweet
Renewal of lost innocence,

The atmosphere of death translated itself in Dowson's heart into an unbearably poignant affection. Dowson always wrote of death with a soft, longing manner, and death inspired tenderness in him as other human events did not. The long evenings of vigil at the unnaturally quiet restaurant in Sherwood Street, with the constant presence of Adelaide in her sorrowful state, exerted a powerful influence over the poet.

Adelaide was displaying alarming changes of mood: sometimes charming, at others hardly speaking to Dowson, which left him distraught and strained to breaking point. He was also acutely aware that Foltinowicz's death would change the structure of the family, though he did not know exactly how. One evening in April when the doctors had despaired of Foltinowicz's life, and there was nothing for the family to do but wait, Dowson and Adelaide found each other alone together. They spoke in lowered tones of her father's condition. The pressure of death in the house, his love for his 'Missie', and his own frustration at his weakness all proved too much for Dowson and he asked her to marry him.

He then realized this was the wrong thing to have said, and immediately begged her forgiveness. Was she angry with him? he inquired. Adelaide must have known this was coming for some time but hardly expected it now, two days before her fifteenth birthday and while her father lay dying. Still, she took it with what Dowson called, 'a great deal of dignity and self-possession' and he added, 'I don't think I have ever admired her more.'[31]

Adelaide reminded him that she was too young, but said that she was not surprised at his proposal, 'and that she was not angry', which he found a relief. He now retreated in confusion from his bold position, as he wrote to his friend Sam Smith, 'Of course I had asked her for no answer – I merely left her with no possible reason to doubt my seriousness in the matter. Finally I suggested that she should forget what I had said for the present – and that we should resume our ancient relations and be excellent friends – and nothing more.'[32]

Dowson left, later confessing, 'I feel as if I had made a hopeless, not very creditable fool of myself,'[33] and spent the night awake, in emotional turmoil. He feared he had destroyed any chance of ever marrying Adelaide by proposing directly to her, in such a clumsy way and at such an inopportune moment.

The following day, however, Mrs Foltinowicz reassured him. She also must have had an eye on the future, as she was now going to have to run the business without her husband. 'Nothing could possibly exceed her extreme kindness and delicacy,' Dowson reported. She did not resent his proposing to Adelaide without her permission, on the contrary, she seemed rather pleased. Ernest Dowson may not have been every mother's idea of a perfect son-in-law, but he was more of a gentleman than any other young man with whom Adelaide might come into contact. Mrs Foltinowicz told Dowson in her imperfect English, which must have made sensitive nuance difficult to express, that Adelaide, 'would like the idea in a year or two' as he paraphrased it in a letter.[34]

Dowson described the funeral with its distressing delays, the slow cortege and the earth falling on the coffin lid. He kept his eyes on Adelaide and said, 'I was amazed to see her during the last difficult week – that immensely trying time which has to elapse between a death and a burial – quite the cruellest part of death – she was intensely distressed and worn out, and perfectly composed. It was the same at the cemetery, when extraneous womankind were dissolved in tears, she stood like a little statue.'[35]

Dowson had gone through a period of torment, three exhausting weeks in which he felt he had been travelling the whole time, sleeping in his clothes and lacking bed and baths. At the end of it he had gained nothing at all or, rather, what he had gained he had immediately given away. He wrote, 'The understanding is that we should not allude to the thing any more for the present, but go on as before.'[36] Adelaide found no difficulty at all in this, and did not refer to the matter again. Dowson said, 'We are both a little embarrassed – I more than she perhaps – and sometimes she drives me to despair by her coldness.'[37]

In a revealing remark, Dowson wished he had a woman friend with whom to discuss his predicament: 'The mind of a girl, of a girl of that age, is such an inexplicable country to oneself; but a woman might give one clues.' He was left visiting Poland nightly in the hope of a kind word or even a chaste kiss from Adelaide, and pondering the conundrum he had constructed: 'I am not very sanguine; if she liked me less or had not known me so long, I believe, my chance would be much better.'[38]

There were other trials for Dowson in 1893: he was mugged while taking a stroll in the area around the dock house, knocked out and robbed of a small sum of money. Early in the year the youngest boy of the foreman at the dock was drowned, and Dowson wrote he had to get away. 'I cannot stay any longer in this atmosphere of dreariness and tears.'[39] It may have been this child he was thinking of when he wrote the poem 'The Dead Child' with its lines,

> Lie still, and be
>   For evermore a child!
> Not grudgingly,
>   Whom life has not defiled,

This welcoming of death is a common theme for Dowson and it could relate to a dead child in general, not one in particular, or could even be a reference back to the same child referred to in Dowson's teenage poems.

Dowson's family moved again in August 1893, having spent only two years at Maida Hill. Perhaps in search of cheaper lodgings, they went to Chadwell Heath, on the edge of Epping Forest, though Ernest Dowson kept his rooms at the dock as his base. He did go to his parents' home, however, that August, when he was 26 years old, to recover from his first attack of tuberculosis. The family was more than well acquainted with the disease and there was no mistaking its symptoms, which were a haemorrhage of the lungs causing violent coughing and the spitting of blood. The only treatment was rest, which would allow the injured tissues to heal, though the bacteria which caused the disease would still be steadily working to damage the lung still further.

Victor Plarr noticed the following year that consumption 'seemed to have got him in its clutches'. His severe colds which he shook off with difficulty were an early sign and Plarr added contributory factors: 'the uncomfortable nights on sofas, the unwise and innutritious dinners he ate, his fondness for fantastic vigils'[40] to which could be added his heavy smoking and, of course, his drinking.

Tuberculosis is a very slow disease, and even in the late nineteenth century could often be kept at bay for so long that the patient was in the happy position of dying from something else. The Dowson family had not the money to provide him with travel to a warmer climate, nor had Dowson himself the inclination to the good food, reduced drinking and rest which he needed. Ernest Dowson must have now known his fate was going to be that of Keats with whom he was so often compared: 'youth grows pale, and spectre-thin, and dies.'[41]

CHAPTER 8

BRIGHT LIGHTS

Dowson made light of his illness, simply confiding to Moore, 'I had a nasty jar on account of my lung,' when he apologized for not producing more of his share of *Adrian Rome*.[1] Most people did not realize he was consumptive until the disease had reached an unmistakable advanced stage, and Dowson always shunned pity. He was secretive about personal matters to an extreme degree, his reticence meaning that even those friends quite close to him who later wrote memoirs, like Edgar Jepson, were incorrect in significant details.

Dowson showed some evidence of a new prosperity at the time of his modest literary successes. He began to dress better, so much so, according to Jepson, that Dowson in his frock coat and silk hat was the best dressed poet he had seen. He had well-made French boots and took to wearing coloured cravats, though this was a short-lived excursion into fashionable neckwear and he later took to fastening his collar with a string of black ribbon. He would take cabs more frequently than in the past, and was able to exercise his habitual generosity with regard to buying rounds of drinks, about which he was insistent, even when others felt he had already paid more than his fair share.

The exact source of his new-found wealth is not clear. Dowson was probably receiving a little money from the dock, though this was soon to cease, and he received some from translations and from the rest of his literary output. Robert Sherard described *A Comedy of Masks* as 'a commercial as well as an artistic success', though the sums of money involved were small.[2] As a matter of conjecture, the most likely source would be that one of the relatives in his extended family had died and he received a small share of the inheritance. It was an unremarkable occurrence for the middle class in Victorian England where families were large and death commonplace.

Whatever the source of his short-lived affluence, it enabled Dowson to spend more time in the Café Royal and at the fashionable music halls. He

often fell into the company of Arthur Symons, fellow Rhymer and liber-
tine, the music hall critic of the *Star* newspaper who dressed to fit the part
with his longish hair, top hat and black cloak. Symons, two years older than
Dowson, was the son of a Wesleyan minister though he had rejected the
strict Methodism of his parents in his youth. He moved to London in 1891
and set up as a literary critic, taking rooms on Fountain Court which
became a frequent meeting place for selected decadents.

Symons wrote:

> Night after night, when I had my window curtains drawn and the light shone
> through them, I was more or less besieged with men and women ... who
> climbed up the steep stairs and began to hammer at my oak door, which was as
> impenetrable as the Gates of Hell. Whenever I heard a knock at the door I
> gazed through the muslin curtains that covered the little window in the narrow
> passage, as discreetly as a woman's veil conceals her face, and if it chanced to
> be Dowson or Yeats or certain other people, I let them in; otherwise never!
> Dowson was always at his best when he came alone: then we talked without
> end, deep into the night. Sometimes we would wander down the deserted
> streets near Covent Garden; where, when one drink had made him unreason-
> able, I had to drag him bodily back from some chance encounter with a
> policeman.[3]

Symons' poetry dealt with London life, the music halls and his sexual
encounters. He wrote, 'Sex, the infernal fascination of Sex – even before I
actually realised the meaning of its stirrings in me – has been my chief
obsession. One's own Vitality: that is a centre of Life and Death.' He
described Dowson as 'morbid and neurotic' sexually but the only evidence
put forward for this, that Dowson told him he was more sexually excited
by a woman's breasts than any other part of her anatomy, shows a pecca-
dillo which falls far short of pathology.[4] John Gray remarked that Dowson
picked up a woman (presumably a prostitute) almost every night.[5]

Symons notes that Dowson did not particularly like the ballet though he
was happy enough to meet Symons' friends among the ballet girls. He
writes of a time when Dowson and another friend of his, the historian
John Addington Symonds on a visit to London arrived, 'then the ballet-
girls, one after another, whose laughter and whose youth always enchanted
me.' They took hashish after their tea and cakes but it had no apparent
effect on Dowson, 'as he sat, a little anxiously, with, as his habit was, his
chin on his breast, awaiting the magic, half shy in the midst of that bright
company of young people.'[6] Symons mentions that hashish had been
Dowson's 'favourite form of intoxication' at Oxford. He is quite mistaken
in this, but may well have been misled by Dowson himself. Symons may
have said he was going to obtain some hashish and Dowson said, 'I used to
take it at college' or words to that effect. Symons has been unjustly blamed
for this simple error, it being said that he gave a false impression that
Dowson was a frequent drug-taker. He was not, but even if he had been,

he would have been contemptuous of anyone who had criticized him for it. His attitude to drug-taking, including the use of opium, was always amused toleration.

Often Dowson would go to a music hall with his acting and literary friends: to the Empire or Alhambra in Leicester Square, more often to the Oxford in Oxford Street, the Tivoli in the Strand, the Mogul in Drury Lane or to Gatti's under the arches of Charing Cross Station. In some of these theatres prostitutes of a higher class than common street-walkers would walk around the promenade at the rear of the dress circle on the second level. It was at the Alhambra that Arthur Symons met Muriel Broadbent who became a member of the circles in which Dowson and Symons moved. She helped him with hospitality when Verlaine visited, for example. They met when Symons had left the promenade of the Alhambra to go to the stalls and he saw 'a shy girl ... evidently very ill at ease'. He invited her to have a drink with him which she did willingly and told him her story. She was the daughter of a physician, but both her parents were dead. She had worked in a laundry but found it arduous and ill-paid, and had come to London to try her luck at prostitution.[7] She became Symons' lover, and also Herbert Horne's. Symons said Horne treated her cruelly, though he did set her up in a flat whose rent he paid, and she continued to see Symons, 'when her men made her exasperated,' he said.[8]

Dowson had a more regular girlfriend than usual at this time too, whose background was probably similar to that of Muriel and who probably met her men friends in a similar way. Dulcie, whose second name is not known, was 'a pretty, dark girl, a lively companion with a girlish sense of humour' according to Jepson.[9] She would often be with Dowson in the Crown and her lively intellect meant she was more than welcome with the poets and artists of bohemian life in London. She may well have been an artist's model as her rooms were decorated with drawings by numerous artists. This is also suggested by her striking manner of attracting attention one time when she felt she was being ignored. She was with some men of Dowson's circle in the artist Charles Conder's rooms in Duke Street where they were talking and drinking burgundy. Among them was a translator of mediaeval romances called Robert Steele, an acolyte of William Morris whose word was holy writ to him on all artistic matters. He had been standing on the hearthrug pontificating on art and literature for a long time and the company were paying Dulcie no attention at all. Perhaps she decided to show them what in her opinion art was all about, or perhaps she just felt like making an entrance. She left the room and went to Conder's bedroom where she took off all her clothes except her shoes, and returned to the company completely naked.

Steele stopped and spluttered in the middle of a weighty pronounce- ment. As if it were the most natural thing in the world, Dulcie went over to Conder and sat on his knee. He smiled and stroked her bare flesh, quite entertained, as were the rest of the group except Steele who burst into a tirade of indignation. Steele's name does not crop up again in records of Dowson's life so presumably he hereafter restricted himself to tamer acquaintances.[10]

Hardly surprisingly, Dulcie resented Dowson's spending the first part of almost every evening at Poland, and she spoke contemptuously of 'la petite' when he arrived late to meet her and his other friends. It is unlikely he was so insensitive as to take Dulcie to Poland but there was an interesting dynamic occurring between the women of the restaurant and those of Dowson's circle. Dowson notes that Adelaide and her mother did not take at all to Gerald Hoole and Marmaduke Langdale's 'irreproachable fiancées' but they were charmed by Marie, one of the women of his group who collapsed in the restaurant after an abortion.[11]

Dowson first laid eyes on Marie when he and several others including Teixeira de Mattos returned to the latter's rooms to resume a game of cards which had taken all night, after which they had gone to the Charing Cross Hotel for breakfast. Back at Plowden Buildings they found an actor of their acquaintance, Lennox Pawle, sitting outside waiting for them with a pretty girl he had met while touring with the Benson company in Scotland in a play called *The Cotton King*. He had brought her to see the bright lights of London, but on that occasion all she saw was the large sofa on which she went to sleep while Pawle joined the card game.

She fitted in well with the group and was present at many of their discussions at the Café Royal, but the gay bohemian life soured when she became pregnant. She took an abortifacient but in her distress did not follow the instructions and took it in a single dose, not four draughts. She collapsed and her friends feared for her life. Dowson was particularly attentive, sitting up with her for two nights, stroking her head and talking to her about France.[12]

She was frail for a long time but eventually recovered enough to plan to go to stay with her sister for a couple of weeks. On the eve of her departure Dowson and Pawle took her to Poland where she was already known. Dowson remarked that 'her charm was really remarkable – it was not only men but women that it struck. She made an immediate conquest of Missie and her mother.'[13] She needed such friends, for she completely broke down, so much so that Adelaide made her go upstairs to the family's own living quarters and lie down. The situation was becoming desperate as Dowson could not get her home alone, and Pawle was imminently due at the theatre to give his performance so he was obliged to leave. Finally Charles Goodhart, who was also in the Benson company, arrived and he and Dowson carried Marie down to a waiting cab. Dowson and Goodhart were again up all night with the ailing woman but she rallied and they took their leave of her, all three of them weeping bitterly as they had been through so much together.

Marie was taken to the station to go north. Dowson was in Pawle's dressing room with Pawle and Goodhart when the telegram came to say she had arrived safely and had been met by her sister. There was great relief that Marie had survived and was in good hands, but there must also have been a release from the anxiety that a woman might die of a botched abortion with Dowson and the other young men in attendance, which would inevitably have led to an inquest and a considerable scandal.

Dowson described the celebration to Jepson: 'We all waltzed around Pawle's dressing room and at the conclusion of the piece indulged so freely in liquor that happening to meet a friend in the Strand we annexed him boldly and carried him in triumph to The Crown. Later on we fell down and Goodhart and I tore our trousers. We slept anyhow (after having tried unsuccessfully to play whist) all about the place. So much for Saturday.'[14] The rest of the letter shows something of the exuberant life Dowson lived with his friends at this time:

> Yesterday Pawle went off to join his company at Derby. Goodie [Goodhart] and I met in the evening. He had a charming man with him, a twenty-ton opium eater, who had run away with his cousin and is now to marry her. We met at seven and consumed four absinthes apiece in the Cock till nine. We then went and ate some kidneys – after which two absinthes apiece at the Crown. After which, one absinthe apiece at Goodie's club. Total seven absinthes. These had seriously affected us – but made little impression on the opium eater. He took us back to the Temple in a cab. This morning Goodhart and I were twitching visibly. I feel rather indisposed: and in fact we decided that our grief is now sufficiently drowned, and we must spend a few days on nothing stronger than lemonade and strychnine.[15]

As he attended Poland at the beginning of the evening, he was rarely or never drunk, but he must certainly have been at the restaurant in states of merriment or the sickness of a hangover which must have led Adelaide and her mother to question his suitability as a husband. They were not the only ones to doubt the viability of a liaison. Now that his infatuation with Adelaide was firmly fixed in his friends' minds, they started observing her more carefully, and particularly as she became older they saw her less as a charming girl and more as a capricious, manipulative young woman.

Many of Dowson's friends were lamentably ignorant of what was happening. Two who wrote memoirs described Adelaide as the daughter of an Italian restaurant keeper and one said she was French.[16] Plarr and Sherard remarked it was through sensitivity (presumably to the poet's memory) that they desisted from revealing more about the relationship. Dowson's Oxford friend Thomas said of the affair at Poland, 'Among his friends, the matter was known to be taboo in the best sense,'[17] though it is questionable how much Thomas saw of Dowson after 1891 and how much he therefore could tell of the relationship as it developed.

Others were less fastidious. The portraitist Will Rothenstein, five years younger than Dowson, had been studying in Paris before he returned in 1893 to join in with the crowd at the Crown, which included Aubrey Beardsley, another artist of the same age who appeared in the Crown at roughly the same time. In 1894 they often shared Beardsley's studio in Pimlico which was within walking distance for Dowson who would call up at the window late at night in the hope of finding a resting place. One night, according to John Gray, Dowson knocked up Rothenstein at about 2.30 am wanting a drink. Rothenstein gave him one and said he should stay there, laying Dowson down and throwing a rug over him. In the morning 'as a penance' he made Dowson sit for two hours to have his portrait done,[18] Rothenstein producing the picture of an intense, restless man with dark wavy hair and prominent blue eyes staring ahead of him.

Rothenstein was taken by Dowson to pay homage at Poland, as his friends usually were. He described Adelaide as 'a decent, rather plain, commonplace girl, a Dulcinea in fact, quite unable to understand Dowson's adoration, his morbid moods or his poetry.'[19]

Conal O' Riordan, an Irish actor and novelist who wrote under the pseudonym F. Norreys Connell, born in 1874, making him seven years younger than Dowson, said he found Poland sordid, but quite respectable, and seemed to despise Adelaide. He said to an audience (some 50 years after the event):

> That young woman, I do assure you, whatever her virtues, was not the Helen for whom the Greeks burnt Ilion: she was not even so much as the Dulcinea who lured Quixote to defeat by the windmill. She was at most the symbol of a symbol, imaging an ideal as preposterous as Barrie's Peter Pan. In his lucid moments Dowson knew that his union with her if consummated would destroy his notion of her. He might be content to woo her for all eternity: to win her would be fatal. I believe that in his heart of hearts he knew this.[20]

Edgar Jepson was convinced Adelaide did not love Dowson and, had they been in love, they could have overruled the objections of her mother for whom 'a poet made no kind of husband'. This shows Jepson's complete misunderstanding of the situation. Dowson was not a poet by profession, but the son of a dry dock proprietor. All the evidence is that Adelaide's mother, in the early days at least, supported Dowson's suit, though with no great vigour. It was Adelaide herself who made the romance such a desperate struggle.

The one friend of Dowson's who gives the impression of understanding was Arthur Symons. This is doubtless because he had a similar experience himself though in his case, characteristically, it was consummated. He was hopelessly and dangerously in love over the period from late 1893 to early 1896 with a ballet dancer from the Empire called Lydia who is commemorated in his poetry under the name Bianca. Really, he was in love with her for the rest of his life. It was one of those loves where they could not bear to be together or apart. 'There was something evil in both of us, which caused such terrible quarrels,' wrote Symons. 'She was absolutely seductive, fatally fascinating, almost shamelessly animal.'[21] They met when she was 19 and he 28, but after two passionate, troubled years, at the instigation of her mother she married a wealthy old man whom she hated.

Biography has a habit of lapsing into covert autobiography, and Symons' memoir of Ernest Dowson seems to have this tendency when he rails against Adelaide, 'Did she ever realise more than the obvious part of what was being offered to her, in this shy and eager devotion? Did it ever mean very much to her to have made and to have killed a poet?'[22]

Symons relents in his tirade, to give a picture of the sheer tediousness of Dowson's courtship in every night returning to what even Dowson himself referred to as 'the veal cutlet and the dingy green walls of my Eden'.[23] Symons wrote:

> I can always see the picture, which I have so often seen through the window in passing: the narrow room with the rough tables, for the most part empty, except in the innermost corner, where Dowson would sit with that singularly sweet and singularly pathetic smile on his lips (a smile which always seemed afraid of its right to be there, as if always dreading a rebuff), playing his invariable after-dinner game of cards. Friends would come in during the hour before closing time; and the girl, her game of cards finished, would quietly disappear, leaving him with hardly more than the desire to kill another night as soon as possible.[24]

Despite his empathy with Dowson, however, Symons saw too that Dowson's love was an idealization which could not be realized. He wrote that Dowson had, 'a sort of virginal devotion, as to a Madonna; and I think, had things gone happily, to a conventionally happy ending, he would have felt (dare I say?) that his ideal had been spoilt.'[25]

The deep tragedy was that Dowson knew it too. In January 1893 the *Century Guild Hobby Horse* published Dowson's 'Statute of Limitations', a story of great psychological depth which has been convincingly suggested as a major source for Joseph Conrad's *Heart of Darkness*.[26] The story concerns Michael Garth whose business resources had failed him at some distant time, so he was unable to stay in England when a post was offered to him in Chile. As so often in Dowson's stories, most of what is recounted happened in an unalterable past; the characters' room for manoeuvre to take control of their lives is limited to almost nothing. Garth was obliged to leave the girl he loved. The girl was very young, 'little more than a child', so there had been no question of an early marriage, and not even a definite engagement. 'He lived in a dream of her; and the memory of her eyes and her hair was a perpetual presence with him, less ghostly than the real company among whom he mechanically transacted his daily business.'

When his five years were finished, increasingly obsessed with material gain, he settled down to another five, which was then prolonged to seven. He was working with the lust of gain for her sake, the avarice being almost sanctified by it. When his lover sent him a new photograph, showing her as a woman as she now was, 'a dignity touched with sadness: a face, upon which life had already written some of its cruelties,' he hid the picture and returned to the inspiration of the earlier portrait. When he begins to return, 'The notion of the woman, which she now was, came between him and the girl whom he had loved.' His despondency increased as the steamer in which he and the narrator were travelling neared England; he felt he had wasted his entire life, and her youth too.

'Our marriage will be a ghastly mockery,' he says to the narrator in considering his plight, 'a marriage of corpses. Her heart, how can she give it to me? She gave it years ago to the man I was, the man who is now dead.' In the end he writes a long letter to his love, and drowns in an accident, which the narrator is sure is suicide. The narrator grimly remarks that 'he had perhaps avoided worse things than the death he met.' Dowson himself could see those worse things, they loomed before him in his own life.

Yet there was still much to be happy about. Dowson was enjoying literary attention, if not acclaim. Work on *Adrian Rome* was proceeding apace. Dowson said it was 'half completed' in September 1893 and he was already looking for titles, suggesting *A Misalliance, The Opportunist* and *The Interlopers*. Later he thought of *The Arrangement of Life*. Both he and Moore felt it was better than *A Comedy of Masks* but Dowson added it was 'vindictive, savage, spleenful, libellous almost, to the last degree' which is a curious judgement.[27]

Dowson's invitation to *The Yellow Book* launch demonstrated that he had attained a certain position in the life of letters in London. *The Yellow Book* was a quarterly magazine published between hard covers. It had been thought of by the writer Henry Harland and Aubrey Beardsley who had met in the waiting room of a TB specialist. They conceived the literary and artistic magazine one foggy afternoon in January 1894 as a showcase for their own talents and those of the London avant-garde. They approached John Lane and his then partner Elkin Mathews who took on the project at their company, The Bodley Head.

The launch party for *The Yellow Book* took place at the Hotel d'Italie in Old Compton Street on 16 April 1894, and was attended by notables of literary and artistic London including Dowson along with fellow Rhymers W.B. Yeats, Lionel Johnson, John Davidson and Ernest Rhys. Symons was in Italy and Le Gallienne was lecturing in Liverpool.[28]

The quarterly certainly set the tone for the mid-1890s and though it was not explicitly decadent, Beardsley's thrillingly sinister line drawings formed the image of corruption and sensuality which typified the period. The articles were generally less likely to offend the more puritan members of the public, though the magazine took a relaxed line, Max Beerbohm noting, 'There are signs that our English literature has reached that point, when, like the literatures of all the nations that have been, it must fall at length into the hands of the decadents.'29

In 1894 *The Yellow Book* overtook *The Hobby Horse* as the periodical to which many of the Rhymers contributed. *The Hobby Horse* had been taken over by Lane and Mathews from Chiswick Press in 1893 and it appeared twice that year (losing *Century Guild* from its name) then once in 1894, then ceased. Dowson sent Harland his story 'Apple Blossom in Brittany' which had never been published, though it had been completed in 1892. It appeared in *The Yellow Book* in October 1894, and Dowson would doubtless have contributed more but events in his own life and in that of the periodical were to impede him.

The Bodley Head were interested in having Dowson as one of their authors. He was corresponding as early as summer 1893 with John Lane and Elkin Mathews about having a volume of his stories published by the company. The principal reader for them was Dowson's fellow Rhymer Richard Le Gallienne who wrote in his report, 'Mr Dowson applies very delicate literary treatment to somewhat hackneyed themes.' He ran through them, questioning the titles of several stories and finishing,

> On the whole, having regard to the delicacy of the treatment, and the success of *A Comedy of Masks* ... I would advise you to accept these as an instalment of a volume, (they are not big enough to make one themselves) with the promise that the stories to come should be more striking, more original in theme – not less so, not mere makeweights – than those under consideration.30

In fact the only later addition to the stories Le Gallienne had read was 'The Statute of Limitations'. By November 1894 Dowson was wavering for a title for the book between *Blind Alleys* and *Sentimental Dilemmas*.

Dowson's first volume of verse was also to be published by Lane and Mathews under The Bodley Head imprint in 1894 and there were even advertisements for it. In the meantime the *Second Book of the Rhymers' Club* was published in June 1894, with no new poets except A.C. Hillier who had not contributed to the first though he had been a Rhymer. They were criticized in this for becoming a coterie, for having closed their doors to all new contributors. John Gray writing in 1906 remarked on the book, 'It is an interesting relic of all that history. It only means a little in respect of Dowson, Lionel Johnson and Yeats. The rest (excepting Arthur Symons) were preposterous.'31 This is a very fair view.

Dowson contributed his maximum of six poems: 'Extreme Unction', 'To One in Bedlam', 'Cynara', 'Growth', 'The Garden of Shadow' and the poem which begins 'You would have understood me had you waited'.

There is a directness and honesty about Dowson's lyrics which raises them as if printed in relief above the others of his group, excepting those of Johnson. Johnson contributed his masterpiece, 'The Dark Angel' ('Dark Angel with thine aching lust/To rid the world of penitence') meaning that this volume carried some of the finest lyrics of the decade.

It is interesting to see from the Rhymers' second volume how decadent ideas and imagery were gaining ground. John Todhunter, an Irish Rhymer who was far from decadent, contributed 'Euthanasia (fin de siècle)' and even Plarr provided 'Death and the Player'.

The book was questioned on moral grounds with Dowson and Johnson picked out for special blame. *The Times* of 6 July 1894 mentioned the volume but with the usual critical judgement of literary critics, the reviewer failed even to mention Dowson or Johnson, remarking, 'The writer who appears to us to have the most genuine poetic fibre in his constitution is Mr Victor Plarr ... a man with real poetical insight.' The *Athenaeum* of 25 August 1894 said Dowson evinces his, 'customary disposition of dwelling upon the less wholesome aspects of life,' citing 'Cynara' as evidence. The use of the term 'customary' is telling, as it means not just that the reviewer was acquainted with Dowson's themes, but that he expected such knowledge also from the reader.

The Rhymers had largely served their purpose now, it had been difficult to maintain attendance at monthly meetings and the summer recesses had become longer. With the decline of the Rhymers, Dowson was seeing less of Plarr who anyway had other interests as he had married in 1892, taking a honeymoon in Brittany along an itinerary suggested by Dowson. He had moved out of the Hobby Horse lodgings to a house in Humber Road, Blackheath. Nellie Plarr had a daughter, Marion, in 1893 and Dowson wrote a verse to commemorate the occasion, beginning,

Mark the day white, on which the Fates have smiled:
Eugenio and Egeria have a child.

He took his usual keen interest in the little girl, sharing with Plarr the pleasure of seeking names for her and saying he was anxious to see her. He frequently asked about her, 'Is the Infanta short petticoated yet? Or when does this interesting development take place?'[32]

His own family were far from such light-hearted badinage. Alfred Dowson's health progressively deteriorated and his depressive mental state did nothing to lighten his load. Ernest Dowson's description of a wistful, sick, literary shipyard owner in *A Comedy of Masks* is clearly a portrait of his father in his last years.

He read little now, but the mere presence of the books he loved best in rough, uneven cases, painted black, lining the walls, caressed him. As with persons one has loved and grown used to loving, it was not always needful that they should speak to him; it was sufficient, simply that they should be there. Neither did he write on these long, interminable evenings, which were prolonged sometimes far into the night. He had ended by being able to smile at his literary ambitions of twenty, cultivating his indolence as something choice and original, finding his destiny appropriate.

He spent the time in interminable reveries, sitting with a volume before him, as often as not unopened, smoking incessantly, and looking out of the window. The habit amused himself at times; it was so eminently symbolic of his destiny. Life, after all, has been to him nothing so much as that – a long looking out of the window.[33]

Alfred Dowson had probably long since stopped going to the dock by the summer of 1894, leaving whatever labours a proprietor had to perform to Ernest. Apart from his illness, there was insufficient work for three managers: himself, Ernest and the foreman. The dock, anyway, was mortgaged and in debt with the foreman as the major creditor.

It is difficult to establish what the relationship was between Alfred and Ernest Dowson. Plarr said Alfred confided to him in mock seriousness that he was frightened of the younger generation in general, and Ernest in particular, but this is probably merely a jocose remark for the benefit of a visitor to the dock. Ernest jocularly referred to his father as 'the governor' or 'my governor', but despite the sympathetic picture he drew of Philip Rainham, there is nothing to indicate a close relationship between father and son. Dowson did not even show his father his poems; his uncle Lewis Swan told an anecdote of Alfred Dowson for a long time admiring the work of a poet whose verse appeared occasionally in a fashionable periodical, signed only with initials. He eventually found that the unknown poet was his own son.[34] Clearly Ernest felt he could learn no more from his father.

After their move from Maida Hill to Chadwell Heath, Epping Forest, Ernest did not live with them, the small family now being just mother, father and Rowland, now 16. They had four different addresses in the first four years of the 1890s, the last move within a year of their settling in Epping, to Battersea. The diseased family seemed to be struggling to find somewhere cheap enough to live, each time locating themselves in a house just above their means, so another move was inevitable, but with even more of their capital depleted. Flat 7, Albert Mansions, Albert Road, Battersea, near the Albert Bridge, was about the lowest level of accommodation which a respectable middle class family could inhabit.

Annie Dowson's sister Ethel Swan later wrote that the Dowsons contrived to conceal their poverty so relatives, who certainly would have helped, did not do so. It may be that they even concealed from Ernest himself the extent of their poverty – not an impossible task considering he saw them only for Sunday lunch. Plarr wrote that Alfred's hospitality to guests was undiminished by his dwindling income. By spring 1894 the

Dowson family's poverty was no longer relative. Around this time Ethel Swan was in Scotland and sent them some Aberdeen haddock as a treat. It was as well she did, for when the gift arrived they had no food in the house. Alfred Dowson, who had taken Swinburne down the Thames on his boat, who had dined with W.S. Gilbert, and conversed with Stevenson and Maupassant, was now so poor he would go hungry if his in-laws had not sent him food. 'Poor old Alfred couldn't stand that sort of thing,' wrote Ethel Swan.[35]

Alfred had a mortal terror, shared with many other Victorians, that he would end up in the poor house. He also had a stubborn pride which forbade him to accept charity so the cycle of hopeless worry and resistance to any help continued.

Whether Alfred Christopher Dowson, aged 51, intended to die on 15 August 1894 will never be known. He took an overdose of chloral hydrate, which was a sleeping draught he frequently used for his insomnia, and the result was vomiting blood. Death probably resulted from the inhalation of vomited matter which could not be resisted in the semi-comatose state brought on by the chloral, exacerbated by his weakness from tuberculosis.

The chloral may have been taken with no intention other than a quiet night's sleep; it may have irritated an existing stomach ulcer or caused the stomach irritation of itself. Gastric irritation is a well-defined side effect of chloral hydrate and the most authoritative drug reference books advise that the gastric irritation can result in vomiting. Toxic doses range widely, between 4g and 30g, so unintentional overdose is easy, particularly with repeated self-dosing where tolerance will have already built up.[36]

The doctor called to Albert Mansions who certified 'haematemesis shock' did not recommend an inquest should be opened, but this does not prove Albert Dowson's death was not suicide. Doctors can be very sympathetic when faced with a distressed family and no particular reason for suspicion, following death in a man not destined to live for long in the best of circumstances. Ernest Dowson's friends certainly felt the death was suicide, Victor Plarr saying he was expressly forbidden to write of it, when there is no reason at all why this should be so unless it were non-accidental, and Conal O'Riordan explicitly saying Alfred Dowson had taken his own life, 'in despair'.[37]

Whatever Alfred Dowson's intention, the result was that Ernest Dowson of Bridge Dock, Limehouse, registered his father's death at Wandsworth two days after it occurred, and the hesitant poet was now head of the household.

CHAPTER 9

DECADENT DISINTEGRATION

Dowson struggled to comfort his mother and make some sense of the family's affairs but it was no job for him. He fell ill at the time of his father's death and was bedridden for days with influenza. His uncle Stanley Hoole, who worked for Lloyd's the insurers, had a far better business head and was able to provide for his sister-in-law. Hoole was not rich, so it was at some cost to himself that he bought Annie Dowson an annuity to ensure she always had some money. He also took Rowland Dowson, now 17, into Lloyd's, presumably in some clerical capacity.

Rowland was a more approachable nephew than Ernest. Their aunt Ethel Swan wrote:

> Nell and I always much preferred Rowland, he was a dear boy ... Ernest was playing the fool, translating brilliantly and then taking awful drugs, absinthe and other things ... [he] was always able to earn, for his publishers said his English translations were beautiful. He was a queer mixture, clever but fearfully weak character and like a madman when he got drink or drugs. No wonder Rowland hated to be with him.[1]

It is unsurprising that Ernest and Rowland did not get on well – siblings often do not. It is interesting to note that Ethel Swan assumes her nephew took drugs – he may have, but to no significant degree, or it would have been remarked upon by his friends in their memoirs of him. It is also revealing of the family's values that she remarks on his practical, jobbing work as a translator rather than a writer of poetry or prose, despite her writing after his death when he had a world-wide reputation.

With the support of the family, Annie and Rowland Dowson were relocated to 97 Quentin Road, Lee, a curious backwater of suburban

London where red and grey terraced houses lined the end of a road entered by an avenue of houses designed to seem larger than they really were, being constructed just one room deep behind an attractive facade, probably thereby echoing the pretensions of the people who lived in them.

Annie must have found the flat in which her husband died unbearable, but another reason for the move to Lee in particular was that her sister, Ada Swan, lived nearby at 1 St Stephen's Road, Lewisham, and doubtless also because she had warm memories of Gothic House at The Grove in Lee, where her two sons had been born when the family was affluent.

Lee was no great distance from the Plarr family's home in Humber Road and Dowson used to walk over Blackheath to see them. Plarr said, 'On one occasion I remember seeing his mother saying good-bye to him and flitting away, a shadowy figure, near a little grove of trees that fronted our house. She would not visit her son's friends – there was evidently trouble in the air.'[2] This last remark is written with hindsight but Annie Dowson, now 46, had always been remarked upon as a nervous, fretful person and her tuberculosis can have given her little rest. She and Rowland had been alone with Alfred when he died and her sister Ethel Swan said 'it upset her brain which was never very strong I imagine.'[3] There are reports that she felt herself to have been a failure as a wife and mother, and to have personally brought about the family's misfortunes.[4]

Marion Plarr takes this view, perhaps informed by her father, who explicitly would not write of the matter, so presumably he had something to conceal. Marion Plarr writes of Annie Dowson:

> She had begun to think that at some time in her life she must have done something very wicked for everything to be going so wrong with them all. ... She would lie awake at night trying to think what it could have been that she had done: but there was nothing specific that she could remember. Perhaps her wickedness had been so frightful that a merciful Providence had wiped it from her mind.[5]

Annie was seeing a Dr Patrick Cumin Scott who remarked that she 'appeared greatly depressed and complained of not being able to sleep.' Rowland said that she had been depressed owing to sleeplessness and worry, and delay in winding up his father's estate.[6]

Certainly she was in a poor state of nerves on Monday 4 February 1895, some six months after Alfred's death, when Ernest had arranged to visit her at Lee and accompany her to Ada Swan's home. He did not take his responsibilities to his mother lightly – he had refused an invitation to go to the West End with friends that evening. He arrived from the dock at five o'clock that afternoon to find the landlady, Mary Hitt, rather worried about his mother. Mrs Dowson had gone upstairs shortly after three, and an hour later the landlady knocked on the door but received no answer. She thought Annie Dowson was probably asleep and tried the door but found it locked.

Ernest tried the door himself and called out to his mother but there was no reply. With mounting alarm he ran to get a carpenter who splintered the wood of the door frame and broke it open with the anxious Dowson and the landlady standing behind him. In the room, Annie Dowson seemed to be kneeling by the bed. Ernest called but she made no response. He knew what had happened, as he had known since the landlady told him of his mother's silence that afternoon: she had killed herself.

Dowson went at once for a policeman and a doctor. The policeman, PC Tagg, said he found Annie Dowson suspended to the rail of the bedstead with a handkerchief around her neck. He cut the handkerchief and the body fell to the floor. A Dr Burton came shortly afterwards and pronounced life extinct; he judged that when he came she had been dead two hours.

An inquest was held three days later at the Working Men's Institute, Old Road, Lee. Ernest told the court he had heard his mother threaten 'to do herself an injury' in the past. She was still deeply upset by the death of her husband, and troubled also about his estate, which was being wound up in Chancery, though she was not in financial want. The verdict was suicide whilst temporarily insane.[7]

Ernest Dowson's distress can scarcely be imagined. His misery went to literally unspeakable depths: none of his friends record that he ever so much as mentioned the death of his parents to them, and he wrote no letters on the subject. He is recorded as being unable to eat or sleep after his mother's death.[8] Conal O'Riordan remarked, 'I suspect that he was always haunted by the notion (I'm afraid only too well founded) that his unsatisfactory career had added to her torments.'[9]

The family helped as much as they could, clearing Annie's possessions from her last home and looking after Rowland. Ernest's young brother stayed with Ethel Swan and considered his future, untrained as he was for any professional occupation in London. Later that year, when he was still only 17, he sailed off to Canada to start a new life for himself.

Ernest Dowson went back to the sombre, eighteenth-century house at the dock, going up the balcony staircase to his dark rooms with their carved oak mantels, curious alcoves and mildewing wainscot. Doubtless on his own, in these gloomy surroundings with his parents recently dead, Dowson would ponder his image from *A Comedy of Masks*: 'He could fancy that the spirits of his ancestors were returned from the other side of the Styx to finger the pages of by-gone ledgers, and to mock from between the shadows of his incongruous bookshelves, at their degenerate descendant.'[10]

It is from this period that Dowson's only extant business letter comes. It is a pathetic attempt to retain a customer, offering to do some work on a steamer for the cost price to the dock, 'as we are anxious to meet you and retain your business'. It has only survived because it was written on the back of one sheet of the manuscript of his story 'The Eyes of Pride'.[11] Dowson continued to make some contribution to the running of the dock, ostensibly as 'joint manager' with the foreman, Richards, but it was Richards who was in control of such business as there was. Alfred Dowson's will, made in happier times, had made provisions for an annuity of £350 a year for his widow, and for Ernest and Rowland to share the remainder and the income from the dock. This probably produced a sad smile by 1895 when the dock's debts may well have exceeded its value. The Dowson estate was being dealt with in the Chancery Division of the High Court and though Ernest Dowson expected, to the end of his life, to receive his share of the residual sum, he never did.

Dowson must have continued his translations over this period, but the only other literary task which obviously involved him was the editing of *Dilemmas*. He stirred himself from his misery and lassitude to correspond on this subject in the year after his father's death, but on nothing else. One of the letters, a month or two after Annie Dowson's death, is written to Elkin Mathews but in his distress he has also signed it Elkin Mathews, incidentally spelling the name wrong. It concerns the dedication of the book to Adelaide – Dowson was concerned that the size and appearance of the typeface should be right. The stories were eventually published in summer 1895 under the title *Dilemmas: Stories and Studies in Sentiment*. They comprised: 'A Case of Conscience', 'The Diary of a Successful Man', 'An Orchestral Violin' (formerly 'The Story of a Violin'), 'The Statute of Limitations', and 'Souvenirs of an Egoist'. The dedication about which he had fretted was printed on a blank page on three lines: 'To MISSIE (A.F.)'.

Elkin Mathews printed 600 copies which were to be sold at 3s 6d (17½p) each; Dowson was to receive an advance of £7.10s (£7.50). The book was warmly reviewed with Richard Le Gallienne saying it had 'life and charm' in the *Realm* and the *Athenaeum* singling out 'A Case of Conscience' for its 'sharpness and directness'.[12]

Advertisements in *Dilemmas* announced that Dowson's poems would soon be published at 5s (25p) with a quotation from the *Boston Literary World*: 'Mr Dowson's contributions to the two series of the Rhymers' Book were subtle and exquisite poems. He has a touch of Elizabethan distinction. … Mr Dowson's stories are very remarkable in quality.'

In the autumn of 1894 the Rhymers intended to produce a third anthology but the partnership of Mathews and Lane broke up, each publishing separately, with Lane keeping the Bodley Head imprint and Matthews keeping most of the authors. There was disagreement within the Rhymers over who should publish the anthology, but they also seem to have run out of steam. The Rhymers had simply become too preoccupied with their own affairs to be able to commit themselves.

Lionel Johnson, for example, was seeing less of Dowson as he withdrew into lonely alcoholism, having been evicted from Fitzroy Street because he tended to show his departing guests downstairs with a candle which the landlord, Mackmurdo, feared in Johnson's unsteady state might lead to a conflagration. In September 1895 he went to rooms at 7 Gray's Inn Square. He is said to have quarrelled with Dowson, and his drinking had driven away former good friends like Symons and Yeats.

Ernest Rhys gives a miserable picture of Dowson at one of the last meetings, when he noticed Dowson's health was giving out. 'On the last Rhymers' Club night he attended, he came late, and broke three long clays in succession trying to light up. Then, asked if he had any rhyme to read, he pulled one out of his pocket, looked at it, shook his head, as much as to say it wouldn't do, and thrust it back again.'13

Despite the Dowson family's private misfortunes which Ernest disclosed to few if any of his friends, the time of his greatest distress happened to coincide with the decadent high season. *The Yellow Book* was enjoying a succès de scandale and making celebrities of Arthur Symons and Aubrey Beardsley. Oscar Wilde was the toast of London, packing theatres with his spectacularly witty plays. During 1893 to 1895 Wilde had progressed from inspiring other decadents to entertaining and outraging the public. His two West End plays, *Lady Windermere's Fan* and *A Woman of No Importance*, of 1892 and 1893, had been brilliant successes, to be followed by *An Ideal Husband* and *The Importance of Being Earnest*, both produced early in 1895.

Dowson went to see Wilde one evening at the Berkeley Hotel in Piccadilly. It was quite early, but he found Wilde in bed propped up with pillows, pasting newspaper cuttings about himself in a large scrapbook.14 A friend they had in common, the biographer Robert Sherard, said Wilde, 'had a very high respect for Dowson's literary gifts, and showed him actual deference.' This was despite the fact that 'Ernest Dowson was not at all the kind of man with whom Wilde would ever have cared to associate ... for he was untidy, even dirty in his dress. ... He was usually drunk and, at most times, when so, noisy and boisterous. Yet Oscar Wilde, because he admired his genius, was at all times glad to see him.'15

Dowson was never one of Wilde's entourage. The playwright was usually surrounded by fawning disciples who praised him, laughed at his jokes however frequently they had heard them before, and accepted gifts in return for their attentions. He also had close men friends who were nearer to him than these hangers-on in intellect. One of them was Lord Alfred Douglas, a handsome poet who was also friendly with Dowson, though they moved in different circles.

When Lord Alfred Douglas became Wilde's favourite, it drew the playwright into conflict with Douglas' father, Lord Queensberry, the 'mad marquis'. He was an obsessive atheist, devoted to boxing, whose rules were named after him, and was ever ready to horsewhip people of whom he disapproved. He once went to a hotel where the Foreign Secretary (later Prime Minister) Lord Rosebery was staying, whip in hand, to deliver the punishment in person. Rosebery had aroused the ire of the Marquis because of his fondness for Queensberry's son, Lord Drumlanrig, who was his private secretary. Rosebery always liked to be in the company of handsome young men and was one of those who gave justification to the popular conception that the ruling class was irredeemably decadent. There was a strong contemporary suspicion that the punishment meted out to Oscar Wilde was excessive because he acted as a scapegoat, to quell the clamour of those who believed the case had implications for those of a higher rank.[16] Drumlanrig was to die of a gunshot wound, almost certainly a suicide, shortly before his wedding in 1894. Queensberry's next son, Lord Douglas of Hawick, married a clergyman's daughter and the family was subsequently subjected to the obscene abuse of Queensberry, to the point of violence. The third son was Lord Alfred Douglas. When he began to be seen frequently with Wilde, Queensberry described the playwright as, 'a damned cur and coward of the Rosebery type.'[17] At the spectacular first night of *The Importance of Being Earnest* in February 1895 the Marquis of Queensberry prowled outside the theatre with a phallic bouquet of turnips and carrots to award to Wilde. Denied access, he later went to Wilde's club and passed in a visiting card marked 'To Oscar Wilde posing as a somdomite' (sic). When Wilde received this some days later, he eventually decided on an action for criminal libel, even though no one had seen it but the porter. Urged on by Douglas, he went to court to be confronted by various male prostitutes and blackmailers who had been bribed by Queensberry to give details of Wilde's real or imagined sex life. In the face of this overwhelming evidence, Wilde had to withdraw the prosecution and was duly arrested in his turn on 5 April 1895.

He was charged under the 'homosexuality' clause of the Criminal Law Amendment Act of 1885 which had been inserted into the legislation at a late date, and which covered any sexual act between men committed either in public or private. No MP had dared to vote against it for fear of being seen to compromise with vice, but it is as well to note that ten years earlier there could have been no Oscar Wilde trial without evidence far in excess of that which was actually presented. As mentioned in Chapter 6, it was W.T. Stead's circulation-boosting purchase of a girl which led directly to the Act's being passed. The fit of popular morality which produced the climate in which these events took place showed English society reacting against decadence and all it stood for in terms of a more liberal sexual code.

It had taken no time for publishers to take the message to heart that decadence was dangerous. Spurred by a vengeful public, they got their retaliation in first. John Lane was on his way to America when Wilde was taken into custody, but when the ship docked he was handed a newspaper which said, 'Arrest of Oscar Wilde, *Yellow Book* under his arm' and he later learned crowds had stoned the window of his Vigo Street offices where *The Yellow Book* was prominently displayed. Several authors clamoured for the dismissal from *The Yellow Book* of Aubrey Beardsley, his being the most visible decadent presence. William Watson sent a telegram: 'Withdraw all Beardsley designs or I withdraw my books.' Lane responded by pulling back the copy of *The Yellow Book* currently on the presses and having all Beardsley's pictures removed. Lane also sacked Beardsley as art director of the magazine and withdrew all Wilde's books from his catalogue.

Outside theatres where the managements had recently been so proud to produce Wilde's plays, paper was pasted over his name on the bills, as if the words 'Oscar Wilde' themselves were an obscenity. The plays soon closed, Wilde was declared bankrupt and the contents of his house sold in an auction which descended into rowdiness.

Wilde had never written for *The Yellow Book*, probably because of Beardsley's dislike of him. Beardsley was not a homosexual. Wilde had not even been carrying a copy of *The Yellow Book* at the time of his arrest, but a French novel bound in yellow. His plays all dealt with heterosexual themes. It was to no avail: moral panic contaminates, with the most vicious consequences.

Wilde was tried at the end of April, the jury failing to reach a verdict. He was then released on bail which was put up by Rev Stewart Headlam and Lord Douglas of Hawick. The latter urged him to leave the country, despite the fact that he could not afford to forfeit the bail money. Wilde refused all appeals to leave and stayed in London, desperately waiting for the inevitable blow of fate.

Sherard wrote,

> he did not wish to see any of his friends except myself, for he said his nerves could not endure the presence even of those most kindly disposed towards him. But one day I said to him: "Oscar, may I bring Ernest Dowson to see you this evening? He would very much like to come." He said, "Oh, bring him by all means. He is an Oxford man and a fine writer of poetry and of prose, and it will do me good to have a causerie with him."

So Sherard kept Dowson sober all afternoon and in the evening they went to Oakley Street (Lady Wilde's home) where Dowson and Wilde sat together in the front room where the bills were rapidly accumulating in the lacquer letter rack. Dowson stayed till long after dark. Neither of them spoke very much, and when they did it was mainly about artistic matters. Sherard said the evening was one of the pleasantest that Wilde enjoyed during his brief period of liberty.[18]

The second trial began at the Old Bailey on 20 May 1895. The evidence was that of men who had been offered the chance of being prosecuted themselves, or testifying against Wilde. There were six counts against him, and when he was later asked if they were true he said there was some foundation to one of them; the other five referred to matters with which he had nothing to do, but to instruct his counsel of this would mean betraying a friend.[19]

Dowson went to the court with Sherard on 25 May 1895 when the verdict was to be given. As they stepped down from their cab a cry went up from the crowd 'Here are some more aristocrats! Here are some more of them!' which shows how Dowson's very appearance associated him with the decadents, who were compounded in the common mind with the ruling class. The two sat in the courtroom just behind the Attorney General, Sir Frank Lockwood. Sherard looked round and realized that of all the friends who had swarmed round Wilde in his years of triumph, he could see only three there to support him in his hour of most need: himself, Ernest Dowson and Lord Douglas of Hawick.[20]

Wilde was found guilty of acts of gross indecency, and given the maximum sentence: two years hard labour, the judge additionally delivering a moral diatribe. 'And I? May I say nothing, my lord?' asked Wilde from the dock, but the judge, doubtless concerned that his vindictiveness would be shown up for what it was beside a speech of Wilde's, waved the prisoner away and he was dragged down to the cells.

Dowson and Sherard left to the whoops of exultation which those crowding down with them were shouting. When the verdict reached the rabble by the Old Bailey steps, men and women joined hands and danced 'an ungainly farandole where ragged petticoats and yawning boots flung up the London mud in feu de joie, and the hideous faces were distorted with savage triumph.' Sherard noticed the bribed witnesses, laughing and smoking cigarettes, being driven off in cabs, and he said to Dowson, 'This is a trial in which, out of nine people incriminated, eight have been admitted to act as Queen's evidence.'[21]

The courage shown by Dowson in attending Wilde's trial as a supporter of the accused can be contrasted with the behaviour of John Gray who instructed a barrister to attend the trial with a watching brief to note if his name were mentioned, in order that he might be protected from scandal. He later bought up copies of his book of verse, *Silverpoints*, to remove any lingering reminder from the record that he was once a decadent.

It was not only the street people of London who danced for joy at Wilde's suffering. W.E. Henley, a former friend of Wilde, wrote in the *National Observer* when the playwright was first arrested, 'There is not a man or woman in the English speaking world possessed of the treasure of a wholesome mind who is not under a deep debt of gratitude to the Marquis of Queensberry for destroying the High Priest of the Decadents.' He advised suicide for Wilde, 'and of the Decadents, of their hideous conceptions of the meaning of Art, of their worse than Eleusian mysteries, there must be an absolute end.'[22] The linking of the Wilde case with the attempt to crush the decadent consciousness was entirely intentional. As the art critic Harry Quilter said in the *Contemporary Review*, 'the fall of the great high-priest of aestheticism has struck the public imagination' and he welcomed the fact that 'the newest developments of blasphemy, indecency and disease receive only a half-hearted and timid approval.' Writers and artists judged 'morbid, uncleanly and unnatural' by Quilter were fostered by a decadent school of criticism which 'must be detected, exposed and destroyed'.[23] One result of the trial, therefore, was the diminution of markets for work at a time when Dowson needed them as he never had before.

By summer 1895 Dowson was a wretched caricature of himself. He had always been a man of secret, desperate passions, but now the anguish of being himself, the appalling pressure of continued consciousness which he had hitherto restrained, seemed to bubble over and flood his whole personality. It was not a single crisis which caused Dowson's now alarming decline, though observers like Frank Harris put it down merely to the impossibility of his relationship with Adelaide. It was true that she was growing away from him, and was both encouraging and distant towards him as her adolescent mood changed, but this was nothing new. The break-up of his personality at this time was due to multiple factors: the death of his parents in such terrible circumstances, the manifestation of his tuberculosis meaning his days were clearly numbered, and the failure of his attempts to find work which would keep him at more than starvation level. The loss of his family and the imminent loss of the dock also meant Dowson was cast adrift from even the tenuous moorings he had previously known. With the departure of his brother, despite their never having been close, his last link with his near family was severed. As the dock foundered economically he faced the imminent loss of the only home he had ever known. Everything was sliding into decay. Dowson's world was a wasteland and if Adelaide gave no consolation, neither did art: his friend, the finest British dramatist of the century, was now picking oakum with bleeding hands. The load Dowson bore would have broken a strong man, and he had never been anything but frail.

Frank Harris said he 'seemed pathetically weak and dependent on casual companionship, lonely and unhappy.'[24] Robert Sherard remarked that 'already in those days all things on this earth had lost their power of appealing to his heart or imagination.'[25]

Sherard, Jepson, Harris and O'Riordan all record visits to the dock at this time, which shows how desperately lonely Dowson was – he had not previously shown any inclination to have friends visiting. Nor did they have to be close friends – a George C. Williamson who knew Dowson very slightly left a record of Dowson in his dock. They had been introduced at the Café Monico where Dowson was with an 'obstreperous party' and Williamson began to talk about Dowson's poetry, which he admired.

Williamson noted that Dowson 'worried me by his excitement, due partially to the fragility of his own frame, and to the illness that eventually carried him off, and partly to the company with whom he was, and to their foolish indulgence.'

Some time later he was in the docks area on business and called in to see Dowson.

> I found a very curious dock with an office opening out of it, the whole thing in bad repair, showing evident signs of neglect, and I found him sitting at a sort of desk table, at which he had been preparing some nautical papers, about which I understood nothing, and with his head buried in his arms, not asleep but strangely silent and reticent. He was in a far weaker state of health than when I had seen him at the Monico.

> He was full of schemes for the future, he was certain that he was going to succeed to a substantial sum of money which would come to him very shortly.

> I was terribly reluctant to leave him. I asked if there was no one else in the place. He said there was no one, he was alone. There was a boy out in the very disconsolate-looking yard. ... He was shabbily dressed and untidy but, notwithstanding all that, every now and then his voice, far quieter and more full of charm than when I had seen him at the Monico, gave utterance to perfectly beautiful poetic thoughts over and over again, about music, about silence, about the fading of flowers, about Extreme Unction and the use of the Sacring Oil, and then finally there was a certain burst of feeling, and he got up and said that he would not die, and he would not be alone, he would live for many years, and meantime, he would go and have a drink and find a friend [a euphemism for seeking out a prostitute]. It was to me a very distressing interview, one that I have never cared to dwell upon very closely, because I was conscious that it was almost too late to do anything for him, and moreover, that he himself would set up a profound barrier against receiving any assistance from anyone. At the same time I was so drawn towards him by reason of his extreme charm, that I walked away in sorrow, and as I left, he put his arms again on the table and his head dropped down, and I left him in very much the same position that I had at first found him.[26]

Harris described how when he went to the East End with Dowson,

> We dined in a frowsy room behind a bar on a bare table without a napkin: the food was almost uneatable, the drink poisonous, and afterwards Dowson took me round to places of amusement! The memory of it all – a nightmare; I can still hear a girl droning out an interminable song meant to be lively and gay; still see a woman clog-dancing just to show glimpses of old, thin legs, smiling grotesquely the while with toothless mouth; still remember Dowson hopelessly drunk at the end screaming with rage and vomiting insults – a wretched experience.

A week later Dowson asked him out to the East End again but he declined.[27]

Dowson's truculence when drunk is well recorded. It was not just that he was argumentative after drinking – he seemed to take on a completely different personality as many habitual drinkers do. It could be taken as a social indicator of alcoholism that normal people, even though they may drink to excess at times, are still recognizably the same person; alcoholics seem to experience a complete character change. Perhaps it is this which they seek in drink. John Gray remarked that Dowson was run in by the police for being drunk and disorderly so often that he was greeted by the magistrate with, 'What, you here again Mr Dowson?'[28]

Arthur Symons wrote of Dowson:

> Sober, he was the most gentle, in manner the most gentlemanly of men; unselfish to a fault, to the extent of weakness; a delightful companion, charm itself. Under the influence of drink he became almost literally insane, certainly quite irresponsible. He fell into furious and unreasoning passions; a vocabulary unknown to him at other times sprang up like a whirlwind; he seemed always about to commit some act of absurd violence.[29]

On one occasion, Sherard recounted, he and Dowson were riding together in an omnibus in the Strand. 'He had been talking quietly to me, when suddenly his phrases began to precipitate themselves, while he waved his hand in the air. He closed his remarks with, "And this is what I want to say," and, so saying, brought the palm of his hand violently down upon the thigh of a guardsman who was sitting opposite him.' The slap was painful and the guardsman remonstrated, at which Dowson immediately asked the big, strong fellow out to the street for a fight while Sherard tried to pacify him. The Guardsman gallantly attempted to back out of what was clearly a contest unequal in his favour, and told Dowson he could not engage in a fight in the street in uniform, at which Dowson called him a coward. The Guardsman said Dowson could be at Knightsbridge Barracks the next day and they would then see who was the better man. When Sherard had induced him to leave the omnibus and asked why he had so provoked a man who could have felled him with one blow, Dowson said gnostically, 'Well, and if it pleases me to be beaten?'[30]

Another memory of Sherard's is even more disturbing, as it demonstrates the outcome of such a fracas. One night Sherard accompanied Dowson to Limehouse and his host had settled Sherard in the dock house, but then Dowson rushed out again into the dark streets. When he returned some hours later, he was bleeding from a stab which he had received in the forehead. Sherard wrote,

> it was a nasty wound and the striker's purpose obviously had been to stab him in the eye. He said nothing about the encounter, but he seemed highly pleased as he surveyed himself in the glass. I do not doubt now that, having purposely provoked some ruffian in the streets, he felt grateful to him for his ready re-

sponse with a knife. His body had been disfigured; suffering had been awarded to him.[31]

Victor Plarr confirmed this story of the head wound when he recalled letting Dowson pass him on the pavement, when he saw his friend coming out of a staircase in Arundel Street:

> So ill and absent-minded, so pale and, to me, forbidding did he look, that I could not summon up courage to address him. Cui bono? Of course I am quite wrong, but we all know this state of feeling ... who does not know what it is to slacken pace behind someone who has failed in cordiality towards one and has seemed bored by one's advances and reminders? ... He had received a facial injury, easily remediable, which may have partly accounted for his unwillingness to revisit old and faithful friends. He was musing as usual, and seemed to see nothing, his eyes almost bulging from his head. He was wrapped in a heavy coat and had a larger cigar than of old in his mouth.[32]

The debonair Arthur Symons was only partly wrong to describe 'that curious love of the sordid, so common an affectation of the modern decadent, and with him so genuine.'[33] Dowson did plunge into the sordid, but not because he liked it: he did so because it made him suffer, and that suffering answered a deep need in him. The fights, the drinking, the hideous recreations and the awful prostitutes were part of a pattern of self-destructive behaviour which Sherard comprehended, perhaps because he was like Dowson in some ways. Sherard said, 'He hunted after suffering with the same eagerness with which most men pursue pleasure ... neglecting himself utterly, with the deliberation of the penitent seeking in the humiliation of sackcloth and ashes and vermin the absolution of his follies and his sins.'[34]

Yeats, who had said he understood Dowson 'too well for I had been like him' (and gave this as the reason for not making more of a friend of him) used virtually the same words, saying Dowson's piety was a 'penitential sadness'.[35] This gives another reason for Dowson's love of the Catholic religion which has perplexed some: the reality of sin, the necessity of suffering and the ultimate goal of redemption form a deep stratum in Catholicism. It offered Ernest Dowson a meaning and context for otherwise all-encompassing pain.

So sober an individual as Will Rothenstein, who described Dowson as 'homeless, miserable and unkempt', saw without understanding but his testimony is all the more powerful for that. He wrote:

> Poor Dowson was a tragic figure. While we others amused ourselves, playing with fireworks, Dowson meant deliberately to hurt himself. While for Beardsley perversities were largely an attitude he adopted pour épater les bourgeois. I doubt if Dowson wanted to live; he was consumed by a weary hopelessness, and he drank, I thought, to be rid of an aspect of life too forlorn to be faced. ...

Dowson had a beautiful nature, too tender for the rough-and-tumble of the market place, and he punished and lacerated himself, as it were, through excess.

Rothenstein described nights at the Crown:

> At 12.30, "Time gentlemen please!" was called, and we would continue conversing outside. Sometimes I would prevail on Dowson, who lived far away in Limehouse, to spend the night with me at Chelsea. There was a cabman's shelter near Hyde Park Corner where one could get supper of a kind, hot tea or coffee and thick bread and butter. Dowson liked the warmth of the place and the rough company. It was not easy to get him away when he was very drunk, nor past some poor street walker who would seize his arm, and try to inveigle him to her lodging.

> Arriving at my studio he would usually refuse the spare bed, and insist on lying under an old-fashioned piano which stood in the sitting room.

This is not the only example of Dowson's actually choosing the least comfortable sleeping place when others were on offer, deliberately selecting the hard bed of penitence for nameless guilts and consuming sins.[36]

While Dowson's sickness did not admit of a cure, there were certainly lacunae in his self-destructive moods, and his friends were a great comfort. Despite the long periods of storm-tossed night, he could still function, and in his more or less lucid times he became one of the group which resolved to create a new vehicle for avant garde art in Britain. Amazingly, and with some courage, a small number of people including the wrecked and desperate man Dowson had become, determined to keep the flag of decadence flying in the face of their puritan tormentors. They were going to launch their own magazine, *The Savoy*, which was to be the decadents' last stand.

CHAPTER 10

SAVOY DAYS

The new king of the decadents was the large, soft figure of the remarkable Leonard Smithers. He was a Sheffield solicitor and friend of the explorer Sir Richard Burton with whom he collaborated in translating from the Latin and printing the *Priapeia*, a collection of poems on the fertility god Priapus; they also translated and published the love poems of Catullus. Inspired by this, and by his general interest in erotic literature, Smithers travelled to London and set up first as a bookseller then additionally as a publisher. By 1895 he had a bookshop at Effingham House in Arundel Street, off the Strand, from which he sold rare books and a variety of pornography and commissioned whatever translations and new work excited him. In the early years he and his family lived above the shop and he kept up a solicitor's practice at 174 Wardour Street until 1896.

Smithers met Arthur Symons when he agreed to publish his book of verse, *London Nights*, which had been rejected by several publishers on the grounds of its supposed indecency. It was thus that Smithers entered Dowson's circle, probably in June 1895, when Smithers was 33, to become an intimate friend of the poet. Dowson was soon describing him as 'all round the best fellow I know, and it is astonishing to me how many people fail to see this, or seeing it temporarily (instance Conder, Rothenstein inter alios) succeed in quarrelling with him.'[1]

Smithers was described by Vincent O'Sullivan, an American poet and novelist who was also a friend of Dowson as, 'A man whom at first sight you would have deemed insignificant. Pale hair, eyes which looked half at you and half somewhere else, a pasty white face, and the blanched hands which always seemed to need washing, or rather scrubbing to work up the circulation. On one of these was a large wedding ring. How he kept it there was another miracle.'[2] Sexual fidelity was not one of his strong points.

Wilde described, 'His face, clean-shaven as befits a priest who serves at the altar whose God is Literature, is wasted and pale – not with poetry, but with poets, who, he says, have wrecked his life by insisting on publishing with him. He loves first editions, especially of women: little girls are his passion.' He called Smithers 'the most learned erotomaniac in Europe' and 'a delightful companion and a dear fellow, very kind to me.'[3] His book business quickly made Smithers a wealthy man. His son said, 'I doubt if any publisher has ever amassed so much money in so short a time in the book trade alone.'[4] Having made some money, he increased it by investing heavily and profitably – in the theatre and in art sales when his business moved to 4 and 5 Royal Arcade in fashionable Old Bond Street. Beardsley suggested calling the new premises The Sodley Bed.[5]

In this time of prosperity, the Smithers family moved to a mansion at 6 Bedford Square. Vincent O'Sullivan recounted how his publisher had a sluttish servant, generally instructed to let no one in, which instruction she obeyed up to the point of bribery, when she caved in and admitted all who would oblige her. O'Sullivan described how he used to go through huge, high-ceilinged, deserted rooms until at last Smithers was revealed in the gloom of some cavernous place, bending over a game of chess, often with Ernest Dowson, sometimes with Teixeira de Mattos, sometimes with some man or men unknown, and Charles Conder coaching him. O'Sullivan recounts there would be no women but Smithers' pretty, plump, black-haired wife Alice. O'Sullivan believed she stayed with him because Smithers in London could give her more excitement and attention than provincial life. 'She loves me,' Smithers would say with apparent regret. Smithers would sit in the Café Royal, or some other restaurant more or less near Arundel Street, through the long afternoons with Dowson or other of his young poets for company, discussing 'things the farthest removed from practical value' until summoned by a boy messenger to return to his office for urgent business.[6]

Edgar Jepson despised Smithers and called him 'the evil genius of Beardsley and Dowson and Conder. He surely shortened the lives of all three.' Jepson thinks Smithers damaged Dowson through his relentless socializing. The publisher was fond of company, and as their patron he demanded the society of those who worked for him, though one wonders how much encouragement Dowson needed to drink, particularly at this time in his life. Smithers' social life, complained Jepson, 'was a life in which there was so much less food than drink. It began early in the evening in Smithers' drawing room, which was adorned by an electric piano, a rare piece of furniture in those days, or at the Café Royal, or in a bar, and it went on, after the bars were closed, till far into the small hours in that drawing-room or at night-clubs.' Jepson found the nightclubs dull – he visited one called Thalia, which was the name of one of the muses, though Jepson joked he had long thought it was named 'Failure'. He remembered it for the dim light in which young bloods, their women, and army officers, determined to get through another night of seedy pleasure, while Aubrey Beardsley tried to ravish Herbert Horne's girlfriend in the supper room.[7]

Dowson's first commission from Smithers was to translate Balzac's *La Fille aux Yeux d'Or* (The Girl with Golden Eyes) for which Charles Conder was to provide six illustrations. Conder, another habitué of the Crown and a comrade in revelry, was also a comrade in pained amours, being hopelessly in love with Louise Kinsella, an American girl whom he painted in *The Green Apple* (now in the Tate Gallery). He had worked in Paris and exhibited there with Rothenstein so he, like Dowson, was at home in France. They would often trip over to Dieppe together for no particular reason but that Conder said, for example, 'I got tired of the Café Royal and the Gourmets and fancied a ragout in Dieppe' and Dowson quickly acquiesced in the scheme.[8] Rothenstein remembered Beardsley, Conder and Dowson after 'last orders' at the Crown wandering about London, and taking the early boat-train to Dieppe without any luggage – Beardsley and Dowson coming back a few days later looking the worse for wear. Conder stayed on. The people from London's artistic community often ran over to Dieppe which, while being at no great distance, had a picturesque beauty and a freedom from English social values. The town retained much of its original character with its harbour and quays, its beautiful churches and dignified streets. There were faded lawns by the sea and a row of white hotels stretching out behind them, a peppermint-coloured casino with chandeliers and green tables, and a terrace from which patrons could watch people passing. The new decadent enterprise of *The Savoy* magazine was to be largely masterminded from here.

Smithers had gone to Fountain Court to see Symons and ask him to edit a new magazine which would rival *The Yellow Book*, now entering what was described as its 'grey' period following the dismissal of Aubrey Beardsley. Symons agreed and went to recruit Beardsley at 114 Cambridge Street where the artist lived with his actress sister Mabel. It has been claimed they had an incestuous relationship but there is no good evidence for this; there was certainly some cross-dressing but the frequency or meaning of it is not known.[9] It was Mabel who suggested that the new magazine should be called *The Savoy*, somewhat provocatively for the middle of 1895, as some of the testimony about Oscar Wilde's sex life came from his reported activities in the Savoy Hotel. There is a delightful anecdote that Mabel once, when dressed as a man, encouraged Wilde's attentions as a neophyte member of his entourage – to his shock when her gender was revealed.

Aubrey Beardsley, now 23, was severely tubercular and when Symons came in he was lying on a couch 'horribly white' and Symons wondered if he had come too late.[10] The young artist had started drinking heavily after he had been sacked from *The Yellow Book* and his health was in a poor state, but the new magazine infused him with renewed vigour. He agreed with enthusiasm to work on it, and on other Smithers projects. Far from

shortening his life, his association with Leonard Smithers gave him something to live for.

Arthur Symons then travelled across to Dieppe with, as he put it, 'my
cynical publisher, Smithers, with his diabolical monocle; [and] Ernest
Dowson, the fantastic poet, who had the face of a demoralised Keats,
curiously accentuated by a manner that was exquisitely refined.'[11] The three
met several times in Dieppe with Beardsley, Conder, Rothenstein and at
least once with Conal O'Riordan. Symons and Conder stayed in 2 La Rue
de l'Oranger, opposite L'Eglise Saint Jacques. Dowson would probably
have stayed with one of them, or Smithers would have picked up his hotel
bill.

It was not all business: Conder's biographer writes of 'the arrival of
Smithers in the company of a harlot or two – big, florid, noisy creatures
were the kind he favoured', while O'Sullivan was more explicit as to
Smithers' taste in amours, saying he was 'always accompanied by some
appalling Venus, sagging breasts, pouched jaws, varicosed legs, rheumatic
ankles, wall-eyed – hideous to the point that one wondered in what suburb
of Houndsditch he could have gone to seek her.'[12] Smithers would entice
his party into the casino with offerings of brandy. More than once they had
to be removed by the police.

In Dieppe, Dowson 'discovered strange, squalid haunts about the
harbour, where he made friends with amazing inn-keepers, and got into
rows with fishermen who came in to drink after midnight.'[13] Arthur
Symons remembered passing a pavement café at one of whose tables
Dowson and a prostitute were drinking. Dowson, half-drunk, caught him
by the sleeve and confided the secret of their relationship, 'She writes
poetry,' he said, 'It is like Browning and Mrs Browning.'[14]

Conal O'Riordan spoke 50 years later of returning with Dowson and
Smithers to Newhaven from Dieppe in autumn 1895 where, in the company of Beardsley, Rothenstein, Conder and Symons, they had been
planning the lay-out of *The Savoy*. He recalled that on the following day the
steamer, *The Seaford*, collided with a fishing smack and sank immediately.
He remarked, 'I have often reflected that it might have been better for all
three of us had we gone down in that ship.'[15]

For Dowson, though, the clouds were lightening a little: he had a new
direction to his life. In Smithers he had a patron who would pay for any
translations he could do, though scarcely at a high rate. Either now or in
the near future Smithers offered to give Dowson a weekly allowance of
thirty shillings (£1.50) for all the translating work he could manage.
Dowson would soon have a publication in *The Savoy* which had solicited his
work and would welcome anything he cared to offer. He decided to make
the great leap and move out of the dock. He had never wished to live in
that part of London, and the very buildings inevitably held painful memories of his family. In business terms he was really no use there, and

Richards, the foreman who was now running the dock, actually gave Dowson some money 'on account'. 'On account' of what, one might ask: the dock's future earnings, perhaps, or Ernest Dowson's share of the sale price? Reading between the lines of this transaction, it is clear that Richards wanted to give his former employer something – perhaps out of kindness or even a desire to see the back of him. The fact that Dowson gave one of his manuscripts to Richards to remember him by, however, suggests there was good feeling between them and it was a considerate gesture from a man who had been through a lot with the Dowson family, but knew Ernest Dowson could not accept charity unless it were dressed up as a business transaction.[16]

Dowson's tremulous nature was not up to making the bold gesture of leaving the dock alone in the full glare of daylight, and he asked Edgar Jepson to come with him one night to help carry his belongings. In fact there were few things: mostly books, and some clothes, and they carried them away quite easily. Jepson did not see why they had to act under the cover of darkness, as if Dowson were absconding without paying the rent, when he was one of the owners of the dock. Jepson said, 'I never knew why we shot that moon with so romantic a secrecy; I do not believe there was any need for it.'[17] Edgar Jepson gives the impression of living through the whole of the 1890s understanding nothing at all.

Dowson went to live at 6 Featherstone Buildings, High Holborn in August or September of 1895. Plarr thought he might have chosen this location because Thomas Chatterton, another tragic poet, died in Brooke Street, High Holborn, but this is fanciful. It is more probable that he moved here because there were relatively cheap rooms in a location convenient for the West End and Poland, Arundel Street where Smithers still lived, and Fountain Court where Symons and, from October 1895, Yeats also lived.

In his memoirs written 20 years later, Yeats remembered Dowson arriving at Fountain Court one evening with a woman whom he knew because she would sometimes be seen with Beardsley or would come with a message from Smithers in that busy time when they were planning the magazine. Symons called her 'Penny plain and twopence coloured', perhaps because she charged a differential rate for sex depending on whether she was made up and well dressed. She was known as 'Penny plain' for short. One or two other young man of letters dropped in and sat around the fire and, as Yeats tells it,

> presently the harlot, having taken off all her clothes to enjoy better the pleasant blaze of the fire, began to tell her life history: her first perception of sex – she had tried to rub away the first hair from her body – her seduction, and then accounts of this or that man, especially of one old man who got his sexual excitement by watching her wring the necks of two pigeons, which he always brought in a basket. Two or three times she interrupted her story to go into the

bedroom with one or two of the men of letters, Symons alone, who prided himself on his fastidiousness, scorning her.[18]

Yeats thinks of this as an archetypal memory of Dowson's 'never choosing, taking whatever life brought into his vague hands.' Yeats acknowledges Symons as his source when he says that Dowson sober, 'would not look at a woman; did he not belong to the restaurant-keeper's daughter? But, drunk, any woman, dirty or clean, served his purpose.'[19] Yeats's superior attitude is presumably because, while he was suffering his years of unrequited love for Maud Gonne, he restrained himself from sex excepting masturbation and a brief affair with Lionel Johnson's cousin Olivia Shakespear. He moved into what had been Havelock Ellis's rooms next door to Symons over autumn and winter 1895 to 1896 in order to have a place in which to have sex with Shakespear, who was married.

Symons said that when drink gave Dowson respite from his intense love of Adelaide, 'he saw all the other faces, and he saw no more difference than between sheep and sheep.'[20] It is certainly a characteristic of love that all others fade into a uniform grey beside the image of the beloved, but this happens with or without the influence of drink.

Something was going badly wrong at Poland by the autumn of 1895, for Dowson was not even attending the restaurant every evening for dinner. The fact that he ate with Frank Harris in the East End (in an episode already recounted) indicates this, and Edgar Jepson testifies that he and Dowson started dining at Aux Gourmets with Teixeira de Mattos, Rothenstein, Conder, Conal O'Riordan, and sometimes Beardsley, Langdale and other actors of Benson's company. Jepson recalled, 'Dowson talked little: he would eat his dinner in a dreamy, childlike content, and now and then would throw in a word, but more often smile,' though Jepson now noticed sudden mood swings when someone – an interloper out to impress rather than one of the circle of friends – was disparaging about something Dowson cared about, 'his face would twist into an astonishing malignity, and he would snarl out really blasting objurgations.'[21]

Adelaide was never out of his thoughts, but when he was with her it was impossible to make her love him. She was easier to love from afar. She was cold and distant, irritated by his attentions, but doubtless also pitied him sometimes for his pathetic devotion. He made her passionless acknowledgement of his suit almost a poetic virtue, incorporating her disdainful moods into a picture of haughty beauty in his verse:

I would not alter thy cold eyes,
Nor trouble the calm fount of speech
With aught of passion or surprise.
The heart of thee I cannot reach:

In another poem there is the eternal cry of those who fail in love: that if only Adelaide knew more she would love him: 'You would have understood me, had you waited.' This time-honoured plea from the heart avoids the interpretation that Adelaide already knew him very well, which was precisely why she was not going to marry him. Even if his instability and uncertainty had been insufficiently apparent in the previous five years, by 1895 the disintegration of his personality was making itself obvious in his drinking, his neglect of his appearance and his increasing desperation. His pleading for Adelaide to give him just one kind word was simply more evidence of his unsuitability as a spouse. She was well over 17 by the autumn of 1895 and Dowson must have been thinking of her mother's words when she was just 15, that she would like the idea of marriage in a year or two. His prospects were now even worse than they had been then; he did not even have a job at the dock. If he did propose again, the answer was 'no' but it is more likely, in the light of his customary indecision, that he simply gathered from her that a proposal would not be welcomed. As he wrote in a poem about her coldness, reversing the myth of Pygmalion:

Because I am idolatrous and have besought,
With grievous supplication and consuming prayer,
The admirable image that my dreams have wrought
Out of her swan's neck and her dark abundant hair:
The jealous gods, who brook no worship save their own,
Turned my live idol marble and her heart to stone.

Dowson's story, 'The Eyes of Pride', which appeared in *The Savoy* in January 1896, was dedicated 'To A.F.' and it obviously bore a relationship to the recent difficult meetings between himself and Adelaide. Dowson thought it his best story excepting 'Apple Blossom in Brittany'.

It concerns a lover's quarrel between Seefang, a 38-year-old painter, and Rosalind, who is 19. They had met in Ploumariel in Brittany. Again, the girl is an orphan, being looked after by a guardian. They are not betrothed officially but have an understanding. Seefang wanted a woman 'who would cure him of his grossness and reform him.' His relationship with Rosalind Lingard had been 'an intoxicating experience – a delicious torture'. He describes her as, 'proud, capricious, not very sweet of temper and – I suspect – a bit of a flirt'.

If Rosalind sounds like Adelaide, his courtship is unmistakably Dowsonian. He whispers into her hair, 'Rosalind, my darling, I wish we were dead together you and I, lying there quietly, out of the worry of things.' Just the thing to inflame a girl. Back in London, the home of both of them, they find their temperaments are incompatible. They quarrel and he goes abroad to work for several years during which Rosalind marries an elderly, titled man. They meet again at a London function but suffer the same divisions, Rosalind showing her keen delight in her power to hurt him, and he realizing that they can either live to torment each other or die. He leaves again on his travels.

This story maintains the deception Dowson practised on himself in translating his experiences into prose: attempting to believe that Adelaide really did love him, but for obscure psychological reasons they were incompatible personalities. As the verse went: 'from the very first, dear! we were fated/Always to disagree.' The story of their relationship so far suggests this was not the case by any means, but facing the straightforward rejection of his love was simply too much for Dowson to accept.

Unrequited love is the cruellest experience inflicted by people not actually enemies: Dowson was demeaned and humiliated, particularly as he recognized deficiencies in Adelaide – and his friends were ever ready to do so if he did not – but he still could not help but love her. If only he could do something to make himself worthy of her, he thought. If only she loved him it would be so easy to be good, to eschew the drinking and the prostitutes; but it was so hard not to plunge into the oblivion of sensation when she was so cold. All other women paled into uniform insignificance beside her and sex with one of them, far from being a betrayal of Adelaide, became a form of self-abasement. Perhaps even the love of Adelaide itself was a form of self-abasement, and he had it in his nature to love most the woman who would treat him worst. Surely, no seraphs ever envied him this love.

His state of mind is demonstrated by a letter to Plarr at this time. He was not seeing his old friend at all now, though he wrote apologizing for his 'abominable procrastination', in September 1895 and added, 'My excuse for not having come to you on the Sunday I daresay you will find equally inexcusable but it was simply because I was in such a state of nervous and physical disability that I had not the faintest recollection of having any engagement.' Like his character Seefang, he was planning to leave, for he wrote, 'I expect to be in this country, much as it tortures and maddens me, till Christmas or the New Year.'[22]

It was not only his personal suffering which beleaguered him; the respectability of Britain was oppressive, and the baiting of decadents was flagrant. Yeats writes of having to avoid the military type of young man in the street for fear of being beaten up; and jokes at their expense abounded in respectable publications. For example, 'To a Boy-Poet of the Decadence':

> But my little good man, you have made a mistake
> If you really are pleased to suppose
> That the Thames is alight with the lyrics you make;
> We could all do the same if we chose.

> The erotic affairs that you fiddle aloud
> Are as vulgar as coin of the mint;
> And you merely distinguish yourself from the crowd
> By the fact that you put 'em in print.[23]

The bourgeoisie was savouring its spleen for *The Savoy*. *The Globe* had already announced: 'It was hardly to be supposed that the young decadents who once rioted … in *The Yellow Book* would be content to remain in obscurity after the metamorphosis of that periodical and the consequent exclusion of themselves. *The Savoy*, we learn, to be edited by Mr Arthur Symons and Mr Aubrey Beardsley, will appear in early December.'[24]

Editorial meetings on *The Savoy* continued. Yeats memorably describes such a meeting, with Beardsley going to the toilet at intervals to spit blood. He wrote, 'We began a warfare on the British public at a time when we had all against us.' Even those who might have been thought likely to support were against the project. The poet George Russell (A.E.) remonstrated with Yeats for writing in such a magazine, calling it 'the organ of the incubi and the succubi' and in a later letter he wrote, 'I never see *The Savoy* and never intend to touch it. I don't want to get allied with the currents of people with a sexual mania like Beardsley, Symons or that ruck.' Dowson and Yeats's fellow Rhymer Thomas Rolleston also wrote in violent terms attacking *The Savoy*.[25] What they would have said if they had seen the things even Smithers removed from the magazine on the grounds of taste scarcely bears thinking about. Beardsley's design for the first cover showed a proud looking woman with gloves and a riding crop dominating a cupid who is poising his genitals to piss on a copy of *The Yellow Book*. Smithers had Beardsley paint over *The Yellow Book* and emasculate the cupid, who appears androgynous in the printed version.

When the first edition of *The Savoy* was due to come out, Smithers distributed as a prospectus paper copies of the contents page which showed a drawing of John Bull with a masculine bulge at his crotch. Jepson gathered together some of the major contributors at the rooms he now shared with Horne in Kings Bench Walk, The Temple. Present were Herbert Horne, Selwyn Image, George Moore and George Bernard Shaw. The consensus was that something had to be done, though they regretted their attention's being drawn to it, and Shaw was sent to tell Smithers to modify the picture, which he did, emasculating John.[26] Dowson was contacted by the objectors and remarked, 'I have conveyed to them my own opinion in the frankest of terms: viz that they are a parcel of idiots.'[27] He considered Jepson especially asinine, for threatening to withdraw a story which Jepson himself considered so indecent he did not want his name to appear on it in case it might damage his reputation. Smithers was glad to permit him to withdraw the anonymous piece.

The decadents who were published by Smithers were always much disdained in Fleet Street and never given an opportunity to respond to attacks. 'Oftenest there was not even a pretext of impartial judgement or of merely trying to understand' wrote O'Sullivan.[28] Other literary folk were like Alice Meynell who referred contemptuously to 'the Smithers people' and felt that her friend Francis Thompson was the genius of the young generation of poets, though he was an opium addict with a predilection for little girls and his anguished verse shows he was fully imbued with the decadent consciousness.

A frequent objection to Smithers by Yeats, O'Riordan and others was that he sold pornography. Dowson had no such objection: he later translated French pornography for Smithers and anyway was familiar with the Latin erotic writers, as was his publisher. Long before he met Smithers, Dowson's only example of a poem inspired by public events was his outraged 'Against My Lady Burton' of 1891. It savages the wife of Sir Richard Burton for 'a deed of everlasting shame' in burning all her dead husband's pornographic writings including his complete translation of *The Perfumed Garden,* sacrificing it 'to her one God – sterile Propriety'.

In the event, no obeisance to propriety would help *The Savoy.* Indecency could be found in everything by those with a mind to look for it. The buyer for the major station bookseller, W.H. Smith, would not stock it because of its alleged obscenity, instancing a print of a naked Antaeus by William Blake which accompanied an article by Yeats on Blake's illustrations of Dante's *Divine Comedy.* Symons, who had visited the buyer, said Blake was 'a very spiritual artist' but the buyer replied that they had 'an audience of young ladies as well as an audience of agnostics'. He called Symons back to say that if *The Savoy* had a large sale notwithstanding, they would be pleased to see him again.[29]

Finally, after a delay which damaged the credibility of the new publication, issue one of *The Savoy* eventually came out in January 1896, not the previous December as had been announced. It was a handsome looking 170-page magazine with wide margins, attractive type, and was beautifully illustrated throughout. Symons attempted to reassure his readership, 'We have no formulas, and we desire no false unity of form or matter. We have not invented a new point of view. We are not Realists, or Romanticists, or Decadents. For us, all art is good which is good art.' This was rather giving the game away, for it was only decadents who considered that there was no morality or immorality in art – the only values by which it should be judged were artistic values.

As well as Beardsley and Symons, there were contributions by Max Beerbohm, W.B. Yeats, G.B. Shaw, Paul Verlaine, Selwyn Image, Havelock Ellis and two pieces by Dowson: 'The Eyes of Pride' and a poem titled 'Impenitentia Ultima' (Impenitence to the End) in which a lover at death asks God to grant him the one wish of a last look at the face of his beloved,

> I will praise Thee, Lord, in Hell, while my limbs are racked asunder,
> For the last sad sight of her face …

The reception for *The Savoy* was mixed but there were some very positive remarks. *The Sunday Times* said, 'we should describe it briefly as a

Yellow Book redeemed of its puerilities' and went on to add, 'the inevitable "story-teller" of the modern periodical is perhaps best found in Mr Ernest Dowson.'[30] *Punch* reviewed it as 'The Saveloy' remarking sarcastically, 'Here is a charming magazine, written by contributors who have the full courage of their woman's creed.'[31]

Dowson was not in London to see the reviews – he left for Belgium with Conal O'Riordan in the last days of September or early October 1895. Dowson had met the young, crippled novelist, who wrote under the name Norreys Connell, when they both attended a lecture on modern fiction given by Hubert Crackanthorpe in the Royalty Theatre. Something O'Riordan said in the time for discussion interested Dowson and he spoke to the novelist. They went back to Plowden Buildings to play whist and when their partners fell asleep, they talked into the dawn then went for breakfast at Lockhart's in Fleet Street, a lifelong friendship cemented.

O'Riordan used to fuss over Dowson and encourage him to take better care of himself. In the early days of their friendship in 1894 Dowson would turn up at O'Riordan's flat in Southampton Row and the Irishman would say, 'Look here, you must have slept in your clothes last night, you'd better have a tub and I'll find you some fresh linen' in which Dowson would meekly acquiesce. O'Riordan also noted that Dowson was not drinking a large amount by contemporary standards but 'he habitually drank without eating and so the alcohol quickly fumed in his brain.' Doubtless O'Riordan attempted to improve Dowson's eating habits also. He said that although he was Dowson's junior by seven years, he treated him as an older brother might 'properly in a position to lecture him on his shortcomings.'[32]

Once in late 1895 Dowson remonstrated with O'Riordan when the novelist had tried and failed to coerce him to return to their lodgings at some time after midnight and he had gone home alone. He woke at dawn to find Dowson sitting on his bed and saying with some intensity,
'Wake up Conal, wake up. There's something I must say to you.'
'Well my dear Ernest,' he answered resignedly, 'What is it?'
'What I want to tell you,' he said solemnly, 'what I've thought I ought to wake you up to tell you is that you're a bourgeois.'
'But,' said O'Riordan, 'I never was anything else and I hope I never shall be.'
'Oh,' said Dowson, very much put out, 'I never suspected it until you went home without me tonight ... I thought you'd be ashamed.'
'Not in the least,' O'Riordan assured him, whereupon Dowson said dolefully, 'Then I might as well have stayed out.'
But O'Riordan persuaded him to go to bed where he probably stayed until nightfall of the following day, as was his habit.[33]

O'Riordan had little respect for bohemian life. He wrote:

There lies a land in the stormy ocean of life, which fools think is a free country. Its inhabitants are wrinkled youths, callow satyrs, and sad women; its pleasures are joyless; its sorrows desperate; its mirthful feasts are debauches of depravity; its loves are shameful; its marriages are unions of harpies and embryos. It is a sepulchre not whited, but painted in gaudy splashes; its shores are studded with magnetic rocks, and on them sit wailing, singing sirens; and woe! woe! to the Ulysses who stops not his ears, for this is the land of Bohemia, where bleach the bones of lost souls.

This was the epigraph to O'Riordan's novel *The Fool and His Heart*, published by Smithers in 1896. It is dedicated 'To my dear friend Ernest Dowson in memory of a sorrowful journey through Flanders.' Dowson commented it was appropriate his friend should dedicate a book with such a title to him.[34] Dowson was suffering from his latest rejection by Adelaide and he may have supplied some of the inspiration for O'Riordan's slight tale of a young man who arrives in London from Ireland to seek his fortune in literary life, and is deeply in love with an unobtainable woman.

O'Riordan wrote of his friend, 'I'm afraid that Ernest (within my knowledge of him) was completely "captivated" by La Vie de Bohème. He saw only the picturesqueness, though I never heard him give it that name, and was blind to the squalor.'[35] It was with such a protector that Dowson travelled to Bruges in October 1895, then on to Paris, finishing at the Hôtel de Medici at 214 Rue St Jacques, though O'Riordan soon moved out of Paris to Mons-par-Donnemarie to board with Dowson's friend the journalist Noblet and his family.

With his departure for Belgium Dowson began the series of wanderings which were to characterize his last years. It was an important personal landmark, for he was never again to be permanently based in his home country. It was also part of a general trend as the decadents and other artists who made the London scene which Dowson knew in the early 1890s dispersed around this time. Wilde was in prison; Horne in Italy; Conder was in Dieppe then Paris; Beardsley was to spend the next few years of his short life largely on the continent for his health; Johnson was lost to morbid alcoholism; Plarr was lost to marriage. Yeats was increasingly devoting himself to literary nationalism and may not have seen Dowson after 1896. He described his last vision of Dowson, 'pouring out a glass of whisky for himself in an empty corner of my room and murmuring over and over in what seemed an automatic apology, "the first today".'[36]

CHAPTER 11

PARIS NIGHTS

Paris gave back Dowson some sparks of his old fire. He was impoverished, but his correspondence has all the joys of his letters of two years previously. He noted cheerfully that O'Riordan smoked and drank nothing so he could afford his two square meals a day, while 'I tighten my belt in order to allow myself a sufficiency of cigarettes and absinthe.' This was as much luxury as he could manage: female companionship was too expensive. 'As for women,' he remarked, he 'dare not even look at them.'[1]

In the Latin Quarter he was back among the cafés, restaurants, prostitutes, and above all the literary friends from whom he drew his lifeblood. His hotel was doubtless chosen for its proximity to the homes of Paul Verlaine and Henry Davray. Davray was a literary journalist on the *Mercure de France* who was so anglophile he used the English rather than the French form (Henri) of his name. He was Dowson's chief advocate in the French press, having translated several of Dowson's poems and printed them in English next to his French versions. Davray was also a key figure encouraging Les Jeunes, the younger generation of artists, chiefly through conversation and free association at the cafés Davray frequented. Dowson now met, or in some cases became reacquainted with, the poets Pierre Louys, Yvanhoé Rambosson and Jean de Tinan, with the author and journalist Gabriel de Lautrec, and with the novelist André Gide. All these young men were within five years of Dowson's age, with the exception of Tinan who was eight years younger but was still, worn out from disease and drink, to predecease Dowson.

Dowson took the first opportunity to visit Verlaine who was living at 187 Rue Saint-Jacques in an apartment shared with an elderly former prostitute. The old poet, now lame, had lived for too long in Paris like a fly in a pot of marmalade (in his own words) and was enduring the consequences. He suffered from syphilis, acute gonorrhoea, various alcohol-related complaints, and was a diabetic. He was still the toast of bohemian

Paris, however, when he hobbled out with his old overcoat and battered felt hat and his hirsute face lined with sadness, demanding another absinthe. He had long had the same habit of personal neglect as Dowson, to the extent that one young writer introduced to the great master had to get away because Verlaine's clothes were so filthy they made him feel sick.[2]

Dowson visited Verlaine several times, and after the first visit the older poet was so kind as to loan Dowson his 'secretary' to help move into his lodgings. This was the notorious Bibi-la-Purée who was originally named André Salis and who acted as a friend and jester to literary Paris. He was the son of a wine and spirit dealer in Angoulême who had long since disowned him. He used to do services for the lodgers at a hotel in the Rue Broca – running errands for them, blacking their boots and providing them with umbrellas which he used to steal from the cafés of the Latin Quarter. He had no home or means of existence but the 'ragged finery' he stood up in. He was described as being, 'in perpetual masquerade. He usually wore a high hat, and never went abroad without a huge bouquet in his ragged frock coat.' Verlaine was his most important charge, and he would clear a way for the lame poet to find a seat in the Café Soleil d'Or or the François Premier.[3]

Soon after his arrival Dowson was called on by Gabriel de Lautrec who knocked and walked into Dowson's room to be greeted with a blinding flash. It was caused by Bibi-la-Purée attempting to start a welcoming fire. As Lautrec recounted it, 'Crouching in front of the hearth he was in the process of putting new life into the fire by rhythmically and liberally sprinkling it with a bottle of petrol, at the serious risk of setting the whole place alight.' Dowson said nothing but seemed daunted by the pyrotechnics.[4] There is an account of Bibi and Dowson, drunk together late one night on the Boulevard St Michel, with Dowson brandishing his friend's umbrella like a weapon and loudly declaiming one of Verlaine's poems.

Too soon for Dowson, but probably in good time for the suffering poet, Verlaine died on 8 January 1896. Dowson and Vincent O'Sullivan attended the funeral together, and walked in the procession from the church of Saint-Etienne-du-Mont to the Cimetière des Batignolles. O'Sullivan was carrying an enormous floral wreath on which was written in big red letters *The Senate*, the name of a monthly publication in English of whose editorial board O'Sullivan was a member. The general public were impressed by it because they though it was sent by the French Senate. Several of Verlaine's admirers remarked on this little delegation, showing that Verlaine had friends in England.[5]

There was said to be an 'army of poets' following the coffin on the hour-long walk, and crowds lined the streets of the Latin Quarter to pay their respects. At the cemetery, Bibi-la-Purée stole the umbrellas of the dignitaries who came to hear the last rites, so Verlaine was buried as he had lived, amid dignity and squalor.

1. Ernest Dowson in 1868, aged nine months, on his mother's lap.

2. Ernest Dowson, aged three, photographed in Turin.

3. Dowson, aged five, a portrait by W.G. Wills.

4. Dowson with friends at Queen's College, Oxford. From left: Arthur Moore, W.R. Thomas, Dowson and P.L. Andrews.

5. A drawing of Dowson
by William Rothenstein.

6. A drawing of Dowson
by Charles Conder.

7. One of the cabmen's shelters which were frequently used by Dowson. Erected for the drivers of horse-drawn carriages, they are still in use by taxi drivers.

8. The Cheshire Cheese, where the Rhymers' Club met.

9. The house where Dowson died in what is now Sangley Road, Catford. Other houses in the street, which have not been modernised, give a better idea of what it looked like when it was the Sherards' home.

10. The house where
Dowson's mother died in
Quentin Road, Lee.

11. Dowson's gravestone in
Ladywell cemetery before it
suffered vandalism.

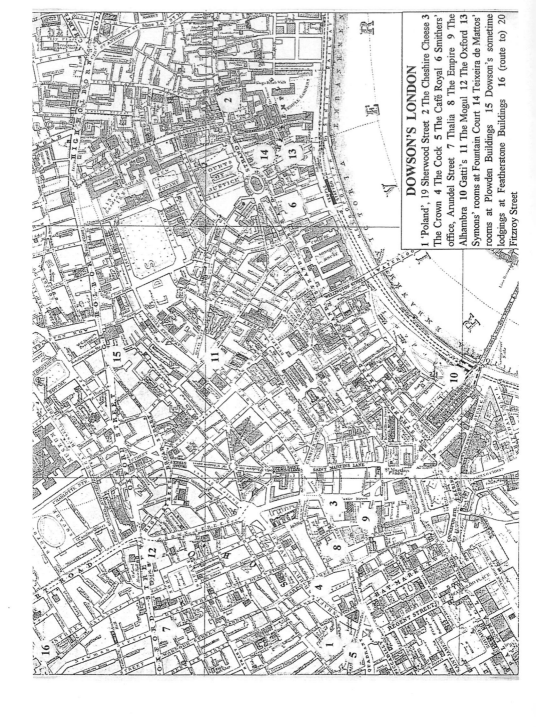

DOWSON'S LONDON

1 'Poland', 19 Sherwood Street 2 The Cheshire Cheese 3 The Crown 4 The Cock 5 The Café Royal 6 Smithers' office, Arundel Street 7 Thalia 8 The Empire 9 The Alhambra 10 Gatti's 11 The Mogul 12 The Oxford 13 Symons' rooms at Fountain Court 14 Teixeira de Mattos' rooms at Plowden Buildings 15 Dowson's sometime lodgings at Featherstone Buildings 16 (route to) 20 Fitzroy Street

Dowson would visit Gabriel de Lautrec for parties and poetry readings at his appartment near the Palais Royal. Yvanhoé Rambosson's trick at these gatherings was to climb out of the fourth-floor window and work his way along a narrow ledge to the window of a woman on whom he had something of a crush. She was never known to let him in. Rambosson was quite a joker; he had a paragraph inserted in two French newspapers announcing an imaginary reception given by Davray in honour of 'les poètes anglais', Dowson and O'Riordan, deliberately spelling both their names incorrectly as such social news items have a habit of doing.[6]

Dowson's evenings were filled with people and light-hearted entertainments. One evening at Gabriel de Lautrec's, with another couple of poets and an elderly academic, they ate dinner then drank rum 'and worked hanky-panky with the planchette', a board supposedly used to receive written messages from the spirit world. They got a message from Satan but, as Dowson remarked, 'he appeared to have nothing of the slightest importance to say, so they gave up and took hashish instead, then fell asleep on sofas and mattresses.'[7]

His letters are cheerful but contain constant appeals for funds – he was clearly living beyond his slender means. His failure to eat properly was also exacerbating his physical condition. In one letter he remarks that his dinner at the time of writing is 'one longish roll 5c [centimes] one Brie cheese 20c. ½ bottle red wine 50c.' He managed also to have an absinthe at the D'Harcourt, a café where he would often meet friends, and had spent something on tobacco and cigarette papers. He had only pennies to buy bread the next day but, mercifully, 'lo there was a letter and £1 and I went out with tears of gratitude in my eyes and had an absinthe and later breakfast.'[8] It was not a life calculated to maintain health, and he fell ill in January, but was adequately recovered in February to receive Smithers who came over to organize the publication of a volume of Dowson's verse.

The debilitating effects of his tuberculosis and lifestyle aside, by the beginning of 1896 Dowson was getting back into his stride as a writer. He had finished *La Fille aux Yeux D'Or* which he dedicated to Pierre Louys to whom, Dowson noted, Wilde's original *Salome* (in French) was dedicated. He was next engaged by Smithers in translating Voltaire's racy mock-epic on Joan of Arc, *La Pucelle*. He had intended to translate the whole work but a change of plan meant he principally updated two old English translations. Parts of the poem, however, had been deemed too indecent to translate earlier, particularly the climax in which Joan of Arc yields to the blandishments of St Denis's ass, and Dowson did service in translating these.

Cupid overlooked the scene,
And with a smile of pleasure watched the Maid,
Twisting her rump and twining close her thighs,
Catching the fire with which her lover sighs,

Hasting the moment when her maid-hood dies.
Nor is her satin crupper loathe to press
The bare sword of her ass with fond caress.[9]

Dowson at last returned to the long neglected *Adrian Rome*, and was
writing a new story for *The Savoy* – eventually to be 'Countess Marie of the
Angels', published in April 1896. It was dedicated to Jean de Tinan, making
it one of only two stories Dowson dedicated to individuals, the other ('The
Eyes of Pride') was to Adelaide. Set in Paris in a winter which still feels like
autumn, it concerns a 50-year-old English officer who had served in India
(as Dowson's maternal grandfather had) and had returned to the city of his
boyhood. His childhood sweetheart, Marie, whom he remembered as a 15-
year-old girl, had been obliged by her family to marry a rich count who
proved to be a fool who dissipated his fortune. The officer had seen her
once again but her sense of duty to her family forced her to send him away
for the feelings he aroused in her were too strong. When they meet again
after her husband's death, he proposes but she persuades him not to marry
her for reasons which are never made clear. He says, 'Yes, very likely you
are right. There is a season for all things, for one's happiness as for the rest,
and missing it once, one misses it forever. ...There are some miseries
which are like happiness.' They part with no expectation of ever meeting
again.

It was like his relationship with Adelaide: everything was such a problem, it was all so difficult, it was better just to move away. As *Punch*
satirized the decadent lover of fiction:

For marriage now I'm too complicated
Too many-natured, too finely strung[10]

Dowson was also writing new verse. It is difficult to tell exactly which
verses were written in the 1895–6 period, except perhaps those which
appeared in *The Savoy* for the first time, but it seems likely that the devas-
tating events of 1895 became a dark muse, once the numbness of shock
had worn off. Because Dowson usually sent copies of his verse to friends,
or published them quickly, most have been dated. There are a number
which are undated, however, and these were among the poems which were
collected in spring 1896 for the volume *Verses*. Several show a depth of
feeling about death and the brevity of life which it is more than tempting to
see as informed by the death of his parents and the insistent intimations of
his own mortality brought on by his disease.

Most clearly this is seen in the verse which he placed at the front of the
volume, before even the dedication. It takes as its title another quotation
from Horace's Odes, 'Vitae summa brevis spem nos vetat incohare longam'
(How should hopes be long, when life is short) and it is a model of Dowson's classical simplicity, conveying the deepest feeling with the minimum
number of words and images. In its entirety it runs:

They are not long, the weeping and the laughter,
   Love and desire and hate:
I think they have no portion in us after
   We pass the gate.

They are not long, the days of wine and roses:
   Out of a misty dream
Our path emerges for a while, then closes
   Within a dream.

Poems which may date from this period and have similar themes are 'Gray Nights' and 'Vesperal', with its refrain taken from the Gospel of Matthew: 'Sufficient for the day are the day's evil things!'

Other verse which seems likely to have been written at this time shows his sense that Adelaide had slipped away from him, though his love, which was always redolent of a sense of death, was now even more insistent. He yearned in one poem to

Reap death from thy live lips in one long kiss,
   And look my last into thine eyes and rest:
What sweets had life to me sweeter than this
   Swift dying on thy breast?[11]

The arrangements for the publication of Dowson's first individual volume were complicated by the unwelcome involvement of Dowson's friend, Edgar Jepson, who made efforts to look after Dowson's affairs in London, something Dowson had neither asked nor encouraged him to do. The root of the problem was Jepson's hatred of Smithers, who was now enjoying an increasing influence with Dowson, and wanted to be his sole publisher.

Dowson had agreed to have his verses published by The Bodley Head when Lane and Mathews were in partnership. Now they had split up, Mathews was taking on Dowson as an author. Mathews had been in a position to make an offer for Dowson's verses for two years, and had been so certain he would be the publisher that the volume had been advertised, but before Dowson left London he was still speaking of trying to get some definite offer from Mathews. Jepson offered to visit Mathews on his behalf, even though he did not know the publisher, and Dowson told him to do nothing of the kind. Nevertheless, Jepson went to see Mathews, and in Paris at the beginning of December 1895 Dowson received a letter from Jepson offering terms for the publication, which he advised Dowson to accept. He was 'generally writing as a recognised go-between between Mathews and myself,' Dowson recounted to Arthur Moore, 'I thought it so impertinent that I have not troubled to answer it.'[12] He must have thought twice about this, for he wrote to O'Riordan (they had by now parted) around the same time, 'Jepson has, I fear, successfully embroiled me with everybody. I have just written to ask what the devil he means by it!'[13]

The letter to Moore who was, of course, a solicitor, continues by asking him to 'as delicately or as forcibly as you like, suggest to Jepson on the first occasion, that by interfering in my affairs he is not assisting me but on the contrary seriously compromising me.' Jepson continued to write 'impudently familiar letters to Dowson to which he did not reply, but he eventually desisted, and the friendship was at an end.'[14]

Dowson was in a quandary about the publication of his poems. There is no doubt that a more assertive man would have pushed for his work to be published far earlier, but it was not Dowson's way. He was now anxious about taking the project from Mathews but convinced himself that he could give it to Smithers because 'besides offering me most munificent terms, he is one of my most intimate friends.'[15] Smithers was doubtless persuasive, and it must have been a rare treat for a poet to be able to say about a publisher that he 'was so very keen' about poetry. Dowson in his turn was 'anxious to do anything I could for him in return for the innumerable services he has done me.'[16] It may also have affected Dowson that Mathews had made a poor production job of his volume of stories, *Dilemmas*, which was not an attractive book.

All Dowson's affairs back in London were as complicated. He had become even more estranged from his relatives whom he was describing as 'bloodsuckers' and in other extreme terms. A specific target was his uncle, Stanley Hoole, which was particularly unfair as all external evidence suggests that Hoole spent his own time and money attempting to sort out the complicated affairs of the Dowson family. Marmaduke Langdale, who knew him, probably through his actor son Gerald Hoole, wrote to Dowson that his uncle spoke 'kindly, of him and was anxious to do everything in his power for him'.[17] Sherard later wrote of Hoole as a 'kind old gentleman'.[18] Yet Dowson took it into his head that his relatives felt 'malice and meanness' towards him and were bent on cheating him of his patrimony about which he would take legal action if he had the means to do so.[19] On another occasion he wrote 'of the monstrous way in which I have been exploited and swindled and ruined by the very people who, from their near kinship to me, I had thought I could depend on – at least not to rob me too flagrantly – I never expected justice or generosity from them.'[20]

The slow speed with which the sum still owing to Dowson was being processed through competing claims was due less to the malevolence of any individual than to the tangled affairs of the Dowson family, complicated by the mortgages on the near-bankrupt dock, the debts to be paid, and the death of Annie Dowson before Alfred Dowson's will had been finally settled.

Ernest Dowson confessed that his resentment 'lights up a sort of intense flame of hatred and loathing which destroys the peace of my days and the sleep of my nights and deprives me of any chance that remains to me of getting cured. For I have been told particularly that my one chance depends on my ability to avoid any strong emotion or excitement.'[21] Wills and inheritance matters frequently stimulate strong passions in people, particularly those with limited business sense, and no great message should be drawn from his remarks about his relatives, but in terms of his own mortality, it shows Dowson was clearly preparing for the end. He wrote in this letter in January 1896 that he was settling his affairs and making O'Riordan and Smithers his executors – a plan he did not in fact put into practice.

One legacy from his ancestors which cursed Dowson was the perpetually bad state of his teeth. His teeth blackened when he was in his twenties, and they started giving him so much pain he had them extracted – presumably one or two at a time. He was probably afflicted by rapidly progressive periodontitis, an inflammatory reaction of the tissues surrounding the teeth. It is characterized by severe and rapid bone destruction which may lead to abscess formation and tooth loss. The jaw pain Dowson suffered which he described as 'neuralgia' in a number of letters was probably caused by a manifestation of this condition, which is hereditary.[22] The nineteenth-century treatment for syphilis by mercurous salts would also damage the gums and result in blackened teeth but there is no evidence that Dowson had syphilis or received such treatment.

Dowson had some kind of skin condition, which cannot have been very serious as it is rarely mentioned. It may have been eczema affecting him intermittently. In May 1896 he wrote to Smithers, 'So far as the malady is concerned I have driven it off my hand and am able to go out without a glove.'[23]

No better for his peace of mind than his various complaints was the situation Dowson had left at Poland when he departed London 'on a sort of mad impulse', which was as complicated as ever. He was corresponding with Adelaide and distance seemed to do their relationship good, as Dowson reported that they were on the most affectionate terms that they had been for years, but he then spoiled the effect of this assurance by writing '– at least I think so –'. Dowson urged his friend Sam Smith to visit Poland to inform Adelaide 'that to get a letter from her is my chiefest pleasure in life' but he begged Smith 'Do not speak of my exile as being so prolonged as I presume it will be. I always write to her with the intention of returning in a month or two – and so I may – for a fortnight! but I doubt if ever I shall make my home in England again.' He held out the hope that the Foltinowicz mother and daughter would carry out a notion they had spoken of and return to Germany, where he would join them. Thus he made the already unlikely event of a union between himself and Adelaide contingent on another unlikely event: their removal to another country. If it can be described as a plan at all, it was one destined for early failure.

Whatever his distress, Dowson was keen not to have his friends think of him as totally irredeemable. He had the lack of self-pity characteristic of a true bohemian. Marmaduke Langdale had written to Dowson that he had 'created a sort of mist of trouble, vague as ghosts in a dream, with which I surround you. It forms a sort of halo of sorrow for you and excites the tears and sympathy of those who love and admire you from afar.' Dowson wrote to Smith that he objected to being wept over.

> I am not remarkably prosperous nor particularly happy – who is? But I do not go about in Paris with a halo of ghosts and tears, having been gifted by God with a sense – common to you and myself but to how many of our other friends? – of humour! occasionally smile, and even in Paris, at a late hour of the night, and Paris is later than London, have been known to laugh.[24]

Dowson shared late nights in Paris mainly with his French friends but he would also see Smithers on his visits to the capital. Conder was also living there, as were Vincent O'Sullivan and Robert Sherard. Beardsley moved to the continent for his health in February 1896, leaving Symons to edit *The Savoy* virtually alone. Beardsley and Dowson moved in the same circles and often came across each other. Dowson had the same admiration as others had for Beardsley's talents and even dedicated a poem to him. Their early contacts in London seem to have been amicable enough, but Beardsley developed an ill-concealed contempt for Dowson which probably tells the observer more about Beardsley than it does about the poet.

Of all the hothouse flowers of the decadence, Aubrey Beardsley was the most curious. He was an infant prodigy but it was not clear whether he was going to be a musician, a writer or an artist. His physical frailty was unquestioned, however: he showed the first signs of tuberculosis at seven and thus lived the whole of his conscious life within the pall of death. His family lived in genteel poverty and he was obliged to start work as an insurance clerk at 16. In 1891 when he was 18 and had developed the hatchet-faced profile with the shambling gait which was to distinguish him, he and his sister Mabel walked into Edward Burne-Jones' studio. Beardsley looked at the pre-Raphaelite master's pictures and showed him some of his own, at which Burne-Jones invited him to stay for tea, where Oscar and Constance Wilde were among the guests. This was his introduction to the artistic life of the 1890s, moving directly into the centre of things. He made his reputation almost immediately as the illustrator of Malory's *Morte d'Arthur* in 1892, then Wilde's *Salome* in 1893; but despite being obviously the best illustrator of his age, he never made enough money from his drawings to live on and always lived in fear of poverty.

Beardsley's distaste for Dowson, who was five years his senior, must be set beside his similarly strong feelings about other decadents. He would not design the cover for Dowson's translation of *La Fille aux Yeux D'Or* because Conder had drawn the pictures for it and, he said, 'my artistic conscience forbids me to add any decoration to a book which he has illustrated.'[25] It was at Beardsley's specific insistence that Wilde should not

be allowed to write for *The Yellow Book*, 'whether anonymously, pseudony-
mously, or under his own name' and he made the same stipulation over *The
Savoy* and a later proposed magazine, *The Peacock*.[26] This was probably
because Wilde had tired of Beardsley's insolence and had made him the
subject of his barbed wit in company, and Beardsley was very sensitive. His
antipathy to Wilde long pre-dated the playwright's trial.

Dowson and Beardsley's situation as 'Smithers people' meant they were
often obliged to collaborate. Beardsley did the binding block for Dowson's
Verses which he designed as two floral, curving lines coming together in a Y
shape. Beardsley joked it meant, 'Why was this book ever written?' Still, he
needed the work and despite his illness which left him frequently spitting
blood, he was glad to be given the commission for a series of drawings to
illustrate Dowson's *The Pierrot of the Minute*, which Smithers decided to
publish in 1897. Beardsley later wrote to his patron André Raffalovich, 'I
have just made rather a pretty set of drawings for a foolish playlet of Ernest
Dowson's'[27] and he later referred to Dowson dismissively as 'the
authorette': 'does the authorette approve?'[28]

Beardsley suggested Arthur Symons should translate *Les Liaisons
Dangereuses*, which he was to illustrate, instead of Dowson, but Dowson got
the job. Within seven days Beardsley was writing, 'Hurry Dowson up over
the translation.'[29] He was waiting to know the first letters of the chapters so
he could do illustrated capitals. He wrote politely enough to Dowson
asking for this information but then wrote to Smithers that the translation
'will want a good deal of touching up, at least it seems so to me', rather
exceeding the boundaries of his responsibilities as an illustrator.[30] He
referred, probably sarcastically, to 'Good old Dowson' in January 1897
when Dowson had completed his work on *La Pucelle*.[31]

Vincent O'Sullivan, another of the Smithers circle who saw a good deal
of Dowson and Beardsley, said:

> In sight of Dowson's appearance and way of life, Beardsley lost all patience and
> tolerance, of which he had not a large stock. He knew he had only a few years
> to live, but he loved life, was interested in lots of things, was not in the least
> morbid. ... The spectacle of a man slowly killing himself, not with radiance, still
> less with decorum, but in a mumped and sordid way, with no decoration in the
> process, but mean drink shops, poisonous liquor, filth and malady, for all the
> accompaniment to the march down under – that, when he saw it in Dowson,
> irritated Beardsley beyond control.[32]

Dowson's appearance gave Beardsley additional cause for complaint.
O'Sullivan wrote:

> Dowson's neglect of his personal appearance went to lengths which I have
> never seen in anybody else still on the surface, and hardly in bums and beats
> and down-and-out tramps forced by hardship to a condition which they have
> not the means to remedy. The thing about Dowson was that he did not want to

remedy it. He was never denuded of money as Wilde was sometimes. But to spend money on baths and clothes and remedies seemed to him to be putting money to the wrong account.[33]

O'Sullivan may be exaggerating, and he is certainly conflating the Dowson of 1896 with the man of 1898, when the poet's decline had reduced him to an even more miserable state, but the general impression is of a person who had never been excessively concerned about personal cleanliness or appearance, becoming more and more dishevelled. Referring specifically to the time they spent in Paris in 1895–6, O'Riordan said, 'In horrible rooms in the Quartier Latin it was almost impossible to keep clean without at least a weekly visit to the public baths; and that was not easy to persuade him to do.'[34]

When Smithers treated his artists they went to good, even fashionable restaurants, where Dowson's appearance did not escape suspicion, but there were no complaints. O'Sullivan felt Beardsley's smouldering resentment, however. He wrote, 'Now that was just what Beardsley could not stand. He said it was unfair to bring a man like Dowson, who looked as if he had slept in the gutter and, what was more, had a very visible malady, among a number of well dressed people who paid a good sum of money for the pleasure of dining in clean and wholesome surroundings.' Is he referring to Dowson's tuberculosis, one wonders? It would be strange to call this a 'visible' malady exactly – 'evident' would be a more appropriate word. Perhaps O'Sullivan is referring to Dowson's skin condition.

When Beardsley did spend time in Dowson's company 'he showed his temper, fell into prolonged silences, and then would answer fretfully in retorts.' Dowson would say pleasant things to him to encourage the young artist to be pleasant but he received waspish retorts in response. 'But Dowson is a great poet,' O'Sullivan said in his defence, in response to one of Beardsley's criticisms. 'I don't care,' said Beardsley. 'No man is great enough to excuse behaviour like his.'[35]

Dowson seemed not to notice, or perhaps not to care about Beardsley's animosity. He wrote to Henry Davray that he would introduce him to Beardsley and remarked on how amusing the artist had been when he took hashish for the first time.

> There was no result for some hours: then suddenly, while we were dining with Smithers at Margery's, the hashish began to work very powerfully. Luckily we were in a cabinet or I think we would have been turned out – for Beardsley's laughter was so tumultuous that it infected the rest of us – who had not taken hashish, and we all behaved like imbeciles.[36]

Dowson reported that he had a 'delightful few days' before he left Paris with Beardsley, Smithers and a girl from the Thalia who travelled with them.[37]

These last days included Dowson's last engagement in Paris, on 11 February 1896, when he went to see Wilde's *Salome* (in the original French) at the Théâtre de l'Oeuvre with Beardsley and Lautrec. He later wrote a long account of the enthusiasm with which it was received to Mrs Constance Wilde, one of a number of examples of the solicitude with which Dowson acted towards Wilde, 'that poor victim of English hypocrisy' and those who had been caught up in the Wilde debacle.[38] One night Charles Whibley, the *Pall Mall Gazette*'s French correspondent, had Ernest Dowson put out of a café on the Boulevards because Dowson took him to task about his censorious attitude to Oscar Wilde. When Dowson's *Verses* was published he sent a copy to Lord Alfred Douglas, Dowson cursing the 'monstrous bêtise' (stupidity) of the people who made it impossible for Smithers to stay in business if he published Douglas's poetry.[39]

The party of Paris had to come to an end for Dowson in the middle of February 1896 because he could no longer afford the prices in the capital. 'It is impossible to live in Paris without sitting in cafés and they mount up,' he wrote.[40] It was cheaper to live in the countryside for Dowson who was now reliant on his small stipend from Smithers for his translation work, plus whatever he could raise by selling stories and poems to *The Savoy*. There would also be fewer distractions in the country and Dowson was keen to get on with his stories, with *Adrian Rome* and his translations. After making inquiries Dowson travelled to Brittany, to Pont-Aven in Finistère which he called 'world's end' from the literal translation of the name (finis terrae, the end of the earth). Here he was to remain for the rest of 1896 and the Dowson legend as the world was to come to know it would be created.

CHAPTER 12

SAVAGE BEAUTY

Dowson made his way across France to the little square of Pont-Aven with a cross in its centre, surrounded by grey stone shops and houses and two hotels. Through it ran a river of spectacular beauty which had brought prosperity to the town as it brought grain to Pont-Aven's mills. The beauty of the port and the surrounding countryside attracted artists, notably Gauguin, who arrived in 1886 to become the central figure in what became called the Pont-Aven School, before leaving for Tahiti. By the time Dowson arrived, the port had already become a magnet for artists and art tourists. The Hôtel Gloanec, recommended to Dowson by Arthur Moore and the Parisian painter Emile Jourdan, offered board and lodging plus cider for 85 francs a month. It was the more bohemian of the two hotels, as Marie-Jeanne Gloanec who ran it had a fondness for artists and was not heavy-handed in pressing for payment of bills. The other residents when Dowson was there were mostly French and American painters. The locals tended to call all outsiders including the French ones, 'the Americans'. Dowson immediately felt at home and wrote, 'I feel I shall do much work here: it is an adorable place and, much as I love Paris, where I have lived now some time, I felt rested and restored to some prospect of reasonable health directly I came here.'[1]

Opposite the Hôtel Gloanec was the more bourgeois Villa Julia where he said the people were 'bête à faire mourir d'ennui' (so stupid as to make you die of boredom).[2] The most interesting guest in the town as far as Dowson was concerned was a small girl, the adopted daughter of an English woman called Agnes Henry whom Dowson described as an anarchist, though he made no distinction between socialists and anarchists.

The poet took the little girl to the circus, and delighted in telling of her reactions to the entertainment.

In the spring he became restless, perhaps finding he was not working as well as he should, and he wanted more quiet than even Pont-Aven would give him. He also felt a change of air might be better for his health which had been poor – he was spitting up blood – so he returned to Le Faouet, perhaps 20 miles away, where he had happy memories of having stayed with Moore in 1892. From there he confided to Victor Plarr that 'constant ill health and depression of spirits have made me a sorry correspondent. ... Faouet is charming in the daytime. One can work without interruption, and, tired of work, one can bask in the blazing sunshine by Sainte-Barbe. But the evenings, the cold, bleak desolation of the evenings!' Nothing was as it had been, even the girls: 'The two little twins, whom Moore and I admired much ... are grown into ugly and farouches girls of twelve.'[3] His letters betrayed there was some serious disturbance in his relationship with Adelaide which he found difficult to admit even to himself. On the one hand his letters gave factual information about her – Missie was studying typing; the restaurant was closed and she and her mother were staying in the upstairs rooms, bored and lonely; they had resumed the restaurant and were trying to sell it as a going concern.[4] On the other hand, Dowson was more depressed about Adelaide than ever before, particularly as the summer wore on and he suffered continued heartache amid the pastoral life of Brittany. 'Why have I wept for a white girl's paleness passing ivory!' he wrote in 'Breton Afternoon'.

He apologized to Plarr in a letter for his miserable tone but said, 'As I have no lungs left to speak of, an apology for a liver, and a broken heart I may be permitted to rail a little sometimes.' He could not even write Adelaide's name but indicated her with a dash, saying she 'writes to me fairly often, friendly letters, which give me sleepless nights and cause me to shed morbid and puerile tears. But she is very kind.'[5] Plarr remarked that Dowson adored the 'savage beauty' of Brittany, noting particularly the granite, the cathedral of Dol, and the walk up the hill opposite Sainte Barbe. Many of his friends record that he was at his happiest in Breton villages; indeed, he became so closely associated with Brittany that he was sometimes known as Douzeuc, the Breton version of his name.

During his stay there he was visited by Arthur Moore, Charles Conder, Vincent O'Sullivan, Leonard Smithers and his old Oxford friend John Arthur Fallowes so he was far from isolated in the summer months. His reputation was much enhanced when *Verses* was finally published in June 1896 in a beautiful volume with a white cover adorned with the gold curving design by Aubrey Beardsley. Smithers published 330 copies, 30 of them on Japanese vellum, and the publisher's generosity as much as his pride in his work led him to give away many copies. It was indeed a slim volume, of less than 60 pages, but it contained most of Dowson's best verse which, in Symons' words 'has the pathos of things too young and too frail ever to grow old, and I think there are a few poems in this book which will indeed never grow old.'⁶

Dowson followed the practice of Verlaine (which was also imitated by John Gray) of dedicating individual poems to friends. Dedicatees included Arthur Moore, Robert Sherard, Victor and Nellie Plarr, Aubrey Beardsley, Hubert Crackanthorpe, Charles Sayle, Teixeira de Mattos, Herbert Horne, Sam Smith, Arthur Cecil Hillier, Conal O'Riordan, Arthur Symons, Vincent O'Sullivan, Yvanhoé Rambosson, Leonard Smithers, Selwyn Image, Marmaduke Langdale, Gabriel de Lautrec and Henry Davray. There was generally no personal reason for dedications – the poems did not relate directly to the individuals concerned.

As well as being a generous gesture, the dedications served the purpose of making the verse seem more exclusive, as if the reader were entering a private world when reading Dowson's verse. The same function was served by the Latin titles of many of the poems: they were addressed to a literary, classically educated audience who needed no translations or footnotes to identify quotations from Horace or Propertius. It was not to everyone's liking. *The Times* in its review remarked on the inappropriateness of 'this curious practice', remarking, 'It may be rather alarming ... for the friends of those mentioned to come across such a heading to a page as "Extreme Unction. For Lionel Johnson" or "A Requiem. For John Gray" when there is no reason to believe that the gentlemen in question are anything but alive and well.'⁷ The *Pall Mall Gazette* reviewer was even more condemnatory: 'One thing, Mr Dowson! Do not, in future issues, put the names of your friends, to whom you dedicate your poems, between the title and the text, especially when they are dedicated "for" and not "to" them. It is generally misleading, sometimes painful, occasionally grotesque.'⁸

This reviewer found little to enjoy in the volume anyway, saying, 'The whole horizon of a poet is not, or ought not to be, confined to an entirely erotic and sentimental region, to a few musk-scented fancies, ranging from a dalliance so innocent that it never gets beyond glances, to phantasmal passions of a somewhat uncomfortable character.'

The *Bookman*'s critic similarly told Dowson to stand up and act like a man, recommending, 'A little fresh strength of nerves, a warmer coursing of the blood in his veins' for the poet, though the writer acknowledged his 'melancholy charm' and charitably admitted 'the legitimacy of depressing verses' which would ensure the book would be liked.⁹ The *Athenaeum* reviewer said Dowson was indebted to Swinburne and Symons but had not the latter's 'spark of genius. ... Mr Dowson knows the language fairly well,' it remarks, 'if only he had something to say!'¹⁰

The *Daily Courier* started in a more positive vein: 'Mr Dowson has a genuine talent. Indeed he has several talents. A classic propriety of epithet, rising at moments to remarkable distinction; a full, rich melody, and even among the wreck of all that is mouldy and unwholesome, an occasional dignity and thought of feeling – all these things are found in his verses and lift them out of the common ruck.' But the reviewer had to assert his masculinity against the poet's apparent lack of the quality. He remarks of 'Cynara', 'to the technical excellence of these lines who could be blind? But for the sentiment, the sentimentality, the nerveless effeminacy, and above all, the affectation, the patent insincerity!'[11]

The main dedication was 'In Preface: For Adelaide' and it read in the authentic tones of Dowson speaking to his love:

> To you, who are my verses, as on some very future day, if you ever care to read them, you will understand, would it not be somewhat trivial to dedicate any one verse, as I may do, in all humility, to my friends? Trivial too, perhaps, only to name you even here? Trivial, presumptuous? For I need not write your name for you at least to know that this and all my work is made for you in the first place, and I need not be reminded by my critics that I have no silver tongue such as were fit to praise you. So for once you shall go indedicate, if not quite anonymous; and I will only commend my little book to you in sentences far beyond my poor compass which will help you perhaps to be kind to it.

There follows a passage from *L'Education Sentimentale* by Flaubert, one of Dowson's favourite authors, in which the hero Frédéric addresses the woman he has always loved but who has never been his lover. They have now both grown old, and he sees with a shock that her hair is white, and in a rare moment of self-knowledge he realizes it would not be right for him to make love to her now; he fears revulsion later on, and the tarnishing of his ideal. The passage Dowson quotes is when the two face each other for the last time and Frédéric says

> Your presence, your least movement seemed to me more than human. My heart fluttered like dust under your feet. Your effect on me was like a moonlit summer night when everything is perfume, soft shadows, whiteness and infinity. The sweetness of the flesh and the soul are held together for me in your name which I repeat to myself, trying to kiss it with my lips.
>
> Sometimes your words come back to me like an echo from far away, like the sound of a bell carried by the wind. It seems that you are there with me as I read any passage about love in books, for whatever is written, however extreme, you have made me feel it.

In Flaubert's book it is a valediction to their love, and there is in Frédéric a sense that perhaps he has been in love with love itself, or with the very words: a nuance Dowson would certainly have appreciated.

Dowson was pitifully anxious about the dedication. He had originally felt he must leave it anonymous, with the dedication but without her name or even initials. He asked Samuel Smith to let him know 'if you think the "Preface" is indiscreet' and was worried in a letter to Gray that it would give the reviewers ('the little yapping puppies of the press') an opportunity to pick at him.[12]

He implored Smith:

> There is nothing in the universe which you can do, which will give me more pleasure than to pay the visit of which you speak. ... Go and see my Missie I beseech you: and tell me how she takes my "Preface" – if she reads it. I only ask that she does not m'en vouloir for it [hold it against me], and that is a little thing to ask for as absolute an adoration as any girl or woman has ever had from anyone.[13]

He begged Moore also to go to see Adelaide: 'I have broken my heart over her, but she remains, none the less, my sole interest in life.'[14] In dedicating *Verses* to her he was hurling his last resources of emotional strength into the relationship. If this brought no effect, what more had he to offer?

He wrote to Sam Smith that he would be 'idolatrous for the rest of my days. Idolatrous to the extent that Keats was when he wrote from Rome to his friend Browne: "the lining which she put in my travelling cap scalds my head" – and like Keats I cannot open her letters for a day or so after they reach me.'[15] Keats was often in Dowson's thoughts, because of the Romantic poet's pained relationship with Fanny Brawne, but perhaps too because Keats died of consumption in the arms of Joseph Severn, who was later a friend of Alfred Dowson, who would often talk of him. These echoes of the life and death of the earlier poet with whom Ernest Dowson was so often compared must have haunted him in his bare room at Pont-Aven.

In the wider world, the reviews for *Verses* were mixed. Yeats was going to review it but seems not to have done so; perhaps he could not obtain a commission. By far the most sympathetic review was from Arthur Symons in *The Savoy*, who wrote 'in these few, evasive, immaterial snatches of song, I find, implied for the most part, hidden away like a secret, all the fever and turmoil and the unattained dreams of a life which has itself had much of the swift, disastrous, and suicidal energy of genius.'[16]

Symons is credited – or blamed – in this three-page article called 'A Literary Causerie: On A Book of Verses', with creating the Dowson legend, though Dowson himself had more than a little to do with the stories which circulated about him. The article did not name Dowson but was said to be about a 'young poet whom I have the privilege to know somewhat intimately.' It has been claimed that Symons hardly knew Dowson, but after the publication of his memoirs in 1977 and those of Yeats in 1972 it is clear that this was not the case. It is also significant that Dowson dedicated a poem to Symons ('Spleen') but did not dedicate verse to Edgar Jepson, who was so scathing about Symons' account of Dowson.[17]

Symons continued, 'He will not mind, I know, if I speak of him with some of that frankness which we usually reserve for the dead, or with which we sometimes honour our enemies; for he is of complete indifference to these things, as I shall assure myself over again before these lines are printed.'

He described how he met Dowson at the Cheshire Cheese, and how Dowson

> first introduced me to those charming supper-houses, open all night through, the cabmen's shelters. There were four of us, two in evening dress, and we were welcomed, cordially and without comment, at a little place near the Langham; and, I recollect, very hospitably entertained. The cooking differs, as I found in time, in these supper-houses, but there the rasher was excellent and the cups admirably clean. Dowson was known there, and I used to think he was always at his best in a cabmen's shelter.

Dowson expressed himself 'especially charmed with the sympathy and tact' with which Symons introduced the subject of Adelaide without naming her. Symons wrote:

> My friend found what was for him the supreme sensation in a very passionate and tender adoration of the most escaping of all ideals, the ideal of youth. Cherished, as I imagine, first only in the abstract, this search after the immature, the ripening graces which time can but spoil in the ripening, found itself at the journey's end, as some of his friends thought, a little prematurely. I was never of their opinion. I only saw twice, and for a few moments only, the young girl to whom most of his verses were to be written, and whose presence in his life may be held to account for much of that astonishing contrast between the broad outlines of his life and work. The situation seemed to me of the most exquisite and appropriate impossibility. She had the gift of evoking, and, in its way, of retaining, all that was most delicate, sensitive, shy, typically poetic, in a nature which I can only compare to a weedy garden, its grass trodden down by many feet, but with one small, carefully-tended flower-bed, luminous with lilies.

Here Symons remarks that a conventionally happy ending, of marriage, might not have brought the anticipated joys.

> But, for the good fortune of poets, things never do go happily with them, or to conventionally happy endings. So the wilder wanderings began, and a gradual slipping into deeper and steadier waters of oblivion. That curious love of the sordid, so common an affectation of the modern decadent, and with him so expressively genuine, grew upon him, and dragged him into yet more sorry corners of a life which was never exactly gay to him. And now, indifferent to most things, in the shipwrecked quietude of a sort of self-exile, he is living, I believe, somewhere on a remote sea-coast.

Symons' memoir of Dowson is unashamedly a piece of journalism and it bears the failings as well as the vitality of that genre. There is certainly exaggeration in it, and the preference for a felicitous phrase rather than the literal truth. It is still both broadly true, however, and has the singular merit of being the only piece about Dowson ever written which was submitted to the poet before publication. If it is inaccurate, therefore, it contains inaccuracies with which Dowson himself concurred. In being so vague about Dowson's 'self-exile' Symons may have been protecting Dowson's whereabouts from the curious, or merely romanticizing the poet's location for effect. Dowson was not so remote that Symons could not send him a draft of the article for approval.

Dowson was generally positive though he suggested a couple of changes: he did not want 'too lurid, an account painted of himself as his friends might be worried' — Selwyn Image had heard stories of Dowson's life in Paris and wrote Dowson a 'grieved and paternal' letter. Dowson was eager to let Symons know he had been 'rusticating' in Brittany and that his 'wanderings in foreign cities are a result of my chronic restlessness — for indeed I have long since outgrown mine old "curious love of the sordid" and am grown the most pastoral of men.'[18]

Edgar Jepson considered that 'one of the worst misfortunes which befell that most unfortunate poet was that he found his biographer in Mr Symons.'[19] Symons, however, did not tell (in later versions of his note on Dowson which were much expanded) the lurid account which Jepson was not above recounting about Dowson and the Pont-Aven baker.

Jepson wrote:

> Only once did he plainly look too long on the wine when it was red, and then in a petulant moment he beat the village baker, and the impudent fellow hauled him before a magistrate. Fortunately, the magistrate, being French, had no patience with such actions, and taking the proper view that if a poet might not beat a baker, what might he beat? censured his fellow-countryman and dismissed the case.[20]

Yeats tells a similar story, saying, 'The French magistrate on being told by some sympathetic villager that he had "an illustrious English poet" before him had said, "Quite right, I will imprison the baker."'[21]

The story gained great currency as part of the Dowson legend but, alas, it is not true. The procès-verbal (official report) of the proceedings taken by the clerk to the Justice of the Peace in the Pont-Aven canton on 21 July 1896 shows the tale was much improved in the telling. On the evening of 11 July, Dowson was drinking with a friend named Raymond Denos, aged 25, who was recorded as being 'sans profession' while Dowson was registered as being, 'homme de lettres'. There is no specific mention of the baker's wife but Dowson and his friend, 'under the influence of alcohol' showed a marked interest in entering the home of the Pont-Aven baker, Louis Limbour. Around one o'clock in the morning they approached the baker's and rattled forcibly on the door. M. Limbour, thinking they were fishermen who wanted bread to take out with them, opened the door whereupon he was struck by the men rushing into the house who grabbed him by the collar and tore his shirt. The baker, doubtless a man of some strength, shoved Dowson and his friend back out of the door at which they resumed their attempts to enter, and finally broke two panes of glass in the window.[22]

The men were imprisoned for the days between the offence and the trial, and Dowson put his emergency plan into effect. He had left a ring with Arthur Symons in London which Symons would use to raise cash if urgently needed by Dowson. His friend received a telegram from him: 'Sell my ring and send money: arrested.' This Symons must have done as Dowson was able to pay his fines which amounted to one franc each for drunkenness, four francs each for disturbing the peace in the hours of darkness, and four francs eight centimes court costs to be shared between them. The baker dropped his charges. Dowson telegrammed Symons gratefully, 'Am free.'[23]

This escapade was still in recent memory when Dowson became acquainted with an American novelist called Gertrude Atherton, a tall, handsome blonde woman ten years older than Dowson, who stayed in the Villa Julia. Dowson was obviously already well known for Atherton described him as 'the most famous person at that hotel [the Gloanec]' who was still 'in dire disgrace' as it was only two months since he had 'got very drunk one night, leaped through the window of a baker's house, and demanded the wife of that pious citizen. He had been haled off to prison by the indignant husband, and compelled to spend two weeks in a cell.'[24]

Atherton's friend, another novelist called Horace Annesley Vachell who was at the Gloanec, was distressed to see the state Dowson was in. He said:

> It hurts me to see him so cowed and wretched. He is really a genius – and what a fate! Only twenty-nine and already an outcast! If one could only keep him from drinking he might pull up and become a brilliant figure in London. He is terribly poor, but what he has written has been received with such acclaim by the critics that anything he wrote would be well paid for, and he could soon reinstate himself. But he won't even write. I am sure.

Vachell inveigled Atherton into agreeing to see Dowson, pandering to her vanity. He said 'It must be years since he has spoken to a decent woman – if he ever knew one! If he thought you took an interest in him ... who knows? ... it might mean a rebirth.'

The notion that the attentions of a respectable woman could be a solution to Dowson's woes is inadequate to the point of comedy. Atherton appreciated the compliment, however, saying, 'I have never looked upon myself in the light of a reformer. But I've read 'Cynara', and his translation of Couperus's *Majesty*. He is one of the most beautiful writers living, and it would be interesting to see what he looks like.'

Vachell was elated and agreed to bring Dowson to see Atherton but he was not sure of his ground. He said:

If I only can. If I can only persuade him. But he's naturally shy, and just now in the depths. He slinks about the hotel with his eyes down, avoiding every one, and I had to pursue him before I could get him even to speak to me. But now I think he is convinced I am his friend, and he talks to me quite freely. Yes! Sooner or later I'll induce him to meet you. The interest of a woman is what he needs to restore his self-respect.

Several days later, as Atherton and her stepsister Aleece Ullhorn were sitting drinking their coffee on the terrasse before the hotel, Vachell crossed the square 'with a sad-looking object shambling beside him'. Dowson was 'a small man with nothing of youth in his bearing. He wore a black sweater, he was unshaven, his hair was long and dusty, his eyes were green, his lips looked like a smudge of red sealing wax, and he had no front teeth.'

Aleece muttered 'Another freak,' raised her parasol and sauntered off. Vachell introduced Dowson to Atherton then left hurriedly. Dowson flopped into a chair. Atherton described how his eyes shifted from right to left and he looked like a trapped wild thing of the forest. She offered him coffee, and he accepted politely, but left it untasted. Atherton tried flattery, 'but he merely flushed a dull red and murmured unintelligible replies.' She talked of other poets and personalities in London whom he must have known, but his eyes grew more hunted, and he looked as if what teeth he had left would chatter. He did not wish to be rude, but he was clearly 'paralysed with fright' at the attentions of this formidable, respectable woman. 'To utter two consecutive sentences was beyond him,' she said, and finally she took pity on him and turned to speak to someone at an adjacent table at which Dowson seized the moment to slink off.

Atherton reported this failure to Vachell who said he had not expected much at first, for he knew how shy and ashamed Dowson was. Atherton fancied trying again – Dowson was a 'lost soul' and as she had never met one before, she found the challenge exciting. The next move in the 'experiment' of Dowson's reform was to invite him to tea in the studio of Mrs Trulow, an American artist living in Atherton's hotel. She sent Dowson a formal note to which he responded with a charming acceptance. When the time came and he crossed the square, the women leaned out of the window gasping at his appearance: his hair had been cut, he was freshly shaven, he had attached a white collar and cuffs to his black sweater, and he wore what looked like a new pair of shoes (in fact donated by Vachell). He looked shy and frightened as he entered the room and the three women paid court to him at which he thawed a little, and in half an hour was not in the least embarrassed.

Gertrude Atherton's blood was up now and, filled with reforming zeal, she determined to reclaim him. She took him for walks, taught him to open her parasol for her and to help her over rough places. She pretended to be frightened when they met cows in the road and he shooed them off valiantly. 'He never neglected to wear his collar and cuffs, shaved himself every day, no longer shambled, and all shyness had fled.' Atherton yearned for the moment when she felt she knew him well enough to persuade him to invest in a pair of false front teeth. She told him of California and he talked of the poets and artists of the day, but he revealed no personal information.

She says she got him to read 'Cynara' which he did in 'a low monotone that never varied for an instant. No accentuation, no rising nor falling inflection. A lost soul intoning in space.' Atherton has this reading taking place on the day he went to Mrs Trulow's but this is surely novelist's licence with the events, which seem more dramatic all taken together when the poet progresses from painful shyness to declaiming his own verse in one afternoon. Dowson, who very rarely recited, would not have done so on almost his first acquaintance with people – certainly not with women. There is another record that he recited 'Cynara' for a small group one evening in the moonlight on the terrasse outside the hotel, doubtless when he had the encouragement of something stronger than tea to drink. Atherton is probably adding a recollection of this evening to her account of Mrs Trulow's tea-party.

Atherton used her relationship with Dowson as the basis for her novel *The Gorgeous Isle*, published in 1908. In it a young woman tries to redeem a drunken poet, the descriptions of whom are close to those of Dowson in his worst phases: 'He looked as if he had never smiled. She pitied him so deeply that she could have wept, for she had never seen an unhappier mortal.'

Whether the remarks she puts into the mouth of her poet are her own insights, or fictionalized renderings of Dowson's speech, it is impossible to know. Of the loss of his self-respect caused by an unhappy love affair, Atherton's poet says, 'I abhorred my body, and would willingly have slashed it off could I have gone on writing without it ... but my inner life was never polluted by my visible madness. I have been vile, but I have never had a vile thought.'[25]

He is redeemed in the novel, and marries the heroine, but he must desist from writing, as his creative gift is linked to his unstable nature, and to write he must drink. After some months of a teetotal marriage in which she has destroyed the poet by forbidding him alcohol, his wife encourages him to drink again.

It suits Atherton's dramatic purpose to picture Dowson as a figure who has sunk as low as a poet can sink. One wonders, therefore, how he managed to enjoy good company, decently clothed, in following years. Partly this is because his appearance depended very much on his state of mind, his income and the company he was in. He was of a cyclothymic temperament, common in creative people, where periods of optimism and industry are frequently interspersed with low esteem and feelings of unworthiness and hopelessness, sometimes in the same day. He was not, therefore, in continuous decline: there would be periods when his spirits were up and his appearance reflected it, though he would never again play the dandy as he had in the early 1890s.

While Atherton's account is subjectively true, less fastidious folk, who were not bent on a mission, saw a different side of him. At about the same time he was seeing the American novelist, he was also friendly with an · English explorer on holiday, Michael Holland, three years older than Dowson, who 40 years later gave his recollection of the poet. 'In 1896 · Dowson was not down and out. He drank too much at times, but when sober was a most delightful companion.' When Holland left Pont-Aven, Dowson was so chivalrous as to go with him some distance, to Rennes, where they entertained a party of French army officers who were on manoeuvres, and Dowson gave the only public speech he is reported to have made – in praise of Anglo-France alliance.[26]

Dowson's relationship with Gertrude Atherton was not to end so merrily. One day on one of their walks, Atherton and Dowson passed a little stone house to let which was referred to rather grandly as a château. 'I could write here,' Atherton exclaimed, 'I've a great notion to take if for the winter.'

Dowson turned to her with sparkling eyes, 'Oh, do!' he said, 'And then I could come and sit by your fireside every day.' Atherton visualized the glowing logs of the fireside while rain beat down outside, with Dowson reading aloud to her his latest poem, and his listening to her read aloud her latest chapter. They agreed they must do it, and Dowson looked at her as if she were offering him paradise. 'Last winter I had no one to talk to,' he confided sadly.

'If Aleece will only consent,' Atherton said, suddenly realizing her obligations. Her travelling companion was looking forward to returning to London. 'Well, you did say she has friends there,' said Dowson impatiently. 'Can't she go back alone?'

But Atherton was afraid she would not. And when she discussed it with Aleece, the other woman said what a fool Atherton would be to bury herself away in a village in France when her novel, *Patience*, was about to come out in London. With this and other imprecations, Aleece persuaded Atherton to leave.

Dowson looked crestfallen when she told him, but he said nothing. She thought he could go to London with her but he could not afford to live anywhere but there. She dared not offer him money for he had already repulsed Vachell who had offered to pay his hotel bills. They said goodbye and he stood watching her carriage disappear in the distance. He did not answer her letters.

Some three weeks later the artist Mrs Trulow wrote to Atherton, 'Your poet has been drunk ever since you left, and no longer sports his collar and cuffs. Too bad your influence was not more lasting.' In a later letter she referred to Dowson's departure, his only luggage an extra sweater.

Dowson had an impressive ability to travel with virtually no possessions at all, and when he did have belongings he usually gave them away to friends. Thus Samuel Smith ended up with Dowson's presentation copy of Arthur Symons' *London Nights* and also John Gray's *Silverpoints*, the latter being one of the few books Dowson had carried with him on his travels. When Dowson left Pont-Aven, it was as a man with nothing to his name but a few manuscripts and his fame. How he managed to travel long distances with so little money is not known, though Jepson writes of at least one ferry-boat crossing on which Dowson won his fare from the captain at the maritime card game of nap.[27]

Dowson had intended to tour the South of France with the painter Gabriel Loiseau in a gypsy caravan and had written enthusiastically about it, but the project came to nought but talk. Loiseau painted his portrait but the picture has never been traced.

Dowson returned to London via St Malo and Southampton at the end of October 1896. The primary reason was that he could not face another winter alone. He first stayed with Sam Smith in Faversham, Kent, then briefly at his old lodgings of Featherstone Buildings, High Holborn.

Superficially, Dowson's prospects looked good. As well as *Verses* which had attracted ample attention, Smithers was soon to publish *The Pierrot of the Minute* with Beardsley's illustrations; 1896 had seen the publication of his translation of *La Fille aux Yeux d'Or*, and the third volume of Muther's history of nineteenth-century painting which he translated with Greene and Hillier. Dowson was also starting on his 'new and monumental translation' of *Les Liaisons Dangereuses* by Choderlos de Laclos and he had other schemes. 'I have seldom felt in more industrious mood,' Dowson wrote to O'Riordan.[28]

There had been some changes in London life, however: his old crowd were dispersed to various locations. Vincent O'Sullivan had been ill and was in a monastery in Wales, and Beardsley was living as an invalid in Boscombe in Hampshire after a severe haemorrhage in Brussels. Dowson had been worried about the artist's health for some time, asking for news of him in letters. Beardsley's farewell to the decadent world was published in *The Savoy* of October 1896. *The Death of Pierrot* shows the enigmatic figure of mime slumped in a bed at the corner of the picture while the rest of the troupe of commedia dell'arte characters tiptoe towards the deathbed, holding their fingers to their lips, staring out of the page at the audience. The death of Pierrot, the character whose enigmatic sadness even in display characterized the early 1890s, gestured towards the death of the decadents in London, both symbolically and, in most cases, physically.

Death was much in the air in *The Savoy*. The August edition which had carried Symons' account of Dowson's life and work also had Dowson's last long story, 'The Dying of Francis Donne', and his 'Venite Descendamus':

Let be at last; give over words and sighing,
  Vainly were all things said:
Better at last to find a place for lying,
  Only dead.

The Savoy too was dying. The attempt to render the magazine acceptable had succeeded too well, and there was little of the decadent sentiment in it, yet this did not endear it to the general reading public. It was tame without being popular.

Symons wrote in the penultimate issue that, 'without the florins [10p] of the general public, no magazine such as *The Savoy*, issued at so low a price, and without the aid of advertisements, can expect to pay its way.'[29] The refusal of W.H. Smith to distribute the magazine, using their position of virtual monopoly to dictate taste, seriously damaged *The Savoy*, and the decision to produce it monthly from July 1896 overstrained the resources Smithers was prepared to invest in it.

The last issue was entirely written by Symons. At the end of it there were advertisements for *The Pierrot of the Minute* – 350 copies at seven shillings and sixpence (37½p) – and for Symons's *The Decadent Movement in Literature*. This book eventually emerged in 1899 titled *The Symbolist Movement in Literature*. The game was not worth the candle.

Another death was that of Dowson's friend Hubert Crackanthorpe, in December 1896 at the age of 26. His wife Leila MacDonald, a poet who also contributed to *The Savoy*, took up with a French artist called Comte d'Artaux. Crackanthorpe also had a lover, Sissie Welch, the sister of Richard Le Gallienne. In the autumn of 1896 all four were living in the Avenue Kleber in Paris. This interesting menage à quatre was disrupted when the Comte discovered he had a venereal disease and accused Leila of infecting him, who accused Crackanthorpe of infecting her and demanded a divorce. Sissie returned to her husband, the actor James Welch, and Crackanthorpe drowned himself in the Seine.[30]

There was another change that Dowson was going to have to get used to: Adelaide Foltinowicz was engaged to be married.

CHAPTER 13

THE DEVIL'S DANCE

At the beginning of 1897 Adelaide was approaching her nineteenth birthday. It was improbable that she would remain unmarried for long. She accepted the suit of Augustus Noelte, a tailor like her father, who lodged above the shop and who helped out in the restaurant, which led to his often being described as a waiter. The only physical description of him is Jepson's: 'a short, cylindrical German, with a large, round head and a large, round, pale, shining face.'[1] What little evidence there is of Augustus suggests he was a decent sort who himself was to be led a pretty dance by Adelaide. Like her father, and like Dowson, he was a weak man who could be easily dominated by Adelaide and her mother.

There is not the slightest negative remark by Dowson against this rival in love, either written or reported, but neither is there any account of how he discovered that these two were to marry. Marion Plarr has him encountering Adelaide and Augustus embracing before he left for Paris in 1895, but though there was some division between Dowson and Adelaide at this time, it was soon resolved, and she has surely concocted this scene for dramatic effect.[2] His remarks about Adelaide having broken his heart in summer 1896 suggest he knew he was not to be her husband. It is a fair presumption, however, that he did not know until his return from France about Adelaide and Augustus's relationship.

Presumably the dishevelled, toothless poet called at Poland some time after his return and was introduced to the situation with as much delicacy as could be managed. A more difficult conundrum than how he got to know of the liaison was: why did he then move in to lodge at Poland? He took a room above the restaurant, where Augustus also lodged, as of course did Adelaide and her mother. The misery of being in such close proximity to the one he loved but had failed to make his own can hardly be imagined. What possessed him to behave this way is scarcely explicable rationally. Perhaps, seeing the state he was in, his old friend Mrs Folti-nowicz took him in out of pity, or he had a haemorrhage and they insisted he stay with them to get the rest and care he needed. Perhaps he wanted one last look at Missie before she was gone forever. Perhaps he just wanted to torment himself and deliberately chose the position of greatest pain.

He had no illusions about what his friends would think. Dowson wrote to Sam Smith:

> I know that you must think me a fool, but I am suffering the torture of the damned. I ought to have drowned myself at Pont-Aven, or having come back to London I ought to have had the strength of mind to have kept away. Now, if I change my rooms or go to the Arctic Pole it is only an increased intolerable Hell, and except yourself, and slightly, Moore, there is not a person I come across who realises that I am being scorched daily, or does not put my behaviour down to sheer ill humour. Quousque tandem, Domine, quousque tandem? [How long, Lord, how long?][3]

Apart from this fragment, here quoted in full, nothing remains to tell what Dowson was thinking over the key period when Adelaide's engagement became known to him. There are only four letters recorded for the first five months of 1897, and the number increases to only eight if the previous five months of 1896 are included, several of them routine business letters. At least one of Dowson's friends, Sam Smith, had letters which were later destroyed but he did allow parts to be copied by the Dowson scholar John Gawsworth, which is how the fragments of the Sam Smith letters have come to be available. On Smith's death at the age of 71 in 1938, his executor acted on his instructions and burned a sheaf of Dowson letters which a witness to the destruction said Smith had 'felt strongly were better destroyed'. This friend of Smith's, L. Birkett Marshall, continued, 'These letters, parts of which were read to me, referred intimately to Dowson's unhappy love affair, and to matters which Smith felt were better unrevealed. He was quite adamant about this.'[4]

There is a temptation to think that the parts of the letters which were not preserved are much more revealing than those which were, which is always the danger when documents are suppressed. The pleasantest gloss to put on this is that Dowson was in one of his rages and said hurtful things which, in his quieter moments, he knew were not justifiable, and Smith did not want to take the responsibility for passing an ugly, one-sided picture of his friend on to the world. We know Dowson wrote in this splenetic vein about his family and it may be that similar remarks are the 'other matters' to which Birkett Marshall refers.

One thing is apparent from the letters: Dowson dealt with the loss of Adelaide as he had dealt with the death of his parents – he did not mention it again, the subject was simply too painful. 'The poet's mouth was for ever closed' on the subject of 'that unhappy courtship', said Sherard.[5]

Sayle and Johnson visited Dowson on 19 April at Poland and he had some contact with O'Riordan but neglected most of his old friends. He said he was 'working furiously' on *Les Liaisons Dangereuses*, now his only source of income, and he was desperately poor. He had some problem with a prostitute called Dollie who was too talkative for Dowson – either prying into his affairs or discussing them with others – and this distressed him. He wrote to O'Riordan, 'Please don't ask me to lunch with her and don't for the sake of my whole happiness give her my address.' It was, he protested, 'only the third occasion since I returned to this sad country that I have dealt with a whore' and as he had been back less than six months, it gives some indication of his usual sexual appetites.[6]

Doubtless Dowson now felt the atmosphere unbearable in London and he escaped once more, this time travelling with Charles Conder to Dieppe, then to Arques-la-Bataille, a village a little to the south of the major town.

Oscar Wilde was released from his imprisonment in May 1897 and immediately went into exile in France, living under the assumed name of Sebastian Melmoth, the first name from the saint, the second from his uncle Charles Maturin's novel *Melmoth the Wanderer*. While some of his old friends were loyal, others were disdainful, and some English tourists in Dieppe saw it as their Christian duty to go out of their way to insult him. Having attracted unwelcome attention in Dieppe, he soon moved to Berneval-sur-Mer, a village a short distance along the coast.

Beardsley snubbed him in public, then visited him, then failed to keep a further appointment.[7] This apparently perverse behaviour is not really so complicated to understand: Beardsley wanted to let Wilde know he was not snubbing him because of a fit of bourgeois morality about homosexuality – his enmity to the playwright had long preceded the trial. He wanted to let Wilde know the insult was for him personally, not given on behalf of society's condemnation.

Dowson was outside any such behaviour: a friend was a friend to him, and as soon as he knew where Wilde was, he arranged to see him. He visited on 3 June 1897 in the company of Charles Conder and the composer Dalhousie Young who had written a defence of Wilde. The playwright was now 42, his face was red and his hands were coarse, understandably for someone who had been doing manual labour out of doors, but friends were surprised to see him looking strong and energetic. His last prison job, as a gardener, had done him good, as had his compulsory abstinence from alcohol and tobacco.

Wilde behaved with his usual generosity and hospitality, as if he had suffered nothing in the past two years, grateful for the visit of the men he called 'The Poet, the Philosopher and the Painter' – presumably to give Young his true title would have been at the expense of alliteration. He wrote to Lord Alfred Douglas: 'Ernest Dowson, Conder and Dal Young come out here this afternoon to dine and sleep – at least I know they dine, but believe they never sleep.' They were up talking till three in the morning.[8]

Wilde wrote to Dowson around 5 June 1897: 'It was most kind of you coming to see me, and I thank you very sincerely and gratefully for your pleasant companionship and the many gentle ways by which you recalled to me that, once at any rate, I was a Lord of Language, and had myself the soul of a poet.'[9]

Dowson had concealed his personal suffering – as he so often did – so as not to impede his friends' pleasure, but he wrote to Conal O'Riordan:

> I had some difficulty in suppressing my own sourness and attuning myself to his enormous joy in life just at this moment – but I hope I left him with the impression that I had not a care in the world. He was in wonderful form, but has changed a good deal – he seems of much broader sympathies, much more human and simple. And his delight in the country, in walking, in the simplicities of life is enchanting.[10]

They were peaceful days, despite Dowson's heartache. Wilde wrote, 'Ernest had an absinthe under the apple-trees!' of another visit, after he had breakfasted with Dowson at Arques, following which Dowson travelled back to Berneval with him and stayed the night.[11] Dowson wrote of Wilde:

> His gorgeous spirits cheered me mightily. I was amused by the unconscious contrast between his present talk about his changed position and his notions of economy and his practise, which is perversely extravagant. He does not realise in the least that nobody except himself could manage to spend the money he does in a petit trou de campagne [a little spot in the country]. He is a wonderful man.[12]

Wilde had some money bestowed by well-wishers and he was excessively generous with it. On the occasion of Queen Victoria's Diamond Jubilee he gave a dinner for 15 children of the Berneval school, and he frequently entertained French poets. He also advanced money to Dowson and paid his hotel bill.

Wilde became very attached to Dowson, writing to him:

> There is a fatality about our being together that is astounding – or rather quite probable. Had I stayed at Arques I should have given up all hope of ever separating from you. Why are you so persistently and perversely wonderful? Do I see you tomorrow? Try to come over. ... Come with vine-leaves in your hair. I suppose I shall see you in ten minutes from this. I am looking out for the green costume that goes so well with your dark hyacinth locks.[13]

When they did meet again, Dowson stayed three days with him.

Around this time Wilde dined with Fritz Thaulow, a Norwegian land-scape artist, and he asked the artist, 'What do you think of our friend, the young poet, with whom I met you the other day?' Thaulow replied, 'It's a pity he drinks so much absinthe.' Wilde shrugged and said, 'If he didn't drink, he would be somebody else. Il faut accepter la personnalité comme elle est. Il ne faut jamais regretter qu'un poète est saoul, il faut regretter que les saouls ne soient pas toujours poètes [You must accept a person for what he is. It is not regrettable that a poet is drunk, but that drunks aren't always poets].'14

Wilde seemed increasingly to rely on Dowson, writing to him through June in the most insistent terms, for example from the Café Suisse in Dieppe: 'Do come here at once: Monsieur Meyer is presiding over a morning meal of absinthe, and we want you,'15 and 'I must see you: so I propose to breakfast at St Martin L'Eglise tomorrow at 11.30 and you must come: take a voiture and be there. I want to have a poet to talk to, as I have had lots of bad news since you left me. Do try, like a good chap, to be there, and wear a blue tie. I want to be consoled.'16 'Tonight I am going to read your poems – your lovely lyrics – words with wings you write always. It is an exquisite gift, and fortunately rare in an age whose prose is more poetic than its poetry.'17

Dowson paid back his friend's hospitality with his company and an attempt to convert Wilde into a heterosexual: a vain endeavour if ever there was one. Yeats is the source for this tale about which he says, 'Dowson claimed to have attempted to reform him at Dieppe' so it may well have been a story Dowson told himself, though there is no record that Dowson met Yeats after 1895.

The story goes that Dowson and Wilde were in a café in Dieppe and Dowson pressed upon his companion the necessity of acquiring 'a more wholesome taste'. Chivvied by this, Wilde consented to visit the local brothel, though they doubted they had the funds for such an excursion. They emptied their pockets on to the café table and, though there was not much, there was enough if both heaps were put into one. Meanwhile the news had spread and they set out accompanied by a cheering crowd. Arriving at their destination, Dowson and the crowd remained outside and presently Wilde returned. He said in a low voice to Dowson, 'The first these ten years and it will be the last. It was like cold mutton.' He then remembered how the Elizabethan dramatists had used the words 'cold mutton' to describe sex with prostitutes and patted himself on the back for his erudition. He said aloud, so that the crowd might hear, 'But tell it in England, for it will entirely restore my character.'18

Dowson introduced Wilde to Smithers who lived up to his boast 'I publish anything that the others are afraid of' when he published Wilde's long poem on the experience of prison, 'The Ballad of Reading Gaol', in February 1898, with only C.3.3., Wilde's prison number, on the title page.

When this edition of 850 sold out in a few days, Smithers printed another 1000 with Wilde's initials on the title page and continued reprinting it as demand grew.

Despite the good company, Dowson was in emotional torment. He used to spend hours on his knees in adoration in a side chapel in the church at Arques. The object of his devotion is worth some attention: it was a painting of a martyred virgin from whose chin a long beard grew.[19] This was the saint known as Wilgefortis, or (in France) as Livrada, whose story the chief authority on saints considers a curiosity of hagiography, hardly worth mentioning 'but for the fact that it has the unenviable distinction of being one of the most obviously false and preposterous of the pseudo-pious romances by which simple Christians have been deceived or regaled.'[20] You could always count on Dowson to be out of the ordinary. St Wilgefortis was one of seven children born at one birth to the wife of the heathen king of Portugal. She became a Christian and took a vow of virginity. Her father wanted to marry her to the king of Sicily and she prayed for divine help which came in the form of a beard and moustache growing on her face. The king of Sicily withdrew his suit and her father had her crucified.

Why did Dowson pick her out of the entire canon of saints? He always had a strong relationship with virginity and with young girls, which sat uneasily beside his desperate sexual promiscuity. Yeats said, to repeat his perceptive remark, that Dowson's religion was 'a desire for a condition of virginal ecstasy'.[21] Adelaide's adulthood and the death of innocence, one of his perennial themes, must have preyed on Dowson's mind at this time. It is tempting to fit the parts of Dowson's personality together to make a modern diagnosis: the paedophilia, sexual promiscuity, inability to form relationships with women who were his equals, self-neglect to the point of dirtiness, and the active seeking of sensations which tormented him would indicate to a psychiatrist some form of trauma in his childhood, probably sexual abuse. As there is no direct evidence for this, it would be wrong to pursue the analysis (and people never are as explicable as psychiatric diagnoses would have us believe) but Dowson was strange even by the standards of other decadents, let alone ordinary society, *something* had affected him to rend his soul so terribly.

Dowson's financial worries were becoming urgent and he had to go back to England to see if he could obtain more money. Whatever Smithers had advanced him had long run out and he must deliver more of his translation to his publisher to be further remunerated. Dalhousie Young was trying on Dowson's behalf to sell some shares in the East India Railway which Dowson owned and which brought him £18 a year but which could be sold for £200, a sum he could live on for over a year. For a man with a limited amount of life left, it seemed a sensible prospect. His share of the dock was still locked up in legal cases, without which he need not have lived in such poverty, but he needed to see his solicitor to try to make sense of it all.

Wilde was now in similar straits. Soon after Dowson's return to London he wrote:

> I hope you will be able to send me what you owe me in a few days, as I have no money. Your bill with Monsieur Bonnet was £11, and then in Dieppe of course there were huge expenses, and I also lent you money. It comes to £19, which I hope to receive within a week, as I cannot pay Monsieur Bonnet [Wilde's hotelier] and he is getting offensively tedious.[22]

Dowson responded, for Wilde wrote back, 'As for the cheque, I know, dear Ernest, you will send it as soon as you can. I scramble on somehow, and hope to survive the season. After that, Tunis, rags, and hashish!'[23]

Back in London in summer 1897, when he passed his thirtieth birthday, Dowson was more interested in seeing old friends again, perhaps under the convivial influence of Leonard Smithers on whom he was even more dependent. His days of walking joyfully in Hyde Park reciting his verse and that of others were behind Ernest Dowson when he next met Frank Harris. He had not seen him for two years, and Dowson was with Smithers when they met again. Harris wrote:

> Dowson had changed greatly: youth and youth's enthusiasms, the lively quick changes of mood had died out of him; he was serious, disdainful; his clothes seemed threadbare and unbrushed; he met me with petulant indifference; a touch of resentment, I thought. Had I omitted some courtesy? or was I one of the many heedless and profane who should have known and helped him and did not? I wondered regretfully.

> The second or third time I saw him he was drunk, hopelessly drunk – and wore – "I don't care" – as a mask. And soon, it seems to me in retrospect, the drinking Dowson obscured for me much of the charm of the younger Dowson. Often he was delightful at first when we met; yet always eager to drink and to get drunk, eager to throw away his hold on life and sanity – to drown the bitter stings of remembrance. I soon found out that his love had jilted him: "chucked him for a waiter" said Smithers grinning.

Harris had no doubt this was the sole reason for Dowson's decline, and that he died of love. 'After a couple of years' courtship – talks at lunch, games of cards after dinner, a kiss or two, friendly on one side and passionate on the other, the illusion of love returned – she married a waiter, and Dowson could never recover his fragile hold on life and hope.'[24]

Frank Harris puts forward a further recollection of Dowson at this time or soon after which cannot be recommended as the truth. It is more likely that, having decided to write a 'contemporary portrait' of Dowson, Harris rounded off his largely accurate account with a final meeting which is, despite the journalist's admitted perception, fictional. He knew Dowson as he knew a great many men who frequented the Café Royal, but he was not

an intimate friend and Dowson would not have confided in him information about his feelings for Adelaide. This account is also simply too
histrionic to be anything but invention. Harris has Dowson finally saying,
"'Ah, God – how did I lose her? Why?" His face froze into despair, wild-
eyed with agonizing remorse. Suddenly I realised that there was nothing to
be done. A desperate gamester, Dowson had risked all on one throw and
lost.'[25]

The knowledge of Adelaide's impending marriage, to be held at the
Bavarian Chapel, Westminster, on 30 September 1897, must have tormented Dowson. He asked Moore to attend on his behalf, and entrusted
him with his wedding gift. He probably did not see Adelaide again, and
anyway sensibly decided to get out of London for the occasion, accepting a
fortuitous offer from a friend to stay with him in Ireland for the whole of
September 1897.

He was in a bad way before he left. It was the last time Victor Plarr was
to see Dowson, when he called on the family to dine and stay the night at
their house in Kensington, a new home in keeping with Plarr's recent
appointment as librarian to the Royal College of Surgeons. There was now
no sign of the 'somewhat comic disfigurement' of his forehead which Plarr
had noticed when he last saw him. But Dowson was like the walking dead.
Plarr recounted:

> Hardly a word could be drawn from him. He seemed frozen to stone. It was
> dreadful. As a family we were longing for sympathy, for congratulations. We
> had a charming new house; our little child was at the pretty age of five; I had
> been appointed to my life's work. He nodded wearily in reply to every question.
> He would tell me nothing of himself. I have no recollection of how we got
> through that evening.

The next morning Plarr left Dowson among his books, returning in the
afternoon. 'He had smoked innumerable cigarettes: they lay all around him
in saucers and trays. And with dreaming eyes he was viewing my little child,
who stood in front of him and seemed puzzled by his demeanour. He
appeared to be looking through her, while she gazed at him.'[26] Marion Plarr
later wrote that while alone with Dowson she drew pictures for him, he
petted her black pomeranian dog, and they talked about brothers and
sisters.[27]

Then he arose 'briskly enough', borrowed a new suit of clothes from
Plarr, 'and announced curtly that he was going yachting off the coast of
Ireland. … He never smiled, seemed to be painfully repressing something –
he had seemed ill at ease and in a state of self-repression throughout his
visit – shook hands briefly, in a most matter-of-fact way, left no exact
indication of his future whereabouts, was gone!'[28]

There was enough to suppress: envy, perhaps, that his friend had the
comfort, love and security which was denied to Dowson. The fact that he

would die soon. The fact that he had lost the only woman he ever loved and that loss would soon be confirmed in a public ceremony. Life was too horrible to bear but there he was, bearing it, as he would continue doing.

Dowson stayed in a house on the banks of the Shannon, at Fairy Hill, Parteen, County Limerick, the guest of a Dublin librarian called J. de Courcy MacDonnell who probably met Dowson in Dieppe. MacDonnell had judged Dowson correctly – the rest and the quiet country manners did the poet a great deal of good. He was living 'amidst an atmosphere of children's voices and the lilting of Celtic thrushes and blackbirds,' according to Rosamond Longbridge, a friend of the MacDonnell family, and herself scarcely more than a child.

Longbridge has supplied one of the most vivid pictures of the poet at one of the most painful times in his tormented life. She wrote:

> I remember perfectly the air he brought with him into the house, as of some gracious gentleness which the buffetings of Fate had beaten back and crushed into himself. He seemed to shelter himself against the friend he had brought with him, like some wind-tortured plant beneath a sturdy tree. His shyness, and that sense of pain he brought with him, made one's heart ache, and I remember now with a mature remorse that as I sat by him I gave vent to some childish "smartness" that made him wince, not because it was aimed at him, but rather because it came from a region of crude flippancy that his bruised soul had shrunk away from long ago.

> He sat crouched down in his chair, and in his face was the luminous pallor of the drug-taker; but in his eyes, the eyes of a woman in pain, there was the light that never shone on land or sea. ... He spoke very seldom, and then in the subdued voice of one to whom the world about him has become a troubled dream; but he listened with shy interest to the table talk and when his buoyant friend broke out into some Celtic witticism, Dowson's face lit up.

> Dowson's hands were frail, but his brilliantly orange thumb and forefinger – he was a prodigious smoker of cigarettes – leapt to the eyes as their most striking characteristic, before one took stock of their fluttering nervousness.

> It was when he laughed – the laugh of a shy boy – under his breath that one made the discovery that this young man with the poet's lips had not a tooth in his head.

Longbridge heard Dowson in conversation later saying that he had possessed a set of false teeth which had been painful to wear, to eat or even to speak with, but he had finally thrown them away when he found he could not hold a pipe in his mouth with them in.

Longbridge, writing 20 years later, concludes, 'That is my Irish memory of Ernest Dowson, an impression of a sensibility so cruelly acute that one was crushed by the perception as though, in some manner, oneself were guilty of it.'[29]

Dowson left after almost two months in Ireland. He had not planned to stop in London, intending to go straight to Paris but his financial affairs were again complicated, by no fault of Dowson's, by the fact that one of the trustees of the fund by which he owned the shares (whose value he was trying to raise) had gone out of his mind. A court order therefore had to be obtained to dispense with his permission for the sale. Dowson persuaded his solicitor to let him have £50 on account, £45 of which he lodged with Smithers with instructions to send him £3 per week. Dowson knew himself well enough, and feared he would ask Smithers for the remainder of his money, so while he was in a settled mood after his Irish rest he begged his publisher, 'Do not send me more than £3 each week.'[30]

Smithers was to send some of this money to Wilde to settle Dowson's debt with him. The money was held up for 12 days in the post, leading Wilde to suspect Dowson had not dispatched it, for which he later apologized: 'I am afraid I wrote irritably to you, but I have been terribly worried by the want of money – the most sordid and hungry of wants.'[31] Dowson later asked Smithers to forward him not £3 but £2, 'unless I specially require it. Time is what I chiefly want and then I believe I can make some money.'[32] He was hoping to arrange more translation work in Paris.

Dowson was in Paris from October 1897 to early January 1898, staying at 214 Rue St Jacques and seeing some of his old crowd including Davray and Beardsley whom he remarked looked better, though the artist actually had only months to live. Dowson's money worries tormented him, he was ill and suffering from persistent insomnia, he was not successful in finding translation work in France, and he was generally unhappy. 'I have spent tonight reading through and destroying old letters, and am in the bottomless pit of depression,' he wrote in November 1897.[33] Presumably the letters were from Adelaide – there is no reason why he should have been saddened by letters from male friends; or why he should have destroyed them; or, for a person who travelled very light indeed, have kept them in the first place.

He handed over Les Liasons Dangereuses in autumn 1897 but Smithers was dissatisfied with it and Dowson agreed to revise the work. Smithers then started him on a translation of The Memoirs of Cardinal Dubois. He had done some more work on Adrian Rome and it was eventually finished in October 1897, largely by Moore. It was sent to John Lane who did not make an offer for it, similarly to Heinemann, then to Methuen who eventually published it in May 1899. Dowson's The Pierrot of the Minute had been published, to no great critical acclaim. The Athenaeum called it a 'pale … pretty reflection' of Keats's La Belle Dame Sans Merci'.[34] Dowson was thinking of compiling another volume of short stories, a plan which was not pursued, and he was still actively writing verse. A note on what is obviously a title page of a notebook (most of whose pages are now lost) describes it as 'Fragments by Ernest Dowson copied out Paris – to be worked up Nov, 1897'[35]

The work was of a morose nature, even for Dowson. Some of it was eventually to be collected in the volume he was going to call *Love's Aftermath* but was in fact named *Decorations in Verse and Prose*. The most bitter of the verses describing the end of his relationship with Adelaide was 'Exchanges':

All that I had I brought,
  Little enough I know;
A poor rhyme roughly wrought,
  A rose to match thy snow:
All that I had I brought.

Little enough I sought:
  But a word compassionate,
A passing glance, or thought,
  For me outside the gate:
Little enough I sought.

Little enough I found:
  All that you had, perchance!
With the dead leaves on the ground,
  I dance the devil's dance.
All that you had I found.

Another work eventually to find its way into *Decorations* was a prose piece called 'The Princess of Dreams'. It deals with what had to be one of the most hurtful facts about Adelaide. As Longaker remarked in 1947, 'Some of Dowson's acquaintances, out of humour with his attachment, reported that her innocence was sullied long before he lost her.'[36] Longaker gives no source, as is often the case, doubtless being tied by an agreement of confidentiality, but he acknowledges the help of only three men who met him and spoke about Dowson who knew the poet over the key period: Robert Sherard, Conal O'Riordan and Arthur Moore. Any of them could, of course, have been repeating things heard from other friends of Dowson, but the most likely source of this remark is Moore, as Sherard knew Dowson mainly in Paris and may never have met Adelaide. O'Riordan rarely went to Poland – he found the smell of garlic there repulsive – and was out of sympathy with Adelaide anyway, so he is unlikely to have found out such information himself. Moore was the only one of the three who was sufficiently close to Adelaide, particularly when Dowson was not there, to make the observations or deductions which would justify this remark.

Dowson's scarcely oblique comment was:

Poor legendary princess! In her enchanted tower of ivory, the liberator thought that she awaited him. ... And he sought her through the countless windings of her forest for many moons, sought her through the morasses, sparing not his horse nor his sword. On his way he slew certain evil magicians and many of his friends, so that at his journey's end his bright sword was tarnished and his comeliness swart with mud. ...

Poor legendary princess.

For he did not free her and the fustian porter took his treasure and broke his stained sword in two.

And who knows where he went, horseless and disarmed, through the morasses and the dark windings of her forest under the moonless night, dreaming of those blue lakes which were flowers de luce, her eyes? Who knows? ...

But there are some who say that she had no wish to be freed, and that those flowers de luce, her eyes, are a stagnant, dark pool, that her glorious golden hair was only long enough to reach her postern gate.

Some say, moreover, that her tower is not of ivory and that she is not even virtuous nor a princess.

The story was the final one in the book, which is significant as Dowson always took special care with the arrangement of his work. It comes after 'The Visit', describing death, which one might logically think should be the last work, but for Dowson what he had suffered was worse than death.

CHAPTER 14

THE VALLEY OF HUMILIATION

Still, there were other gaudy nights for Ernest Dowson. He returned to London in January 1898, presumably to try again to clear up his financial affairs. He was talking about starting a new life in South Africa when his inheritance came through but, like most of Dowson's plans, it came to nothing.

Dowson's real genius was for making friends. He lodged at 1 Guildford Place, Bloomsbury, with the writer Matthew (M.P.) Shiel, already known for his collections of stories, *Shapes in the Fire* and *Prince Zaleski*, the latter a series of crime stories featuring a decadent detective. Shiel was born in the West Indies, of partially negro descent, the son of a Methodist minister. He had studied in London, including six months medical training at St Bartholomew's Hospital, but left without taking a degree and entered the world of literature. Shiel described Dowson in a character whom the hero of his novel *The Weird O'It* encounters. He is 'a poet in a small, but very select, way, well known in certain so-called "literary" circles: a fellow who, with his like at that time, kept night-hours, awoke at 7 pm, drank deep, died young, and associated as comrades with the commonest people.' The character ate at a green cabmen's shelter where he was well known; he had been jilted by a 15-year-old Italian waitress, and subsequently had 'taken worse than ever to drink (really hereditary, like his consumption) and had written to the girl a poem more exquisite, in our opinion, than anything done by Horace.'

Shiel described the rooms where they lived: 'A low light burned on a shaky table, giving a smell; there was a fire, and an old easy-chair with decadent bottom.' Other boarders included a railway porter and a girl who strung beads for three-farthings a gross.[1]

Rather than the Crown or the Café Royal, Dowson was now more often at a public house in the centre of the Strand called the Bun House which was kept by an old actor who had once played with Ellen Terry and was reluctant to allow his customers to forget it. Another of Smithers' authors, named Ranger Gull, referred to the types who frequented this area of the West End as the 'Stranded gentry', almost a dying breed who inhabited the place 'when Bohemia had not quite vanished and the Street teemed with celebrities who used its tavern and restaurants like clubs and knew every inch of it as a sailor knows his ship.' Other characters who used the bar and were known to Dowson were Lionel Johnson and John Barlas.

Gull remarks that it was here that

> poor Ernest Dowson the poet was constantly to be seen towards the end of his short and tragic life. I knew him well. Very few of us had then read his poems nor suspected the hidden genius which was to flower in such dainty splendour after his death. He seemed a lost creature, a youthful ghost strayed amongst the haunts of men, an object of pity. Pale, emaciated, in clothes that were almost ragged, poor Ernest frittered from bar to bar in search of someone with whom to talk. When he found a friend, his face would light up with a singular and penetrating sweetness that made one forget his untidiness – to use no other word – that verged upon offence. He was never penniless, was always the first to pay for others, and when the drink was served he would sometimes furtively take a little gold cross from his waistcoat pocket and dip it into his glass before he drank.

Someone who did not know the circumstances once said, 'Ernest, were you ever in love?' The poet answered in the words of Voltaire, 'Vous me demandez si j'ai aimé; oui! c'est une histoire singulière et terrible! [You ask me if I have loved. Yes, it is a story both remarkable and terrible.]' Gull said, 'While I live I shall never forget the wan smile, the haunted look in the poor fellow's eyes.'[2]

When he had money to spend, he was the soul of charity, particularly to poor streetwalkers to whom he would pass coins with no expectation of favours in return, simply because they were cold and hungry. His generosity was the stuff of London legend. Newman Flower, a journalist and another habitué of the cafés where Dowson drank, wrote:

> He would discover, through the comradeship of drinking, some literary derelict in a wine shop, and give him all the money he had. Once he emptied his pockets to such a creature whom he had never seen before. And some nights afterwards he came back to the bar and asked for his erstwhile friend in order that he might pour into his hand the money he had just received for a literary effort. The beneficiary was absent. The proprietor of the wine shop offered to take the money and hand it over. "But," he inquired, "what is the man's name?" Dowson did not know, he had never bothered to inquire.[3]

Smithers was in financial difficulties himself, so Dowson's slight relative prosperity at this time must mean that his solicitor had eventually succeeded in selling his railway shares though the sum eventually raised after solicitors' fees cannot have been great, particularly as he had already received £50 of it and some of the remainder was already promised to repay debts. The sum owing to him from his parents' estate continued to elude him.

Dowson was able to afford another luxury, a regular girlfriend, at this time. He was going to visit Oscar Wilde in Naples with Smithers, then Wilde moved to Paris and Smithers went to see him alone. Wilde referred archly to Dowson's lady-friend on 18 February 1898: 'I am glad you are coming over alone. I don't want to be bored with Mrs Dowson. Ernest is charming, but I would sooner be with you alone, or with him along with you.'[4]

Smithers set Dowson to work on editing Ben Jonson's *Volpone* which he intended to publish with Aubrey Beardsley's illustrations. For this Dowson worked in the British Museum library, outside which he encountered his old Rhymers' Club colleague Ernest Rhys. Rhys wrote, 'My last glimpse of him was on the steps of that rendezvous of scribes, the British Museum. He looked three shades further gone in ill health; his clothes were dusty, and a small red stain of blood on his collar emphasised the pallor of his face.'[5]

It was a time of the passing of friends and Dowson stood as if in a spectral line waiting his turn. He said Hubert Crackanthorpe's ghost was calling him from the other side of the Styx.[6] Beardsley died on 16 March 1898 in Menton at the age of 25. In his last days he was still, pathetically, trying to draw when he was too weak even to hold a pen. He had converted to Catholicism the previous year and was seized with a fit of conventional morality in the fortnight before his death, writing to Smithers that the publisher must destroy all copies of the drawings he had done to accompany Samuel Smith's translation of Aristophanes' sex comedy *Lysistrata*. Smithers ignored the request.

Dowson attended a Requiem Mass for Beardsley at the Farm Street Church in Mayfair. Here he was observed by Gertrude Atherton, who wrote, 'He looked more like a lost soul than ever as he drifted past with his unseeing eyes. And very shabby, very poor. I half rose to follow him, but sank back with a mental headshake. He was a sensitive creature and could have no wish to meet again one who had known him during a brief period of regeneration.'[7]

Dowson's feelings at the death of his friends – and particularly a death from consumption – must have been like that of his character Francis Donne, who 'had lived so long in the meditation of death, visited it so often in others, studied it with such persistency, with a sentiment in which horror and fascination mingled,' that it was with a shock that knowledge of his mortality dawned on him.

In 'The Dying of Francis Donne', one of the most powerful evocations of mortality in literature, the protagonist is 35, a man of letters, a popularizer of science. He is going to die soon, perhaps in a few months. He promises himself a holiday but realizes that rest and relaxation are

> as it were, some tardy sacrifice, almost hypocritical, which he offered to powers who might not be propitiated.

> His burning sense of helplessness, of a certain bitter injustice in things, a sense of shame mingled; all the merely physical dishonour of death shaping itself to his sick and morbid fancy into a violent symbol of what was, as it were, an actual moral or intellectual dishonour.

He strains for the certainties of the Church but finds an afterlife no more than a possibility. He stops thinking of it.

> And he gave it up, turning his face to the wall, lay very still, imagining himself already stark and cold, his eyes closed, his jaw closely tied (lest the ignoble changes which had come to him should be too ignoble), while he waited until the narrow boards, within which he should lie, had been nailed together, and the bearers were ready to convey him into the corruption which was to be his part.

Dowson was long tormented by insomnia and he had more than adequate time for such reflections.

Donne feels 'Since Death is coming to me ... let me meet it, a stranger in a strange land, with only strange faces round me and the kind indifference of strangers, instead of the intolerable pity of friends.' In this he had a definite Dowson characteristic, for the poet always shrank from pity and often refused the material assistance of friends. Frank Harris remarked, 'There was in him an uncomplaining almost stoical independence curiously akin to hopelessness: for months at a time he was half-starved; yet he would not appeal to his relations who could and would have helped him, still less to his friends whose aid would only have been limited by their means.'8 Harris is quite correct, Dowson's aunt, recorded only as Mrs Holford Secretan, said, 'Without any shade of a quarrel or disagreement he dropped away – till his relations never knew if he were dead or alive – or he need not have been in the state he was.'9 The refusal to ask for assistance, even while in mortal difficulty, was of course one of the traits Ernest shared with Alfred Dowson.

He describes the mood of resignation he must often have endured in the poem 'Dregs':

> The fire is out, and spent the warmth thereof,
> (This is the end of every song man sings!)
> The golden wine is drunk, the dregs remain,

Bitter as wormwood and as salt as pain;
And health and hope have gone the way of love
Into the drear oblivion of lost things.
Ghosts go along with us until the end;
This was a mistress, this, perhaps, a friend.
With pale, indifferent eyes, we sit and wait
For the dropt curtain and the closing gate:
This is the end of all the songs man sings

This went into the volume he was preparing for Smithers, *Decorations in Verse and Prose*, on which he was working in the winter of 1898–9. In most cases the verses were second pickings from what Dowson called his Poésie Schublade (poetry drawer), a manuscript book (or books) which had already yielded material for *Verses*. A few, however, showed evidence of having been written recently and from this evidence, and the accounts of observers, it is clear he was still straining after verse up to the end of the century.

It was probably in the preparation of *Decorations* that Dowson met Althea Gyles, one of the few women associated with decadence. She was a poet and painter who 'sacrificed herself with an Asiatic fanaticism' to her art, according to Yeats, living on bread and shell-cocoa so that her food never cost her more than a penny a day.[10] She was a year younger than Dowson, a fiery woman with red-gold hair whom Smithers engaged to design a cover for *Decorations*. Gyles became Smithers' lover – perhaps this had been the case as early as 1898. The design for Dowson's book was a double rectangle in gold on white, enclosing a stylized flower with thorns on the front with another pattern, of thorns and foliage, on the back. Gyles also designed covers for Yeats and illustrated Wilde's *The Harlot's House* which was published by Smithers.

In early 1899 Dowson returned to Paris, now staying at the Hôtel Saint Malo in Rue d'Odessa. Here he worked on his verse and his translations and ventured forth to meet friends or to encounter the night alone. Whatever money he had had was now gone and he was again dependent on payments from Smithers in return for bundles of completed translation.

Smithers would sometimes visit. O'Sullivan recounts he was once asked, 'What has brought you to Paris this time?' He replied, 'I have come to Paris to kill Dowson.' The joke was that Dowson was quite clearly three-quarters dead already, drifting around the Latin Quarter and the marketmen's bars about the Halles, where he could drink all night. Vincent O'Sullivan said he was 'little able to resist a possibility of endless drinking, endless souses from the fall of night.'

When Smithers was told that Jean de Tinan (Dowson's friend and dedicatee of 'Countess Marie of the Angels') was dead at 23, he asked what he died of. O'Sullivan said, 'The doctors declared he was worn out by the life he led.' Smithers laughed sardonically. 'Damned puny Frenchmen! They can't stand anything. Look at Dowson. Is he dead? Is Conder dead? Am I dead?'[11]

Charles Conder and Dowson went together to La Roche Guyon, a picturesque town on the Seine, in March 1899 as a rest from Paris. Dowson's state of health alarmed his old friend who wrote to Will Rothenstein, 'Dowson was taken very ill on Saturday and wanted one's whole attention. He had a fit in the morning which left his mind in a most confused state and with a most extraordinary series of hallucinations. I left him there as he refused to come to Paris and ... has promised to let me know if he gets any worse. I only made him worse and I fancy he will quiet down in a day or two.' Of course, if Dowson were ill again he would hardly be in a position to summon Conder. The poet had probably emphatically rejected help in his usual manner and Conder had become irritated by him. On 31 March 1899 the artist wrote, presumably in response to an inquiry by Rothenstein, 'Dowson is all right again but I haven't seen him for a couple of weeks.'[12]

One common cause of such convulsions as Dowson experienced (presuming he was not epileptic, which seems reasonable as this is the only description of a seizure) is sudden withdrawal from alcohol. These 'rum fits' which afflict some alcoholics in the mornings in particular are caused by alterations in the levels of glucose and calcium in the blood after heavy drinking.

Another, linked cause of Dowson's malady at this time, was the poet's prodigious intake of absinthe. The ability of the liqueur to cause seizures mimicking an epileptic fit had been described in the medical literature since 1864. Its other deleterious effect was the development of hallucinations. The disease known as 'absinthism', probably caused by the thujone constituent in the drink, was described as leading to a dazed condition, intellectual enfeeblement, and terrifying hallucinations. The extent of brain damage was related to the intake of absinthe, in volume and over time, and the drinker's age, nutritional status and general health. On all counts except his comparative youth, Dowson was a bad case.[13]

Dowson's predilection for the turbid drink is well attested by his night-time companions. A medical student called Thurston Hopkins claimed to remember his rhapsodizing on it: 'absinthe for poets ... absinthe has the power of the magicians; it can wipe out or renew the past, and annul or fortell the future.'[14]

He was more equivocal when he hymned the drink in *Decorations*, in a piece called 'Absinthia Taetra' (Hideous Absinthe):

The man let the water trickle gently into his glass, and as the green clouded, a mist fell away from his mind.

Then he drank opaline.

Memories and terrors beset him. The past tore after him like a panther and through the blackness of the present he saw the luminous tiger eyes of the things to be.

But he drank opaline.

And that obscure night of the soul, and the valley of humiliation, through which he stumbled were forgotten. He saw blue vistas of undiscovered countries, high prospects and a quiet, caressing sea. The past shed its perfume over him, to-day held his hand as it were a little child, and to-morrow shone like a white star: nothing was changed.

He drank opaline.

The man had known the obscure night of the soul, and lay even now in the valley of humiliation; and the tiger menace of the things to be was red in the skies. But for a little while he had forgotten.

Green changed to white, emerald to opal: nothing was changed.

Dowson was by no means permanently drunk; his drinking was much tempered by his poverty. He was writing to Smithers in summer 1899 that not only had food been scarce, but 'even tobacco' so he must have been in dire straits indeed.[15] Even a two and a halfpenny stamp (1p) was more than he could afford at some times.

His friends were concerned about him and Victor Plarr wrote that an unnamed old friend (almost certainly Sam Smith) went to visit him as 'a kind of rescue party' in May 1899. He found Dowson 'lying in bed all day, and dining, as he was perversely fond of doing, at a wretched little gargotte.' His chief associate was Bibi-la-Purée.[16] Plarr's notion that this visitor came to tell Dowson there was money available from his father's estate is wrong. Dowson died expecting this money. It may have been that some money was forthcoming on the publication of *Adrian Rome* which took place at this time.

It must have been after being in receipt of funds from some source that Robert Sherard found him, slumped over a table sticky with absinthe. Sherard was a colourful character, a descendant of Wordsworth as he was fond of reminding people, and formerly a friend of Verlaine. A duelling scar on his leg gave testimony to his eventful life. Dowson had previously described Sherard as 'charming but the most morose and spleenful person I have yet encountered. His conversation is undiluted vitriol.'[17]

Sherard, at this time working as a journalist, later recalled his impression of Dowson, when he found him in the café. 'His nerves were all gone,' he wrote. Dowson told him he was afraid to enter the room in the hotel near the Gare Montparnasse where he lived for nameless horrors obsessed him. Sherard recounted there was 'a statue on his mantelpiece which filled him with terror. "I lie awake at night and watch it," he said, "I know that one night it means to come down off its shelf and strangle me." He was so nervous that he could not enter a shop to ask for anything. He was ever haunted with the perpetual dread of falling down paralysed.'[18]

Sherard was moved by Dowson's state and his obvious inability to look after himself. He took the poet to his own rooms at 105 Boulevard Magenta. As he had no bedroom to give him, he offered to have a bed made up for the poet on a large comfortable couch. Dowson was still sufficiently himself to refuse the offer. As Sherard tells the story:

> At the same time there stood in my study another sofa, which was covered with American cloth, and which was the hardest and most uneasy couch that upholsterer ever devised. I had bought it on this very account, so that I should only seek repose upon it during my labours, when extremest fatigue compelled me. Dowson refused the soft couch and insisted on sleeping on the hard one. He would allow no bed to be made up for him, but just threw himself upon the sofa in his clothes. He would not even remove his boots. In this uncomfortable way he spent most of the nights during the six weeks that he remained with me.

Sherard remarks on 'many other examples of the deliberate way in which he used to inflict pain and discomfort on his body, as though his soul wished to revenge itself upon its earthly coil for what it had suffered through its agency.'[19]

Dowson's host described him as 'the most complete case of neurasthenia that I have ever witnessed', instancing that the poet could not even summon up the energy to open any letter that came for him.[20] Once he asked Sherard to go to the Hôtel d'Odessa for him and see if a letter which might contain a cheque had arrived from Smithers. Sherard received the letter from the hotel keeper and took it to Dowson, who was waiting a long way down the Rue de Rennes. Sherard remembered:

> He was very anxious to know if the money had come, but he was too nervous to open the packet and assure himself. He put it into the side pocket of his jacket, and gradually, as we walked along, worked the envelope open. At last he cried out, "It's all right! I feel the frill of the cheque!" Some time later, having written to some friends in London for money to enable him to discharge his hotel bill and to return to London, he left the registered letter which came in reply unopened for four days. Part of the time it was lying on the floor of the room which I had assigned to him. "I am frightened to open it," he said.[21]

Dowson was able to repay his host to some extent, later writing to Smithers that he had lent Sherard money, 'borne with his temper, stood him and his wretched little w[hore] of a mistress innumerable meals and been rewarded with nothing but insolence and abuse.'[22] This outburst is typical of Dowson in his worst moods and should not be taken to represent actual events; it may have been that he felt ashamed of receiving help and wanted to deny that he had ever been in need of it.

Oscar Wilde had returned to Paris and he and Dowson once ran into each other in a Paris street, probably their last meeting. Wilde was with

Rowland Strong, an English journalist, who refused to drink with Dowson on account of his relations with Sherard because Strong had argued with Sherard over the Dreyfus affair, Sherard supporting the Jewish captain, Strong the anti-semites. Wilde felt this behaviour was childish, and went to another café with Dowson but the poet's desperate amusements were not to his taste. He wrote to Smithers that Dowson 'forced me to go to the Pantheon at midnight. It was dreadful, a Café-Pandemonium.'[23] Later in the summer he sent a copy of the published play *An Ideal Husband* to Dowson.

To anyone ignorant of the man, and looking at the publication record alone, 1899 seems a very good year for Dowson. *Adrian Rome* had been published by Methuen in May. It was more widely reviewed than any other work of Dowson's, if poorly received: reviewers said that despite some good writing the novel failed to engage the reader sufficiently, it was too artificial.[24] Reginald Turner, Oscar Wilde's friend, was the one exception, writing in the *Daily Telegraph* that 'not one page in the volume is dull. ... Adrian Rome can be strongly recommended to every novel reader. The authors write well, and write life as it should be written, while one of them at least, is a sweet singer, whose poetry comes out markedly and delightfully in his fiction.' He remarked that the heroine of the book 'recalls those sweet maidens of whom Mr Dowson has sung in his beautiful verses.'[25]

Decorations in Verse and Prose was published at the end of 1899, though Dowson was mercifully not to live to see the reviews. The *Athenaeum* unenthusiastically said it could not measure up to *Verses*, the poet possessed 'neither sustained thought nor sustained passion, but he could set an exquisite moment to music.'[26] The *Academy* said the verse 'is in substance agnosticism unsustained by the joy of life; in style it is exceedingly craftsmanlike and perfect, with a sense of form that lends appropriateness to the title.' While saying Dowson borrows too much from Verlaine, the reviewer says the work has 'an almost morbid grace and delicacy, which can only be conveyed by Rossetti's word gracile, and a decadent melancholy.'[27]

La Pucelle d'Orléans was also finally published this year, and Dowson's translation of *The Memoirs of Cardinal Dubois*. In 1899 Dowson had also finished his translation of the De Goncourt Brothers' *The Confidantes of a King: The Mistresses of Louis XV* but Smithers could not afford to publish it and it did not appear until 1907. The next translation was *The Memoirs of the Duc de Richelieu* which was never published. Smithers, desperate to keep his business afloat, then had Dowson translate what was probably pure pornography (as opposed to salacious memoirs), as Sherard's wife, whom he later saw in London, referred to seeing him with 'a French book with some evil pictures, which he said he was translating for a very fine gentleman.'[28]

Smithers had been a good friend indeed to Dowson, advancing him money on translations yet to be done, holding his own money for the improvident poet, and even having him work on books Smithers himself could not afford to publish. Victor Plarr's remark that he was a 'parasite on the genius of others' and that he and Verlaine 'were, in great measure [Dowson's] perverters'[29] is surely wrong. Dowson spent much of the latter part of his life in France, where Smithers visited only a few times a year and for a few days at a time. His principal contact with Dowson was in forwarding him money. His influence on Dowson was far more likely to have been that described by Vincent O'Sullivan: 'If he had been St Francis de Sales and John Wesley rolled together instead of the man he was, he would not have succeeded in prevailing upon Dowson to see any charm in a sober, godly and tranquil life.'[30]

In late summer 1899 Dowson returned to London, perhaps for another attempt at settling his parents' financial affairs, or perhaps because, as he said to Frank Harris on an earlier occasion, 'Poverty can hide in London better than anywhere else.'[31]

He was coughing desperately and suffering from haemorrhages of the lungs which required complete rest to help them heal. He knew his state would appall people. A friend (probably Sam Smith) met him in London when he was ill and coughing and offered to take him to a restaurant where they had been before, but he said despairingly he could not face dinner there.[32] He returned to the cabmen's shelters for warmth and nourishment, and the familiar hazy, beer-smelling interior of the Bun House.

R. Thurston Hopkins, a medical student at University College, wrote that he used to see Dowson there. He described the poet as 'thin, small-boned, [with] light brown wavy hair which was always curiously upstanding, blue eyes, a tired voice and nerveless, indeterminate hands, with thin fingers, such as are in the habit of letting things fall and slip from them.' His collar was held together with a piece of black moire ribbon tied in a bow. Hopkins remarked that Dowson seldom smiled: 'His face was lined and grave, and yet it was the round face of a schoolboy and sometimes one might catch a gleam of youth in his blue eyes. At such moments a ghost of a smile would flit over his sombre features and wipe out the fretful expression which generally lurked there.'[33]

Hopkins reported that Dowson, 'an absent-minded dreamer', carried a small silver-plated revolver in his hip pocket which he would produce and hand round for inspection in bars and cafés for no apparent reason. He had presumably won it in a card game and later lost it the same way, or pawned it, for there is no further mention of it.

Hopkins said he became an occasional companion of Dowson's, sometimes walking round with him and playing a game they called Blind Chivvy which consisted of finding short cuts from one part of London to another by way of the alleys and byways which abounded in the city before it was remodelled in the mid-twentieth century by the Blitz and the planners. Hopkins tells a story of their encounter with a sinister character whom they met in a bar and later observed entering the house where

Dowson lodged, 152 Euston Road, opposite St Pancras church. Dowson would not stay under the same roof as the man and so went home with Hopkins to Crouch End. The story takes on a fanciful character when Hopkins recounts that the man died in the lodging house leaving no possessions but a bag of soft earth or mould. Dowson, he said, told him the stranger's name was Lazarus and 'that mould in the bag was graveyard mould.'[34] It is a tale well told, and of interest not so much because of the undoubted accuracy of many of Hopkins' observations (which may have come from other accounts, like that of Edgar Jepson who was known to Hopkins), but because it gives the fantastic flavour of evenings spent with Dowson and shows how, even in his wrecked and sometimes deranged state, Dowson could be fascinating company for the right companion.

Someone else who saw Dowson and recognized the attraction of the poet, even in his worst states, was Newman Flower, at this time a young journalist but later to become a distinguished publisher. He wrote that there was a picture of Dowson 'seared in my mind' from October 1899 which was a period of heady excitement in London because the Boer War had just broken out in South Africa. Oblivious to such events, Dowson sat in a bar.

> He had before him, I remember, a high tumbler of claret. His eyes were half closed ... he seemed only partly conscious of the passing and re-passing of people about him. His long, thin fingers worked in painful travail over the marble top of the table at which he sat.
>
> He fascinated me. He seemed like a piece of wreckage salvaged from some vast destroying stream. His hollow cheeks, his pallor, his thin lips pressed tightly together, the ceaseless writhing of his fingers presented to my mind a picture of acute agony. I wonder why it was that one whose written thoughts had so impressed me could sink down to this hell.
>
> Presently he opened his eyes, but he really saw no one. His lips began muttering things – stupid, incoherent things – and I saw him grope in his vest pocket for a stub of pencil which he ultimately produced. Then he searched as painfully in his coat, and pulled out a wad of letters, from which he selected one and began to scribble wildly on the back of it. He wrote something, crossed it out, scribbled feverishly on again. When he had filled the whole of one side of the paper with writing, most of which he had crossed out afterwards, he turned it over and began writing in pencil across the ink address of the letter.[35]

Such is the picture of Dowson at the end: a drunken, diseased and impoverished man, without a home, cruelly disappointed in love, unable now even to scrape a living from his career; desolate, toothless, shunning his friends, ravaged by pain and neglect. Yet Ernest Dowson was still struggling with his last coherent thoughts to write verse.

CHAPTER 15

THE DYING OF ERNEST DOWSON

The new century dawned in a cold London as Ernest Dowson dragged himself past the bright displays in shops and the flocks of revellers. We know now that Dowson's self-destructive despair was a more appropriate welcome to the arrival of the twentieth century than the easy optimism of those doing the Dawn of the Century two-step at garish celebrations.

Robert Sherard had heard that Dowson had been ill and that he was living in a garret on the Euston Road. He visited one Sunday morning and found his friend in a sorry state. He was in bed, though it was past noon, and he told Sherard that he had been lying there since the preceding Friday. He spent whole days and even couples of days without leaving his room or procuring food. His landlady supplied him with a small breakfast but, he confided in Sherard, 'I don't think that she will let me have that for very long, for I am in arrears with my rent, and they are pressing me for it. Every morning now there is a note on my tray from the landlord asking me whether "I consider myself a gent".'[1]

Sherard brought him some food and a bottle of wine, but when he returned the next afternoon, he found Dowson just as he had left him – he had not stirred from his bed. Sherard remarked, 'He was just too wretched and depressed to make any effort on behalf of himself.' He induced Dowson to get up, and the poet showed him a small confectioner's shop where, he said, 'I get my meals when I get any, I thought at that shop one could buy only such things as buns and glasses of milk.' He was working for Smithers who paid him weekly when he sent in work, but for weeks he had been too feeble to do any writing. Sherard saw him several times, but

164

each time he was lying in bed, often without having eaten anything for 24 hours.[2]

Sherard did not see Dowson for several days. Then, in about the second week in January 1900, he went to a wine shop in Bedford Street to write some letters in the downstairs room which was used for that purpose. Someone touched him on the shoulder and he turned and started, 'For it was as if a being from the grave were standing by my side.' Dowson was looking pale and wretched. Sherard bought him two brandies and the poet told him he had been driven by the landlord's threats to go to his publisher to appeal for money. Smithers meanwhile had gone off to Dieppe leaving a sarcastic note for Dowson. The poet was trying to screw up the courage to return to face the landlord empty-handed. Sherard had himself fallen on hard times financially but he gave him half a sovereign. As he passed it over he felt Dowson's quivering hand. 'It was in an abominable state,' he said, and he felt he must take Dowson home with him.

Sherard was hardly living in luxury. He and his wife and their adopted son were in a small house in Catford, the bottom half of which they let to a bricklayer and his family. Dowson agreed to come, as he had not the courage to return to his landlord but, he said, 'You must take me down to Catford first-class, for I cannot bear to be with people.' He was so weak that Sherard had to take him in a cab to Charing Cross station and from Catford station to his home less than a mile away at 26 Sandhurst Gardens (now 159 Sangley Road) up a lane which Sherard described as 'a mud swamp'.[3] Sherard's only work at the time was the production of a leaflet about a new process of making white lead which was written while Dowson was with him.

Sherard's wife, Marthe, said she was at home and her little son was playing with the tin toys he had been given for Christmas when she heard a racking cough and her husband brought in 'a sick young man' who was 'nothing but a skeleton'. Dowson apologized at the imposition, and said he was getting over influenza. She remembered how kindly he stroked Paul's head, and how he looked into her eyes, 'as if he were frightened'. He spoke in French, which Marthe Sherard understood well, and she remarked, 'After he had finished what he was saying, he would often burst into a sort of laugh, as if the sound of his voice amused him.' He later took to speaking English, probably so he could be understood by Paul, who was too young to be frightened by his appearance.[4]

Marthe Sherard put Dowson to bed in the most comfortable room in their small house. His clothes were very old and dirty, though she noted his waistcoat bore the label of a French tailor. His coat was frayed at the lapels and threadbare at the sleeves. He had a black hat which she recognized as like those worn by artists in Paris. Robert Sherard considered it proof that Dowson's previous neglect of his clothes had been wilful and that, 'I could

give him no greater pleasure than to bring back home to our cottage a new
shirt or a clean collar for him, and to put it on him.'⁵

Mrs Sherard knew they were too poor to provide Dowson with the
medical attention he needed, but he refused any attempt at medical inter-
vention anyway. She pressed him after he had been staying with them a
short time and he said if he were not much improved in a few days she
could call for a doctor. When he was not improved in a few weeks, he was
still refusing permission for a doctor to be called. She hit on the ruse of
inviting round the doctor father of one of Paul's schoolfellows, but when
Dowson heard him in the house he became agitated. Marthe Sherard said
she found him, 'half-dressed, pacing about the room, his eyes burning with
fear and anger. "Mrs Sherard", he said, "if you bring that man in to see me,
I'll leave you and go out and die in the street."' He also refused to see a
priest, staring at the ceiling a long time when Marthe Sherard asked him,
then turning over in bed with his face to the wall, his hand over the covers
clenching and unclenching, saying, 'No, no, no one is to see me.'⁶

Mostly Dowson sat in an armchair looking through two sunny windows
over the green fields behind the house. Robert Sherard said Dowson ate
well and was cheerful. He used to read his invalid friend passages from his
work about the white lead process and they would laugh together 'on the
pass to which the Parnassians had come. Towards the end we used to sit
together all day talking of literature and les journées de Paris. At times he
put out his hand and touched mine and said that he was happy that he had
met me.' As night fell one grey evening, looking over the Kentish countryside, Dowson said, 'Literature has failed for me. I shall look somewhere
else in the future.'⁷

They talked of people they both knew, like Smithers, and Dowson read
every book Sherard had in the house – Thackeray's *Henry Esmond* was his
favourite. He also took to reading Dickens, which he had not done before.
Sherard wrote, 'I think that those last days of peace and quiet were as
happy as any that had been allowed him in his life.'⁸

After he had been four weeks with Sherard, his host had to go to
France on urgent business which he could not neglect – he desperately
needed the money it would realize. He left Dowson in his wife's hands and
went to Catford Station to get his train to Waterloo and then France. As he
was walking up and down the platform, thinking of Dowson

> a prompting came to me to return to him. I tried to resist the feeling, for it was
> urgent that I should not postpone any longer that work which I had undertaken
> to do. But the feeling grew stronger and stronger. At last I threw my ticket away
> and returned home. He was pleased to see me. He said he had been almost
> expecting me to come back.⁹

Sherard contacted Conal O'Riordan who lived in nearby Bromley, and
who sent Dowson money. He wished to take over the care of his friend,

and when Dowson was well enough it was intended that he should stay with O'Riordan. The novelist said that Dowson 'imagined his surviving relatives were seeking power to lock him up as a lunatic.'[10] Dowson's last letter, written in a shaky hand to O'Riordan around 20 February 1900, refers to avoiding 'the necessity of lunatic proceedings' but also says he will soon ask his uncle Stanley Hoole to see him, so he was more reconciled to his family than he had been previously. Another visitor, whom O'Riordan met on his way out of Sherard's house was Charles Conder who was accompanied by his current comrade in revelry, Augustus John.[11]

Dowson used to send Sherard out to get medicines made up from prescriptions he found in *Health in the Home* and other such publications, and for ipecacuanha wine which would loosen a cough but had no curative properties. He continued to insist he was suffering from the after-effects of influenza, and that as soon as his strength returned he would be quite well. He knew that he was still due the sum of £600 or £700 and he talked eagerly of what he would do with the money. He was hoping to find some companion who would share expenses and go to the South of France with him. He was full of hope for new literary projects when he made 'a fresh start'.

Dowson told Marthe Sherard his dream was to go to the Riviera and asked her what her dream was. She replied, 'I would like nothing better than to go to the West End and have a fine dinner with fine people at a brightly lighted restaurant,' for Marthe Sherard was an educated woman of some refinement and was irritated by the life of poverty she had found in being a writer's wife. The poet asked Paul's dream, and he said he would like a wind-up train, which would run by itself, better then the tin train which he was pushing round the floor. The sunlight flooded into the room and Dowson put his hand on the little boy's head and said, 'You shall have your train, Paul, and you,' and he smiled kindly at Marthe, 'shall have the finest dinner at the finest place in the West End when my ship comes in.' He lay back, staring at the ceiling, repeating, 'When my ship comes in.'[12]

On 22 February Dowson tried to dictate his last letter to Arthur Moore but could not form the opening phrase, saying he was too tired. Still, that night he sat up talking with Sherard till five in the morning, and even after he had gone to bed, kept shouting for Sherard not to go to sleep but to keep talking to him. Thus insomnia tormented him to the very end, and Sherard lay on a sofa rather than go to bed so he could keep Dowson company. Marthe Sherard recalls their voices: her husband's a deep bass and Dowson's 'high-pitched tone like a wail'. He would not let Sherard sleep, calling him in at 6 am to drink some port in his room. Sherard remembered that they discussed improbabilities in the plot of *Oliver Twist*: whether Bill Sikes would really have murdered Nancy with Fagin's word alone against her, which Dowson doubted.

At eight he was coughing badly, and sent Sherard to the chemist's to get some ipecacuanha wine. He was still coughing after this, and Sherard said the doctor must be fetched. Sherard went downstairs to ask the bricklayer's wife to fetch a doctor and as he was coming back up he called out, 'You had better get up, Ernest, and sit in the arm-chair. You will breathe more easily.'

Marthe Sherard held Dowson in her arms and for a moment he seemed to catch his breath. 'You are like an Angel from heaven,' he said, 'God bless you.' They were the last words he spoke. When Sherard returned to the room he was trying to say something but it was the end. Sherard took the limp body in his arms to lift him to a sitting position and wiped his brow but as he did the head fell on his shoulder.[13]

What was it like? Of all writers who have lived, perhaps Ernest Dowson has written most profoundly of the actual moment of death. If anyone could describe his own death in advance it was he. In 'The Visit' the narrator looks at his 'old body on the bed, and the room in which I had grown so tired, and in the middle of the room the pan of charcoal which still smouldered' and he says to Death, 'I have wanted you all my life.'

The death of Philip Rainham in his novel is, 'as if, in his great weakness, the ache of his old desire, his fever of longing, had suddenly left him ... as though the literal wasting away of his body had really given freer access to that pure spirit, its prisoner.'

For Francis Donne, 'An immense and ineffable tiredness had come over him that this – this was Death; this was the thing against which he had cried and revolted; the horror from which he would have escaped; this utter luxury of physical exhaustion, this calm, this release.'

Insofar as it is ever possible to tell such things, Dowson was right. As he died in a writer's house, we have an account of his death too. Robert Sherard wrote, 'There was no struggle, there was no agony; and the only sign that was given to me ... was the beautiful calm that settled down, like a brooding dove, upon his tired face ... one never saw peace more reposeful on features more ravaged.'[14]

The bricklayer's wife, who acted as servant to the Sherards, laid out the body. She told Sherard there was no point in his crying, 'now that the gentlemen was gone.' Sherard reflected miserably that Dowson had 'worked well and with genius, for ten years but probably never received remuneration equivalent to that of their lodger the bricklayer.'[15]

Sherard wired Stanley Hoole at Lloyd's, but before his arrival a coroner's officer came, presumably at the suggestion of a doctor who was called to certify death. As the dead man had not seen a doctor prior to his death, an inquest might well be indicated, but the arrival of Stanley Hoole with his assurances that Dowson's death could not possibly benefit the Sherards financially satisfied the police. Hoole made the necessary arrangements and provided for the funeral. He replaced the pennies with which the servant had covered Dowson's eyes with silver coins, telling the woman she should have them after they had served their purpose and Dowson was laid in his coffin.[16] Hoole registered the death of his nephew, whose profession was described as 'author' with the cause of death as 'tuberculosis. Pulmonary syncope' meaning the lungs had ceased functioning.

Sherard informed those friends of Dowson with whom he was in contact and wrote a lurid account for the newspapers of Dowson's last months. 'In an indifferent and callous London,' he wrote, 'haggard, emaciated and forlorn, he dragged his poor, weary, tottering limbs from garret lodging to publisher's shop disregarded, unheeded, neglected ...' and so on in the same vein.[17] Nellie Plarr saw the account and ran in to her husband, shocked. Victor Plarr was distressed at the implication that Dowson's friends had knowingly let him die. 'Ye gods!' he exclaimed, 'Our doors had stood open for him, our lamp had been trimmed for him for years! He had stayed many days with us in the dear old seasons: why had he not died with us?'[18]

As a result of the newspaper announcement, the cottage was soon flooded with wreaths and messages of sympathy. The funeral was held on 27 February 1900 at the Catholic chapel in Lewisham which stood on the site where the large Roman Catholic church of St Saviour's (which still stands) was soon to be built. It is a few hundred yards from St Stephen's, where Dowson's parents were married, and less than a mile from the place of his birth in Lee. Ernest Dowson had come home at last.

There was a long cortege following the hearse as it wound its way up the hill towards Ladywell Cemetery to the triangular plot set aside for Catholic burials. Several relatives attended in addition to Stanley Hoole, almost certainly Ada Swan (his mother's sister). It may have been at her request that the grave was dug especially deep: 15 feet, in fact, for when she died at the age of 87 in 1939 she was buried in the same grave, as was her servant, Betsy Fraser, who died two years later.

Among his friends at the funeral were Robert and Marthe Sherard, Arthur Moore, Edgar Jepson, Teixeira de Mattos, Nellie Plarr who represented her husband who was ill, Herbert Horne and several actors. Lennox Pawle, one of Dowson's actor friends from the glorious days of the early nineties, burst into tears at the graveside. 'The most exquisite poet of the age to have died thus,' he wept.[19]

The obituaries were brief. The *Daily Telegraph* called Dowson 'a writer of verse which had the true poetic touch. Since he went up to Queen's College, Oxford, some fourteen years ago, he proved an inveterate Bohemian, without any attempt at posing in that uncomfortable role. He was quite genuine and simple, loved by his friends, but difficult to live with by reason of his vagabond temperament.'[20] The *Kentish Mercury* called him 'a well-known minor poet and litterateur ... full of promise, [who] was only thirty-two, and might have achieved greatness.'[21] Arthur Symons wrote in the *Athenaeum* 'The death of Ernest Dowson will mean very little to the world at large, but it will mean a great deal to a few people who care passionately about poetry.'[22]

Symons then set about preparing a long piece on Dowson for the *Fortnightly Review* which was based on *The Savoy* article on Dowson and later formed his introduction to *The Poems of Ernest Dowson*, published in 1905. After the *Athenaeum* obituary appeared, Sherard wrote to Symons who visited Catford to hear Sherard's version of Dowson and visit the grave. Later Symons wrote to his wife Rhoda, 'The man just such another wreck as Dowson, half drunk and half maudlin.'[23]

Symons' *Fortnightly Review* article was not a quick work of hack journalism – he obviously showed it to many of his friends who doubtless knew Dowson. He wrote to Rhoda Symons:

> Read the Dowson very carefully and tell me how it strikes you, and if anything seems too strongly sad – about drink etc. Some of my friends want me to tone it down. It seems to me that I have not said a word too much and that I could not tell the truth in any other way. You will see I have woven in bits of the *Savoy* article – which Dowson read and thoroughly liked.

Rhoda responded that it was 'simply splendid. In my opinion there is not one word too much about the man's personal character.'[24]

Symons wrote to Edmund Gosse who must have inquired about the circumstances of Dowson's death:

> This hysterical, misleading, and quite untrue note on Dowson was written by Sherard, in whose cottage he died, and who certainly was very kind to him at the last. Dowson was never really in want of money; he had at least a dozen attached friends (many of whose names you must know well) any one of whom was ready to do anything he could to help him. But with a thousand a year he would have lived and died exactly the same. I am bringing out all this in my *Fortnightly* article. Which at the same time tells everything without disguise – if they will print it as I write it. I have worked eight hours on it yesterday, and have already done most of the personal part. I shall annoy my friends and please my enemies (always so gratifying) by pointing out that his note of delicate charm owed nothing to the disorder of his life, as, also, it was uncontaminated by it.[25]

At some time in the first half of 1900, Symons had an urgent message to go to see Althea Gyles. He found her lying in bed in a room bare except for five books (one a presentation copy from Wilde) and the extravagant costume jewellery she used to wear. There was a bottle of chloral hydrate by her side and the bed was strewn with manuscripts. She was very pale and she lay back with her red hair strewn across the pillow, asking Symons to compile a book of her best verse. She was convinced she was going to die. She asked to see his article on Dowson, still in draft, and said, 'When I meet him, I'll tell him about it.'[26]

Gradually the literary world came to hear of the death. Yeats wrote to Lady Gregory, 'Poor Dowson is dead. Since that girl in the restaurant married the waiter he has drunk hard and so gradually sank into consumption. It is a most pitiful and strange story.'[27]

Robert Sherard now took his long-delayed French trip and took the opportunity to visit St Germain-en-Laye where Dowson had urged him to go to write. He there wrote his account of Dowson's last days which has been quoted here, summing up his view with the remark, 'I cannot conceive Ernest Dowson otherwise than supremely unhappy. He was not of this world or for it.'[28]

He stopped in Paris and went to visit Oscar Wilde at the Hôtel d'Alsace in the Rue des Beaux-Arts. Sherard was first turned away by a hotel porter who told him Wilde was too tired to see anyone – he had been drinking very heavily. Later that day Sherard returned and sent up a message: 'Sorry to hear you are tired, Oscar. I have come to Paris from Ernest Dowson's deathbed – he died in my arms – and I thought you might like to hear about him and the messages he bade me take to you.'

He was allowed in and found Wilde in a dressing gown in a squalid room. A bowl was full of ashes and cigarette ends, some books were heaped in a corner, there was a pile of letters on the mantelpiece and a bottle of absinthe by the wash stand. Sherard remarked that the playwright was 'in a dreadful state of nerves ... he was shaking and groaning.' The table was littered with papers. Sherard inquired about Wilde's work. He said he was still writing but added, 'One has to do something. I have no taste for it now. It is a penance to me but, as was said of torture, it always helps to pass an hour or two.' Sherard told him of Dowson's death, about which he did not seem to Sherard to be too interested. The reason is probably that he found it too painful to come to terms with immediately.

'It is all so sad,' was all he said, 'Ernest was an enfant voué au noir [a child of the night]. ... Much of what he has written will remain.'[29]

Later, Wilde wrote a more considered view of his friend to Leonard Smithers:

> I am greatly distressed to hear of Ernest's death: how sudden it must have been! Poor wounded, wonderful fellow that he was, a tragic reproduction of all tragic poetry, like a symbol, or a scene. I hope bay leaves will be laid on his tomb, and rue, and myrtle too, for he knew what love is.[30]

That was true, and all the more sad because he did not know what it was to be loved.

CHAPTER 16

FRIENDS OF ERNEST DOWSON

The muffled echoes of Dowson's death reverberated through the dwindling decadent community. Many of his friends were not to survive him for long. Oscar Wilde followed Dowson within the year. He wrote nothing after 'The Ballad of Reading Gaol' and his drinking and increasing penury blighted the end of his life. An ear infection, which an operation did not rectify, was the immediate cause of death, though his biographer Richard Ellmann is sure the underlying cause was syphilis. He died in Paris in November 1900 at the age of 46 having been received into the Catholic Church on his deathbed.[1]

Wilde thus died after his enemy, the Marquis of Queensberry who also, like those he so reviled and so resembled, eventually came to the Catholic faith. Lord Alfred Douglas was one of many of Dowson's friends who never forgot the poet, and he remarked in his biography in 1931 how he regretted he did not do what he might have to help Dowson in his years of need. He married the poet Olive Custance in 1902. He passed the rest of his life in argument and litigation, dying in 1945.[2]

Lionel Johnson, who had a small private income and so was saved the added burden of poverty while he suffered his decline, lived in a series of rooms in the Fleet Street area. He spent all his time between his rooms and nearby bars. He developed a persecution mania, saying he knew detectives were after him. His laundress, who also cooked his meals, testified that he was drinking two pints of whisky every 24 hours.[3] On Monday 29 September 1902 he walked unsteadily along Fleet Street to the Green Dragon. He perched himself on a barstool which he then fell off. He had obviously lost consciousness, so he was taken to St Bartholomew's Hospital where he died two days later at the age of 35. The post-mortem revealed he had suffered a stroke – a ruptured blood vessel within the skull, which is a frequent symptom of heavy drinking.

Henry Harland, former editor of *The Yellow Book*, died of tuberculosis in 1905 at the age of 44. Charles Conder died in 1909, at 40, his drinking having long been the despair of his friends. In his last years he contracted what the *Dictionary of National Biography* calls brain disease, which may be a euphemism for syphilis. He spent his last years in Virginia Water Asylum in Surrey, obsessed with the prospect of imminent death, reproaching himself for wasted time and talent.[4]

Leonard Smithers' business was declared bankrupt on 18 September 1900. His son Jack said he had been suffering from 'muscular rheumatism' (perhaps a euphemism for venereal disease) which made it difficult for him to work. Smithers kept himself going by issuing pirated editions of Wilde and selling batches of letters from Beardsley, Wilde and Dowson for which he has been pilloried as some kind of literary pariah, but these were all men he had helped when he was able to and no one else would. They would not have denied him the assistance had they been alive to give it. The great days, anyway, were past, and he and his wife both took to drinking heavily. Ranger Gull, one of his former authors, wrote of a time when a friend and he 'found Smithers in the gutter of Oxford Street – starving. We made a little purse to put him on his legs. It was of no use. Six months afterwards he died, absolutely alone and in circumstances of extreme horror.'[5]

On 19 December 1907 (which coincidentally was Smithers forty-sixth birthday) his wife and son, who had not seen Smithers for some time, were sent for. They went to a house in Fulham near Parson's Green, where the publisher had been found. The house was completely bare of all furniture except a wicker hamper. There were some 50 empty bottles of chlorodyne in the house, which was a preparation containing chloroform, morphine, ether and ethanol, to which Smithers had doubtless been addicted. He was found lying there dead, completely naked, with his clothes and even his monocle gone.[6]

John Davidson's misery lasted longer. He was tormented by the lack of recognition of what he saw as his genius. He spent an increasing amount of his time working out a personal cosmological theory which explained the existence of the universe, and the non-existence of God, Hell and Heaven, in which matter is forever striving to reach self-consciousness. He wrote a great deal of verse on the subject with lines such as:

It may be Matter in itself is pain,
Sweetened in sexual love

In 1909 at the age of 52 he drowned himself in the sea in Cornwall, where he had lived for the previous two years. When his body was found in the bay at Mousehole after months in the water it was too badly decomposed for the cause of death to be determined, but suicide was never doubted.

Charles Goodhart, the actor who had looked after the stricken Marie with Dowson when she collapsed at Poland, ran through a considerable fortune and fell on bad times. On Christmas morning 1917 he went into a butcher's shop, took up a knife, and cut his throat from ear to ear.[7]

The revolutionary poet John Barlas found love of a sort: he lived with a 'weird young female' who 'professed anarchy' and 'wore flannel under-things of a blood-red hue to show the colour of her convictions.'[8] He went mad at least as early as 1898, when Davidson wrote to Gosse that he was in Gartnavel Asylum near Glasgow.[9] According to Sherard he was 'to linger on for years, a physical wreck with a mind diseased,' until he died in the asylum in 1914 at the age of 54.

Arthur Symons at least was a survivor. He was trying to work towards a universal theory of all art when he first suffered a nervous breakdown in 1908. He was believed to be suffering from an advanced stage of syphilis, but this was an unreliable diagnosis, given the circumstances of his condition.

He lived on, and his wife Rhoda was obliged to keep him by going on the stage and begging money from his friends. He continued to write, but his work was mainly re-arrangements of previous material. His new, original writing was incoherent.[10] He survived his breakdown to recover and function reasonably well, though with none of his former power. In his sixties his mental condition deteriorated progressively. Rhoda, herself dying of leukaemia, wrote that Symons had cried because Bessie (their maid) had given him nothing for his birthday, so she had to go to the village and get him two green pencils. 'He was enchanted and wrote the names of all the cats with them – Setebos Symons – Zambellino Symons – Beelzebub Symons! He was perfectly happy! but it is pitiable to watch the wreck of a brain such as his was.'[11] He outlived her, however, and died in 1945, at 79, eight years after Rhoda.

Trial and disease did not spare those who had lived what was far from a life of pleasure. Rowland Dowson travelled to Western Canada and walked vast distances in his quest of fortune but without success, though he married and the couple had a daughter called Annie, after his mother (later Annie Glanville of Vancouver, British Colombia). He was the sole beneficiary of his parents estate (in excess of £1000) when the lawyers had finally finished with it in 1902, so he must at least have enjoyed some comfort before the family curse caught up with him and he died of tuberculosis in 1913 at the age of 36.

Not all Dowson's friends of the 1890s came to a sorry end. Herbert Horne spent most of the rest of his life in Florence on his art studies, though dying in 1916 at the age of 52. Selwyn Image became Slade Professor of Fine Art at Oxford and died in 1930 aged 81. John Gray went into the priesthood and was appointed to the parish of St Peter in Edinburgh in 1905. His friend André Raffalovich joined him there and resumed his life of lavish hospitality. They lived together until their deaths – within a few months of each other – in 1934. M.P. Shiel's work was influential, on Arthur Conan Doyle among others, but it was Sherlock Holmes, Doyle's detective of the 1890s who was to endure, not Shiel's Prince Zaleski. He wrote little of note after 1901, and died in Chichester in 1947. The adventurer Michael Holland, who knew Dowson in Pont-Aven, went to the Gold Coast of Africa in 1897 where he fought for the Empire, returned to his home in Sussex and took to collecting books, including first editions of Dowson's works. He died in 1956 at the age of 86.[12] Charles Sayle worked as a university librarian in Cambridge until his death in 1924 at 60. Arthur Moore retired as a solicitor in 1937 and died in 1952 aged 85, having often spoken to researchers about Dowson in his later years.

Will Rothenstein became one of the most important portrait painters of his age and a significant member of the art establishment, Principal of the Royal College of Art and a war artist in both world wars. He was knighted in 1931 and died in 1945 at the age of 73. Two of Dowson's friends won the Nobel Prize for Literature – W.B. Yeats in 1923 and André Gide in 1947.

Yeats never did win the love of Maud Gonne, who said she had 'a horror and terror of physical love' though she had two children by a French journalist.[13] In 1903 she married John MacBride, 'a drunken, vainglorious lout', according to Yeats, though he was to redeem himself by fighting in the 1916 Easter Rising and later being executed by the British.[14] Yeats became one of the greatest poets of the twentieth century, founded the Irish National Theatre, became a senator in the Irish Free State, and died aged 74 in 1939.

As the most successful – and prolific – of Dowson's friends, Yeats was the one who chiefly defined the 1890s, not least in his editing of the *Oxford Book of Modern Verse* where Dowson and many other of Yeats's friends found a place. Yeats called the writers of the nineties 'the tragic generation', citing as one reason for the tragedies that 'unlike the Victorian poets, almost all were poor men, and had made it a matter of conscience to turn from every kind of money-making that prevented good writing'.[15]

It is true that many of the artists of the nineties evinced a heroic dedication to art amid cruel poverty, but this is inadequate as an explanation of their respective fates. Johnson was not poor, yet followed a similar trajectory to Dowson, who usually was. Wilde was only poor because he was profligate: what money he had, he wasted. A reasonable amount of money, paid weekly to Dowson would undoubtedly have helped the poet to eat, but it would also have enabled him to drink more which would not have been to the benefit of his health. Even given sufficient income he might well have died at roughly the same time of some accident or alcohol-related condition.

Ernest Rhys complained personally to Yeats of his compounding the Rhymers wholesale into the 'tragic generation', though to be frank all the best poets, Yeats excepted, did have lives which could reasonably be called tragic. Such an assessment has to exclude Rhys, who lived to the age of 87, and Le Gallienne who lived to 81, but they were hardly poets of even the second rank. Their longevity at least shows that the Rhymers were not merely a decadent coterie, dedicated to living fast and dying young. Of the 13 core Rhymers whose death dates are known (Hillier's is not) only two failed to reach their fortieth birthday: Dowson and Johnson; the same number as passed their eightieth. Ten of them reached 60.

So it was Dowson's bourgeois friends who lived to tell tales of him, like Edgar Jepson whose memoirs show no trace of the disagreement which divided him from Dowson, though the poet may well have been reconciled with Jepson after their differences had died down. Samuel Smith wrote to Jepson in 1937 that some of the letters he possessed (now destroyed) referred to the novelist: 'E. D. had his sudden fits of fury, but they died down rapidly and finally he "hoped to live with you in amity".' Smith confided to Jepson that, 'I may as well observe that I haven't made a success of my life – nor did I ever expect to. Quite apart from defects of intellect and character, a queer nervous derangement which has dogged me from the start finally did me in altogether, and I am now what my house-keeper calls a "perfect harmlet".' To add to his troubles, an operation on his right eye and the removal of the other left him almost completely blind at the end of his life. No one whom he knew was interested in his souvenirs of Ernest Dowson and he was writing to Jepson, whom he had not seen for over 40 years, to ask if there was anyone 'among the younger generation' who would appreciate those of Dowson's books, letters and photographs which he had.[16]

Jepson died the following year, in 1938, at the age of 74. He had traded artistic freedom for financial security, having written a good novel, *The Passion for Romance*, published in 1896. He found it made him little money so wrote a popular novel, *The Dictator's Daughter*, 'and have gone on writing it ever since' to the extent that he eventually wrote some 50 novels, none of which have survived a century on.[17]

Conal O'Riordan, addressing an audience about Dowson in 1946, remarked that it would have been better if Smithers, Dowson and himself had died in an accident as they travelled together from Dieppe in 1895. This is understandable as it relates to the other two, for they both came to sad ends in a short time, but it is revealing that he includes a retrospective death wish for himself. He said it would have been better for Smithers and Dowson, but 'Best for myself because I should have been spared long years of suffering and humiliation.'[18] He was to die two years later at the age of 74.

Victor Plarr found it salutary that he became known and pointed out by a younger generation as 'the man who knew Dowson.'[19] He stayed friendly with men of letters, associating with Ezra Pound around 1910. Pound satirized him lightly in 'Hugh Selwyn Mauberley':

> For two hours he talked of Gallifet;
> Of Dowson; of the Rhymers' Club;
> Told me how Johnson (Lionel) had died
> By falling from a high stool in a pub ...
>
> Dowson found harlots cheaper than hotels

Plarr died in 1929 at the age of 66.

Vincent O'Sullivan continued to write and publish to defend the memory of Wilde, Dowson and the other decadents he had known. He died in poverty in Paris in 1940 at 71 and was buried in a communal grave.

Robert Sherard continued his social investigation work on behalf of the poor and suffering with such books as *The Child Slaves of Britain* in 1905. He divorced Marthe in 1906, writing *After the Fault* the same year about the failure of the marriage. He had two more marriages, but 'he was a difficult man to live with, violent, alcoholic and syphilitic.' A biography of Guy de Maupassant led to some relief from his poverty and to his being honoured by France in 1929 as a Chevalier of the Legion of Honour. He died in London in 1943 at the age of 83.[20]

As always, it is far easier to trace the lives of men than of women in the Victorian period. Mabel Beardsley died of cancer in 1916 aged 44 after a successful acting career. Her death is commemorated in Yeats's poem 'Upon A Dying Lady'.

Symons' and Horne's lover, Muriel Broadbent, married W. Lewellyn Hacon, co-director of the Vale Press, in 1899, in future using the name Phylis Hacon. Dowson's girlfriend from 1893–4, Dulcie, was reported to have married into brewing, and was still living when a Dowson scholar tried to see her in the early 1940s, but one of Dowson's surviving friends would not disclose her address for fear a reminder of her wild past would haunt her respectable old age.

After Marthe Sherard's relationship with Robert Sherard ended, she seems to have taken up with a man called Dillon-Jones, as this is the name under which she was seen by Mark Longaker in 1939 in a Poor Law hospital in Poplar. She hated being in such an institution with the 'lowest scum of humanity' and pleaded, 'You can pity me, a Latin and Greek scholar, surrounded by such people.' She was able to recite Dowson's verse, and contrasted her acquaintance with him with the straits to which she had come – 'I have known great poets: Ernest Dowson died in my arms.'[21] She died in 1942 at the age of 82.

Arthur Symons tried to have Althea Gyles's verses published and found a publisher for her. The book was being set up when the publisher discovered she insisted on having it dedicated 'to the beautiful memory of Oscar Wilde'. The publisher was prepared to compromise – he would have accepted a dedication to Wilde, even, but not the word 'beautiful'. With true Celtic defiance, Gyles demanded all or nothing, so the manuscript was returned and there never was a volume of Althea Gyles's poetry.[22] Althea Gyles lived on, however: her flaming hair now grey, her independence an old woman's eccentricity, her punctilious craftsmanship becoming mere fussiness about domestic trivia. She lived in bedsits in Tulse Hill and then Sydenham, casting horoscopes as the new century wore on, until she became a ghost from the 1890s in war-shattered London. She died in a nursing home near Crystal Palace in 1949 at the age of 81.

There is just one other terrible story to tell. Adelaide Noelte had three children, all girls. Bertha was born in July 1898, Amelia in August 1900, and Catherine in December 1902.

Adelaide's does not seem to have been a happy marriage. Augustus did not want to manage a restaurant, preferring to keep to his trade of tailoring, which he endeavoured to carry on in a room above the restaurant, without great success. In August 1903 Adelaide and Augustus had a week's holiday at Hastings and it was here that Adelaide told her husband she had recently had an abortion, performed by a German midwife, whom she refused to name, at her home. He was upset at this and, as she could have gauged his reaction, one wonders why she told him at all. Perhaps their being on holiday meant Augustus wanted to have sex with her, and as this would have been painful given the recent operation, she had to give him a reason why she would not comply.[23]

Adelaide's mother (also named Adelaide) had died at the age of 61 at the end of 1900. Probably Adelaide's flirtatious nature asserted itself after her mother's death, for she had at least one male companion, the friendship of whom led her into duplicity. This was Joseph Kaiser, an unemployed German waiter, who had rented a room on the third floor at 19 Sherwood Street early in 1903 and was working as a racing tipster. She was said to be 'on very friendly terms' with Kaiser. A woman called Winifred Harris, who had known Adelaide for seven years and had been in her service, presumably as a maid, was once prevailed upon by Adelaide to write a letter to Augustus to say that she had slept at Sherwood Street one night when she did not. The reason for this was that Augustus had caught Adelaide alone with Kaiser and was suspicious of their relationship. Augustus must have been away, perhaps looking for work, or he would have known whether or not his wife was alone in the house with no other adult but Kaiser.[24] One rumour about the couple was that Augustus was working in a mill away from London, and this would fit with the other known facts.[25]

The tale seems to be one of commonplace sordidness: married life and the needs of the children held insufficient excitement for Adelaide and she started having sex with the lodger. When pregnancy resulted, the product of this relationship was aborted by the agency of one Bertha Baudach. She was a 53-year-old German midwife who lived in Drummond Street, behind the Euston Road. She seems to have been a prolific abortionist, or perhaps just a very unlucky one – all we have to go on is the record of the courts where she made frequent appearances. In 1895 she was sentenced to five years' penal servitude for performing abortions, and had been acquitted of the same offence at the Old Bailey on 24 July 1903 after the death of a woman. Post-mortem examination found the marks of an instrument used to procure the abortion, but there was insufficient evidence to connect Baudach with the crime.[26]

The next time Baudach was mentioned in court was in connection with the inquest into Adelaide's death. It seems that late in 1903 Adelaide became pregnant again and sent Winifred Harris to Bertha Baudach's home over a barber's shop in Drummond Street on 23 November to tell the midwife Adelaide wanted to see her. In evidence Harris said Baudach told her she was a good woman and would 'do the same for her at any time'.[27] Baudach went with Adelaide into her bedroom and remained an hour and a half with her, then came again in the morning two days later.

Harris said Adelaide paid Baudach either £2 or £3 and said, 'It is all over.'[28] Adelaide's experience fitted in with a pattern of abortion from the early twentieth century: most women who had abortions were in their mid-twenties, many already had children. They turned to abortion not to postpone having children, but to limit their numbers as they could afford no more. The means used by Baudach (in as much as it can be gathered from the court report) was also the most common: a catheter or other instrument introduced into the cervix.[29] Court records accuse Baudach of inserting a syringe into Adelaide's vagina, 'abrading' the neck of the womb and syringing with hot water.[30]

After the operation Adelaide became ill with chills and a fever, and a Dr Groth was called. He visited twice on 30 November and suggested she might be suffering from septicaemia (blood poisoning). She showed some improvement, for on 5 December she wrote telling the doctor she was better and asking for the account. Joseph Kaiser was reported to have been in constant attendance on Adelaide, doing his writing in her bedroom, and giving her medicine. The reason given to the inquest for his presence was that Mrs Noelte was not to be left alone. She must have suffered a relapse for she died on 13 December 1903. She had been suffering from inflammation of the stomach and liver and had been vomiting blood. Kaiser told the inquest he was not present at the death, though the death certificate explicitly stated the information had been given to the registrar by 'Joe

Kaiser; present at the death.' He said he registered the death and attended to other matters as her husband was so upset.[31]

Dr Ludwig Freyberger, a pathologist, said death was due to blood poisoning from an abortion probably performed within a fortnight of her death. It was possible that the deceased had undergone a similar operation in August, for he found signs of an instrument having been used. The inquest report noted, 'the cause of the death was failure of the heart following severe anaemia while she was suffering from blood poisoning in consequence of the decomposition of a portion of the after birth in the womb, the result of an abortion.'[32]

The inquest jury brought in a verdict of manslaughter against Bertha Baudach, and a Detective Inspector Edward Drew, who had been sitting in court awaiting this decision, was given a warrant for her arrest by the coroner. She had been summoned to appear but had not done so. The jury also wished to charge Kaiser with manslaughter as an accessory both before and after the fact but the coroner, John Troutbeck, declined to accept this. The jury foreman said, 'We think it a case of very strong suspicion.' But the coroner said, 'We must have facts, not only suspicion.' The jury foreman also said Winifred Harris was deserving of censure, but no action was taken against her, either.[33]

At her subsequent trial it was explained how Baudach tried to evade arrest by hiding, then fighting so vehemently it took six or seven policemen to control her. The defence said she was in Germany at the time of Adelaide's death, though witnesses said otherwise, and that she did not know Adelaide and had never attended her. On 25 March 1904 she was found guilty of procuring an abortion on Mrs Noelte and was sentenced to seven years' penal servitude.[34] Thus Adelaide Foltinowicz – Ernest Dowson's 'Missie' – departs from the public record. It is as well he never lived to know of her fate.

There were no reports that ghosts walked, and the dock prospered under its competent new owner, who refitted it. An application before the Building Acts Committee of London County Council of 1904 shows the owner seeking planning permission to install two new dock doors. It also shows that the name had been changed; whereas it used to be named Bridge Dock, it had always been known by the name which it now bore officially: Dowson's Dock.[35]

CHAPTER 17

THE DOWSON LEGACY

ndrew Lang sneered 'What is a decadent in the literary sense of the word?' The journalist and poet was responding to Arthur Symons' obituary essay on Ernest Dowson. 'I am apt to believe that he is an unwholesome young person, who has read about "ages of decadence" in histories of literature, likes what he is told about them, and tries to die down to it, with more or less of success.'

Lang continued that the ideas of life on which Dowson ruined himself, 'have been the ideas of hundreds of boys, of whom the majority laugh at their past selves in a year or two. If this kind of existence, if these sorts of productions, be decadent, surely even boys must see that decadence is rather a mistake. With all its faults, there is more to be said for muscular Christianity.'[1]

Also in response to Symons' essay, this time when it was published as a preface to Dowson's collected poems in 1905, a reviewer summed up Dowson with the following: 'Born in 1867, he died in 1900, having thrown away his life in such reckless and foolish dissipation as comes to few – Dowson had the best of life before him, and he chose the worst.'[2]

Such unkind accounts are a failure of arithmetic as much as of compassion. If the amount of work is divided into the time available, the result is a prodigious demonstration of industry. Even if we are generous with the time scale, and take Dowson's working life as being the 15 years from the age of 17 to 32, he still achieved a remarkable amount. Despite being in increasingly serious states of consumption and depression from the mid-1890s, in his short life he produced two volumes of poetry, one verse play, a volume of short stories, three novels in collaboration and one alone, and nine translations, some very lengthy. Much of the time he was doing this work, he was also holding down a full-time job. In one so ill, and so injured as he, such industry is astonishing.

It was not, however, matched by a commensurate income. 'He affords altogether the most discouraging example of the inutility of conscientious-ness in modern English literature that one can find,' wrote Robert Sherard.[3]

Dowson wrote for love, not money, so his work should be judged on its own merits. At least few of his contemporaries doubted his immense talent. Ernest Rhys wrote in 1931: 'Probably if any surviving Rhymer were asked today which of all the poems evoked by the club had most affected him, he would say Dowson's "Cynara", with Lionel Johnson's noble lines on the statue of Kings Charles the First, or one of Yeats's poems in close se-quence.'[4] In a letter to his father, Yeats wrote about the Rhymers:

> The doctrine of the group, or rather of the majority of it, was that lyric poetry should be personal. That a man should express his life and do this without shame or fear. Ernest Dowson did this and became a most extraordinary poet, one feels the pressure of his life behind every line as if he were a character in a play of Shakespeare's.[5]

Dowson's life was also an inspiration for prose writers. Somerset Maugham may have partly based *Of Human Bondage* on the Dowson-Adelaide story. The story was much in currency in the circles in which he moved and, though Maugham is always thought of as a distinctively twentieth-century writer, he was born only seven years after Dowson. Whether or not he borrowed from Dowson's life (and he claimed to have based the work on his own) there is a rich field of material in the book describing scenes in bohemian London and Paris which were common to both Dowson and Maugham.

Some books which Dowson inspired directly have been mentioned earlier. Marion Plarr, the daughter of the man who knew Dowson and, incidentally, one of Dowson's adored little girls, wrote a book called *Cynara: The Story of Ernest and Adelaide*, published in 1933. Gertrude Atherton's *The Gorgeous Isle* of 1908 is based on Atherton's reading of Dowson's character. May Sinclair's best-selling *The Divine Fire* of 1902 is said to be based on real and imagined aspects of Dowson's life but if this is so, the novelist has digested them very well. *The Swan of Lee* by Laurence Dakin, published in 1972, is an unmemorable account of the poet's life.

Desmond Flower described his position in the group of artists of the 1890s as 'the purest and at the same time the most representative poetic genius that it possessed'. He makes no attempt to deny that Dowson 'had but few strings to his poetic bow' but asserts that 'from this limited instrument he wrung every note of which its small compass was capable'.[6] Ifor Evans said that Dowson, 'in his short lyrics seems to gather up the oldest symbols of which poetry has been made, and to use them afresh.'[7]

Yet Dowson does more than simply capture the spirit of the age (not that this is an insignificant achievement): he points forward to the future with a further layer of pessimism in addition to the lassitude and weariness which is obviously apparent. As Chris Snodgrass perceptively noted:

> Late-Victorian Aestheticism had always implicitly assumed that if the world of Art were ever proven to be primarily disguised egoism, a mere projection of desire, arbitrary fiction rather than distilled essence, then its efficacy as life's sanctifying Truth would be shattered. It was a very twentieth century reality that Dowson continually sought to deny, even as the integrity of his art continually confronted it. His work intensified the inherent contradictions in the fin de siècle, pushing traditional Romantic and Victorian solutions to their logical conclusions and thus acting as an ironic harbinger of ensuing Modernist alternatives.[8]

Certainly T.S. Eliot, high priest of the Modernists, respected Dowson as a poet whom he called 'the most gifted and technically perfect of his age' and recognized his own debt to Dowson, 'whose technical innovations have been underestimated.'[9] Eliot acknowledged that his line 'Falls the Shadow' from 'The Hollow Men' was derived from Dowson's 'falls thy shadow', which lines, he said, 'have always run in my head.'[10]

Ezra Pound too found Dowson, an influence, as is apparent from his first volume of verse, *A Lume Spento*, published in 1908.[11] Philip Hobsbaum remarked that it was the 'semi-dramatic projections of Ernest Dowson' in his verse which helped Pound to bridge the gap between himself and Browning to form a 'lyrical-descriptive form of monologue' which Hobsbaum applauds as a creative endeavour.[12] Kelsey Thornton also convincingly places Dowson in a creative and evolving tradition of verse, seeing him taking from Swinburne and giving to Eliot and Pound.[13]

Another of the next generation of poets to be inspired by Dowson was Rupert Brooke who tried to follow some of Dowson's experiments in metre and wrote of 'learning Ernest Dowson by heart'.[14] Brooke led debates on the merits of Dowson and Swinburne in the Eranos Society at Rugby.[15] D.H. Lawrence also admired Dowson's technical skill and said 'Cynara' inclined him to weep.[16]

It was the lyrical sadness which attracted Edward Thomas, too, to Dowson: 'to us, he seems to have rediscovered regret and all the emotions which the inaccessible and irrecoverable arouse, since he expressed them with a beauty and simplicity which no contemporary equalled.'[17]

Despite these critical plaudits, it is true that Dowson's gift was undoubtedly limited – he cannot stand next to the four greats of mid-to-late Victorian poetry: Tennyson, Browning, Arnold and Swinburne – but Dowson has a good case for a placing in the front rank of the second league. What he did, he did to perfection, and not only in his exceptional command of the language, but also in the depth of his feeling and the facility with which he expressed it. 'Always through the music and the singing runs a chill undertone,' said Rupert Brooke, 'the thought that the night awaits.'[18]

The enduring potency of Dowson's message is shown by the number of artists through the years who have borrowed his imagery. King Vidor's film *Cynara*, released in 1933, opened with the words that it was 'Inspired by Ernest Dowson's immortal lines, "I have been faithful to thee, Cynara, in my fashion".' It was based on a successful play also called *Cynara*, by H.M. Harwood and Robert Gore Brown. The subject matter – a barrister has an affair with a shop-girl and lives to regret it – is hardly Dowsonian, but the tribute to Dowson implicit in the title is impressive; likewise Margaret Mitchell's use of Dowson's line 'Gone With the Wind' for the title of her romantic novel, and of course the title of the subsequent film. *Days of Wine and Roses*, released in 1962, was another film which took its title from Dowson. The poet's name is also invoked as a symbol of kinship in Eugene O'Neill's *Long Day's Journey into Night*, first performed in 1956, where the poetry the brothers love shows their closeness and their distance from the values of their father. Michael Moorcock explicitly credits Dowson's influence in his *Dancers at the End of Time* trilogy and uses two titles from Dowson: *The Hollow Lands* published in 1974 and *The End of All Songs*, in 1976. They also explore Dowsonian themes of decadence and ennui.[19]

The extent to which Dowson's melancholy vision had permeated images of the turn of the nineteenth century is demonstrated in historian George Dangerfield's famous book *The Strange Death of Liberal England* where he remarks, 'When I first thought of writing this book I had in mind a mixture of Cynara and Sophocles – the madder music, the stronger wine, the approaching catastrophe of which the actors themselves were unaware.'[20]

Dowson was not unaware of the coming catastrophe. As Victor Plarr commented, 'The "tomorrow one dies" phrase recurred constantly in Dowson's talk. … The young men of the Decadence were for ever acting and speaking as though after their time all would be chaos, and yet that period is twenty years ago, and they are many of them dead, and everything goes on as usual.' Thus wrote Plarr early in 1914.[21]

At the distance of more than a hundred years, it is possible to view what stood for 'wholesomeness' at the turn of the nineteenth century with some scepticism. The Victorians and Edwardians have not enjoyed favour in the judgement of history: their glorious empire became the butt of jokes, their sexual morality regarded as at best hypocritical, and at worst disgusting.

Worst of all, and challenged by such poets of the period as Wilfred Owen and Siegfried Sassoon, was the obscene assumption that to cast their sons into the mud of the Western Front in some way gave them a noble death. Is a life dedicated to art, although riven with disease and drunkenness, truly 'wasted' in some way when compared to a life ended in disease

or shrapnel wounds in Flanders? Dowson and his friends of the 1890s
lived and died by their own creed and for their own beliefs; it is questionable whether the same could be said for the boy soldiers of the First World
War. As Rudyard Kipling (born only two years after Dowson) wrote as an
epitaph to the 'defrauded young':

> If any question why we died,
> Tell them, because our fathers lied.

The decadents chose their lives, came to an inevitable fate, and took the
consequences without remorse.

It is not merely the passage of time which makes it easier to regard
Dowson's life of pyrotechnic suffering with sympathy. The end of the
twentieth century finds, like the end of the nineteenth century, whole
generations in Europe who have not known war. The luxury and indulgence of late twentieth century life bears a closer parallel with the tenor of
the 1890s than any other time since. Brilliant stars who flared and died
became a commonplace; 'live fast, die young' a cultural motto.

With the advent of AIDS, love and death were locked in an embrace
which Dowson would have instantly recognized as his own territory, and
the artistic society of the late twentieth century was devastated as it had
been at no time since the 1890s.

Much could be said against Dowson: of his drunkenness, tendency to
get into brawls, his bizarre attachments to little girls, his consistent failure
to be decisive; but a man has a right to be considered at his best. It is as a
supporter of Oscar Wilde when almost all turned against him that Dowson
should be seen; as a brilliant craftsman of English verse; as a dedicated and
hard working writer, who worked even when racked with the disease which
was to kill him at such an early age.

Life presented him with suffering, and he returned it as beauty.

APPENDIX

DOWSON'S MAJOR WORKS

STORIES, POEMS AND PLAYS

1892 *The Book of the Rhymers' Club*
1893 *A Comedy of Masks* (with Arthur Moore)
1894 *The Second Book of the Rhymers' Club*
1895 *Dilemmas: Stories and Studies in Sentiment*
1896 *Verses*
1896 Work in every issue of *The Savoy*, published throughout 1896,
        except the last
1897 *The Pierrot of the Minute: A Dramatic Phantasy in One Act*
1899 *Adrian Rome* (with Arthur Moore)
1899 *Decorations in Verse and Prose*
1902 *The Poems of Ernest Dowson*, edited by T.B. Mosher
1905 *The Poems of Ernest Dowson*, with a memoir by Arthur Symons
1934 *The Poetical Works of Ernest Dowson*, edited by Desmond Flower
1947 *The Stories of Ernest Dowson*, edited by Mark Longaker

Two unpublished novels: *The Passion of Dr Ludovicus* (1889, with
Arthur Moore); *Madame de Viole* (1890)

TRANSLATIONS

1894 Emile Zola, *La Terre*
1894 Louis M.A. Couperus, *Majesty* (with Teixeira de Mattos)

1896   Richard Muther, *Geschichte der Malerei im neunzehnten Jahrhundert* (with G.A. Greene and A.C. Hillier)
1896   Honoré de Balzac, *La Fille aux Yeux d'Or*
1898   Choderlos de Laclos, *Les Liaisons Dangereuses*
1899   Voltaire, *La Pucelle d'Orléans*
1899   Paul LaCroix, *Memoirs of Cardinal Dubois*
1907   Edmond and Jules de Goncourt, *The Confidantes of a King: the Mistresses of Louis XV*

Unpublished: *The Memoirs of the Duc de Richelieu* (MS in Princetown Library)

LETTERS

1967   Desmond Flower and Henry Maas (eds), *The Letters of Ernest Dowson*
1984   Desmond Flower (ed), *New Letters of Ernest Dowson*

NOTES

INTRODUCTION

1. Arthur Symons, 'Ernest Dowson: A Memoir' in *The Poems of Ernest Dowson* (London, 1905), p vi.
2. Frank Harris, 'The Swan-Song of Youth: Ernest Dowson' in *Pearson's Magazine*, March 1917.
3. William Butler Yeats, *Memoirs* (London, 1972), p 92.

CHAPTER 1: THE PAGAN CHILD

1. Griffin W. Hall and H.C. Minchin, *The Life of Robert Browning* (London, 1910), pp 81–2. There are no further records to hand about Joseph Dowson so it may be that he too died of tuberculosis when young.
2. Victor Plarr, *Ernest Dowson 1888–1897: Reminiscences, Unpublished Letters and Marginalia* (London, 1914), p 40.
3. Desmond Flower and Henry Maas (eds), *The Letters of Ernest Dowson* (London, 1967), p 6. This invaluable work is not the only source of many of Dowson's letters, but because it is the most comprehensive and easily available collection, almost all references to his letters will be to this volume. In all cases of collected letters, the reference will be to the date of the letter rather than the page number.
4. Mark Longaker, *Ernest Dowson* (Philadelphia, 1967), p 4.
5. Private letter to Desmond Flower from Conal O'Riordan dated 14 January 1939 now in the possession of the author.
6. Ernest Dowson and Arthur Moore, *A Comedy of Masks* (London, 1893), p 2.
7. Bradford A. Booth and Ernest Mehew (eds), *The Letters of Robert Louis Stevenson, Vol 1, 1854–74* (New Haven, 1994), 22–29 November 1873.
8. *Ibid.*, 9 December 1973.
9. Dowson and Moore, *A Comedy of Masks*, pp 13–14.
10. Longaker, *Ernest Dowson*, p 164.
11. Dowson, *Letters*, p 7.
12. Plarr, *Dowson: Reminiscences*, p 21.
13. Edgar Allan Poe, 'The Philosophy of Composition' in *Essays and Reviews* (New York, 1984), p 19.
14. Plarr, *Dowson: Reminiscences*, p 21.
15. *Ibid.*

16. Letter from Lewis Swan to his daughter Madeleine, quoted in Longaker, *Ernest Dowson*, p 17.
17. Frederick Fitzroy Hamilton, *Bordighera and the Western Riviera*, translated by Alfred C. Dowson (London, 1883), p 7.
18. Dowson and Moore, *A Comedy of Masks*, p 116.
19. Dowson, *Letters*, to Arthur Moore, late November 1888.
20. 'It is Finished', published in Desmond Flower (ed), *The Poetical Works of Ernest Dowson* (London, 1934; republished 1967). All quotations from Dowson's verse will be taken from this, the definitive text, except where indicated. The analysis of the manuscript book also comes from Flower who once had it in his possession. It is now in the Pierpont Morgan Library in New York.

Chapter 2: The Pessimistic Student

1. W.R. Thomas, 'Ernest Dowson at Oxford', *The Nineteenth Century*, April 1928.
2. *Ibid.*
3. Longaker, *Ernest Dowson*, pp 25–6.
4. *Ibid.*, p 30.
5. Thomas, 'Ernest Dowson at Oxford'.
6. Desmond Flower (ed), *New Letters of Ernest Dowson* (Andoversford, Gloucestershire, 1984), to Charles Sayle, c. 1 October 1888.
7. Walter Pater, *Studies in Art and Poetry: The 1893 Text* (Berkeley, 1980), pp 188–90.
8. Dowson, *Letters*, to Arthur Moore, 28 March 1890.
9. Victor Plarr, 'An Informal Epitaph on Behalf of a Young Poet', *Poetry and Drama*, June 1913.
10. Thomas, 'Ernest Dowson at Oxford'.
11. Henri Murger, *Scènes de la Vie de Bohème*, translated by George B. Ives as *Bohemian Life* (London, 1926), pp xvii and xx.
12. Arthur Symons, 'A Literary Causerie', *The Savoy*, August 1896.
13. Edgar Jepson, *Memories of a Victorian* (London, 1933), p 219.
14. Ernest Dowson, 'The Cult of the Child', *The Critic*, 17 August 1889, quoted in Dowson, *Letters*, pp 433–5.
15. Plarr, *Dowson: Reminiscences*, p 79.
16. Dowson, *Letters*, to Victor Plarr, 6 September 1890.
17. Dowson, *New Letters*, to Charles Sayle, c. 1 October 1888.
18. Conal O'Riordan, 'Bloomsbury and Beyond', in *Essays by Divers Hands: Transactions of the RSL of the UK*, vol 24, London 1948. Lecture given 11 September 1946.
19. Thomas, 'Ernest Dowson at Oxford'.
20. Longaker, *Ernest Dowson*, pp 3–4.
21. Dowson, *New Letters*, to Charles Sayle, c. 1 October 1888.
22. Frank Harris makes such a remark, though he may be following Arthur Symons in his preface to Dowson's collected poems of 1905. Thomas, 'Ernest Dowson at Oxford', says the same.
23. Dowson, *New Letters*, to Charles Sayle, c. 1 October 1888.

Chapter 3: Dowson and Son

1. Dowson, *Letters*, to Arthur Moore, late November 1888.
2. Dowson, *New Letters*, to Charles Sayle, late April 1889.
3. Victor Plarr, *The Globe*, 21 May 1889.
4. Plarr, *Dowson: Reminiscences*, p 33.

5. Dowson and Moore, *A Comedy of Masks*, p 1.
6. *Ibid.*, pp 2–3.
7. Dowson, *Letters*, to Arthur Moore, 13 November 1888.
8. Plarr, *Dowson: Reminiscences*, pp 12–13.
9. *Ibid.*, p 46.
10. Dowson, *Letters*, to Victor Plarr, 26 October 1890.
11. Richard Le Gallienne, *The Romantic '90s* (London, 1993), pp 112–13.
12. Dowson, *Letters*, to Arthur Moore, c. 15 February 1889.
13. Plarr, *Dowson: Reminiscences*, p 17.
14. Dowson, *Letters*, to Arthur Moore, c. 11 January 1889.
15. Letter from Arthur Moore to Mark Longaker dated 10 October 1939, printed in preface to Mark Longaker (ed), *The Stories of Ernest Dowson* (London, 1949), p 5.
16. Dowson, *Letters*, to Arthur Moore, 3 February 1889.
17. Dowson, *New Letters*, to Charles Sayle, 8–14 June 1889.
18. Dowson, *Letters*, to Arthur Moore, 26 May 1889.
19. *Ibid.*
20. Dowson, *Letters*, to Arthur Moore, 11 February 1890.
21. Dowson, *Letters*, to Arthur Moore, 1 June 1890.
22. Dowson, *Letters*, to Arthur Moore, 7 July 1889.
23. Dowson, *Letters*, to Arthur Moore, 5 March 1889.
24. *Ibid.*
25. Dowson, *Letters*, to Arthur Moore, 10 March 1889.
26. Dowson, *Letters*, to Arthur Moore, 24 March 1889.
27. Dowson, *Letters*, to Arthur Moore, 29 June 1889.
28. Dowson, *Letters*, to Arthur Moore, 31 October 1889.
29. Dowson, *Letters*, to Arthur Moore, 13 November 1888.
30. Booth and Mehew (eds), *The Letters of Robert Louis Stevenson, Vol 1, 1854–74*, 7–13 December 1873. The passage continues: 'However, I forgave him, and read him that bit of Walt Whitman about the widowed bird, which I thank God affected him quite tolerably.' Reading the aria from *Out of the Cradle Endlessly Rocking* was Stevenson's test of a personality; if they were not emotionally affected by it he considered them beyond redemption. Alfred Dowson asked him to read it again a few nights later.
31. Dowson, *Letters*, to Arthur Moore, 28 March 1890.
32. Dowson, *Letters*, to Arthur Moore, probably 3 January 1889.
33. Dowson, *Letters*, to Arthur Moore, 11 November 1889.
34. Dowson, *Letters*, to Arthur Moore, 7 November 1889.
35. Dowson, *Letters*, to Arthur Moore, 24 December 1889.

CHAPTER 4: THE SERIOUS RHYMERS

1. Dowson, *Letters*, to Arthur Moore, 5 March 1889.
2. Dowson, *Letters*, to Arthur Moore, 27 January 1890.
3. Dowson, *Letters*, to Charles Sayle, c. 25 November 1890.
4. Dowson, *Letters*, to Arthur Moore, probably 4 December 1890.
5. Bruce Gardiner, *The Rhymers' Club; A Social and Intellectual History* (New York, 1988), p 9.
6. Dowson, *Letters*, to Arthur Moore, 2 February 1891.
7. Plarr, *Dowson: Reminiscences*, p 28.
8. Arthur Lynch, 'Le Gallienne' in *Our Poets* (London, 1894).
9. Arthur Symons, 'The Decadent Movement in Literature', *Harper's New Monthly Magazine*, November 1893.
10. *Ibid.*
11. Dowson, *Letters*, to Arthur Moore, 20 March 1891.

12. Gardiner, *The Rhymers' Club*. Some eight members of the Rhymers were involved in the London Irish Society inaugurated in May 1892 for the promotion of Irish literature. At least two early meetings of the Irish Literary Society were hosted by the Rhymers, at the home of one of them or at the Cheshire Cheese.
13. William Butler Yeats, *Autobiographies* (London, 1961), p 300.
14. Lynch, 'Le Gallienne', p 48.
15. Jepson, *Memories of a Victorian*, p 236.
16. Morley Roberts in *John O'London's Weekly*, 30 September 1933.
17. Ernest Rhys, 'Lines on Marlow', in *The First Book of the Rhymers' Club*.
18. Dowson, *Letters*, to Arthur Moore, 16 and 18 November 1889.
19. L. Birkett Marshall, 'A Note on Ernest Dowson', *The Review of English Studies*, April 1952, p 162–4.
20. Sam Smith, letter to Edgar Jepson, c. 1937, copied by John Gawsworth and now in the possession of the author. Smith was unsure whether the last name was Pater or (George) Moore. Given this choice, I am sure it would have been Pater.
21. Ernest Rhys, *Everyman Remembers* (London, 1931), p 106.
22. Le Gallienne, *The Romantic '90s*, p 110.
23. Yeats, *Autobiographies*, p 312.
24. Yeats, *Memoirs*, p 93.
25. Dowson, *Letters*, to Charles Sayle, 1 April 1889.
26. Yeats, *Autobiographies*, p 318.
27. *Ibid.*, p 304.
28. Rhys, *Everyman Remembers*, p 113.
29. Le Gallienne, *The Romantic '90s*, p 113.
30. Lionel Johnson, 'In Honorem Doriani Creatorisque Euis', translation in Ian Fletcher (ed), *Complete Poems* (Oxford, 1953).
31. Yeats, *Memoirs*, p 94.
32. Longaker, *Ernest Dowson*, p 108.
33. Arthur Symons, 'Ernest Dowson, A Memoir' in *The Poems of Ernest Dowson* (London, 1905), p xxv.
34. Dowson and Moore, *A Comedy of Masks*, pp 3 and 47.
35. *Ibid.*, p 296.
36. *Ibid.*, p 231.
37. *Ibid.*, p 234.

CHAPTER 5: DOWN AMONG THE DAUCADONGS

1. Jepson, *Memories of a Victorian*, p 219. This is actually a description from 1893, there being no earlier ones.
2. Dowson, *Letters*, to Arthur Moore, 16 February 1890.
3. Dowson, *Letters*, to Arthur Moore, 28 March 1890.
4. *Ibid.*
5. Dowson, *Letters*, to Arthur Moore, 8 April 1890.
6. C. Smart, *The Works of Horace Translated Literally into English* (London, 1885), p 94.
7. Flower (ed), *The Poetical Works of Ernest Dowson*, p 249.
8. Arthur Symons, *The Café Royal and Other Essays* (London, 1923), p 5.
9. Dowson, *Letters*, to Samuel Smith, March 1891.
10. Dowson, *Letters*, to Arthur Moore, 10 April 1891.
11. 'Testudo' i.e. Mostyn Piggott in *The World*, 8 May 1895.
12. Grant Richards, *Memoirs of a Misspent Youth* (London, 1932), p 339.
13. *Ibid.*, p 342.
14. Dowson, *Letters*, to Victor Plarr, c. 14 February 1892.

15. Plarr, *Dowson: Reminiscences*, p 22.
16. Ian Fletcher, 'Neo-Jacobitism in the 1890s' in *W.B. Yeats and his Contemporaries* (Brighton, 1987). Johnson, Crackanthorpe, Texeira de Mattos and Marmaduke Langdale (who was descended from a famous royalist family) were also Neo-Jacobites.
17. Yeats, *Autobiographies*, p 301.
18. 'Log-Roller', *The Star*, 11 February 1892.
19. Dowson, *Letters*, to Arthur Moore, 3 April 1891.
20. Yeats, *Autobiographies*, p 311.
21. Dowson, *New Letters*, to Charles Sayle, 10 March 1890.
22. Dowson, *Letters*, to Arthur Moore, 19 October 1890.
23. Dowson, *New Letters*, to Charles Sayle, 30 August–1 September 1890.
24. Harris, 'The Swan-Song of Youth'.
25. Dowson, *Letters*, to John Gray, February 1892.
26. *Pall Mall Gazette* review, 4 May 1893.
27. Longaker (ed), *The Stories of Ernest Dowson*, p 106.
28. Dowson and Moore, *A Comedy of Masks*, p 301.
29. Dowson, *Letters*, to Arthur Moore, 19 October 1890.

CHAPTER 6: MORAL TORTURE

1. Dowson, *Letters*, to Arthur Moore, 5 March 1889.
2. Dowson, *Letters*, to Arthur Moore, 26 November 1889.
3. 'Walter', *My Secret Life* (New York, 1988). For example, pp 544–5: 'most poor girls are fucked before they are sixteen. It is immaterial who does it but they will be fucked. She is quite as willing to have it done as he is to do it, and probably it is the female who incites the male (unwittingly perhaps) following simply the law of nature – quite as much as the male incites the female to pleasure. What rot then this talk about male seduction, when it is nature which seduces them both.' Like the rest of the memoir, this is filtered through Walter's single-minded view of the world, but there is no doubt that he had the experience to justify his statements.
4. It is to be found in Bruce Loughton, *Philip Wilson Steer 1860–1942* (Oxford, 1971), pp 113–21.
5. Fraser Harrison, *The Dark Angel: Aspects of Victorian Sexuality* (London, 1977), p 147.
6. *The Times*, 20 August, 27 August and 3 September 1891.
7. *The Times*, 19 September 1891.
8. Dowson, *Letters*, to Arthur Moore, 3 September 1891.
9. Dowson, *Letters*, to John Gray, 3 September 1891.
10. Dowson, *Letters*, to Arthur Moore, 22 September 1891.
11. Plarr, *Dowson: Reminiscences*, p 30.
12. Le Gallienne, *The Romantic '90s*, p 110.
13. Dowson, *Letters*, to Charles Sayle, July 1892.
14. Dowson, *Letters*, to Arthur Moore, c. January 1892.
15. O'Riordan, 'Bloomsbury and Beyond'.
16. Desmond Flower manuscript copy of interview with John Gray headed 'Extract from Diary April 19 Edinburgh'. Probably 1932. In author's possession. Hereafter: Gray interview.
17. Gray interview.
18. Harris, 'The Swan-Song of Youth'. A vindication of Harris's general accuracy is in Gray interview.
19. Dowson, *Letters*, to Victor Plarr, February 1892.
20. Dowson, *Letters*, to Victor Plarr, c. 13 February 1892.
21. Dowson, *Letters*, to Sam Smith, early May 1892.

22. Dowson, *Letters*, to Victor Plarr, c. 13 February 1892.
23. Dowson, *Letters*, to Sam Smith, early May 1892.
24. *Ibid.*
25. *Ibid.*
26. Dowson, *Letters*, to Sam Smith, April–May 1892.
27. Dowson, *Letters*, to Victor Plarr, c. February 1892.
28. *Ibid.*
29. Dowson, *Letters*, to Victor Plarr, 10 February 1893.
30. Dowson, *Letters*, to Victor Plarr, 17 February 1893.
31. Ernest Dowson and Arthur Moore, *Adrian Rome* (London, 1899), p 44.
32. *Ibid.*, p 5.
33. *Ibid.*, pp 49–51.
34. *Ibid.*, p 54.
35. *Ibid.*, p 132.

CHAPTER 7: THE ADVENTURE OF LITERATURE

1. Dowson, *Letters*, to Victor Plarr, c. 26 October 1892.
2. Dowson, *Letters*, to Arthur Moore, c. 10 November 1892.
3. Edgar Jepson, 'The Real Ernest Dowson', *The Academy*, 2 November 1907.
4. Jepson, *Memories of a Victorian*, p 248.
5. *Ibid.*, p 265.
6. *Ibid.*, p 247.
7. Jepson, 'The Real Ernest Dowson'.
8. Jepson, *Memories of a Victorian*, p 259.
9. Harris, 'The Swan-Song of Youth'. All events described by Harris must be regarded with suspicion but he certainly moved in the same circles and, it is reasonable to suppose, had observed Dowson closely enough to make these perceptive remarks with adequate authority.
10. Graham King, *Garden of Zola: Emile Zola and his Novels for English Readers* (London, 1978), p 241.
11. Dowson, *Letters*, c. 9 April 1894.
12. Plarr, *Dowson: Reminiscences*, p 96.
13. Robert Harborough Sherard, *The Real Oscar Wilde* (London, 1916), p 81.
14. Jepson, 'The Real Ernest Dowson'.
15. Harris, 'The Swan-Song of Youth'. It is worth remarking that Desmond Flower, a better linguist than I and therefore in a better position to judge, considered Dowson's translations of Verlaine to be very good.
16. Symons, 'The Decadent Movement in Literature'.
17. Arthur Symons, *The Memoirs of Arthur Symons: Life and Art in the 1890s*, edited by Karl Beckson (University Park, Pennsylvania, 1977), p 129.
18. Dowson, *Letters*, to Victor Plarr, c. 28 November 1893.
19. Dowson, *Letters*, to Victor Plarr, c. 20 September 1893.
20. *The Bookman*, November 1893.
21. Dowson, *Letters*, to Victor Plarr, late October 1893.
22. *The Athenaeum*, 23 December 1893.
23. *The Spectator*, 23 December 1893.
24. *The Critic*, 17 February 1894.
25. Plarr, *Dowson: Reminiscences*, p 72.
26. *Ibid.*, p 69.
27. Dowson, *Letters*, to Victor Plarr, 17 January 1893.
28. Dowson, *Letters*, to Victor Plarr, c. 23 February 1892.

29. *Ibid.*
30. Dowson, *Letters*, to Victor Plarr, April 1893.
31. Dowson, *Letters*, to Samuel Smith, late April 1893.
32. *Ibid.*
33. Dowson, *Letters*, to Victor Plarr, April 1893.
34. Dowson, *Letters*, to Samuel Smith, late April 1893.
35. *Ibid.*
36. Dowson, *Letters*, to Victor Plarr, April 1893.
37. Dowson, *Letters*, to Samuel Smith, late April 1893.
38. Dowson, *Letters*, to Victor Plarr, April 1893.
39. Dowson, *Letters*, to Victor Plarr, early April 1893. The poem 'A Dead Child' could only relate to the foreman's child if the date ascribed to this letter is wrong, as the poem was published in *Atalanta* in February 1893. An incorrect date on the letter is possible, as Dowson almost never dated his personal letters.
40. Plarr, *Dowson: Reminiscences*, p 101.
41. John Keats, 'Ode to a Nightingale' in *Keats' Poetical Works* (Oxford, 1970), p 207.

CHAPTER 8: BRIGHT LIGHTS

1. Dowson, *Letters*, to Arthur Moore, 27 August 1893.
2. Sherard, *The Real Oscar Wilde*, p 81.
3. Symons, *The Memoirs of Arthur Symons*, p 112.
4. *Ibid.*
5. Gray interview.
6. Symons, *The Memoirs of Arthur Symons*, p 117.
7. Karl Beckson, *Arthur Symons: A Life* (Oxford, 1987), p 93, quoting 'Pages from the Life of Muriel Broadbent', unpublished MS.
8. Symons, *The Memoirs of Arthur Symons*, p 127.
9. Jepson, *Memories of a Victorian*, p 283. Regrettably, Jepson is not to be trusted on names; he seems to have changed all the women's names in his memoir out of excessive fastidiousness, even though he was writing 40 years later. Longaker had at least one other, verbal source, however, who also called her Dulcie, perhaps after Jepson.
10. *Ibid.*, pp 283–4.
11. Dowson, *Letters*, to Edgar Jepson, 30 July 1894.
12. Jepson, *Memories of a Victorian*, p 266.
13. Dowson, *Letters*, to Edgar Jepson, 30 July 1894.
14. *Ibid.*
15. *Ibid.*
16. These were Yeats, O'Sullivan and Harris, in the works cited elsewhere here.
17. Thomas, 'Ernest Dowson at Oxford'.
18. Gray interview.
19. William Rothenstein, *Men and Memories, Vol 1, 1872–1900* (London, 1931), pp 237–8.
20. O'Riordan, 'Bloomsbury and Beyond'.
21. Symons, *The Memoirs of Arthur Symons*, p 157.
22. Symons, 'Ernest Dowson, A Memoir', p xiii.
23. Dowson, *Letters*, to Arthur Moore, 20 July 1891.
24. Symons, 'Ernest Dowson, A Memoir', p xiv.
25. *Ibid.*
26. Ruth Y. Jenkins, 'A Note on Conrad's Sources: Ernest Dowson's 'The Statute of Limitations' as source for *Heart of Darkness*', *English Language Notes*, March 1987.
27. Dowson, *Letters*, to Victor Plarr, c. 20 September 1893.
28. Arthur Waugh, *One Man's Road* (London, 1931), pp 254–5.

29. Max Beerbohm, *The Yellow Book* II, July 1894.
30. Dowson, *Letters*, pp 263–4.
31. Brocard Sewell, *In the Dorian Mode, A Life of John Gray* (Padstow, Cornwall, 1983), p 55. Gray was sending a copy of the book to Mrs (later Lady) Maclagan in February 1906.
32. Dowson, *Letters*, to Victor Plarr, late October 1893.
33. Dowson and Moore, *A Comedy of Masks*, p 45.
34. Longaker, *Ernest Dowson*, p 63.
35. *Ibid.*, p 164.
36. *ABPI Data Sheet Compendium 1985–6* (London, 1986); *British National Formulary* (London, 1984).
37. Plarr, *Dowson: Reminiscences*, p 102. Plarr had written to Dowson's surviving relatives about his intention to publish his reminiscences and it is doubtless they who forbade him to write of Alfred's death, and of Annie's. See also O'Riordan, 'Bloomsbury and Beyond'.

CHAPTER 9: DECADENT DISINTEGRATION

1. Longaker, *Ernest Dowson*, p 164.
2. Plarr, *Dowson: Reminiscences*, p 102.
3. Longaker, *Ernest Dowson*, p 164.
4. *Ibid.*, p 163.
5. Marion Plarr, *Cynara: The Story of Ernest and Adelaide* (London, 1933), p 163.
6. *Kentish Mercury*, 8 February 1895.
7. *Ibid.* The newspaper report says that Rowland found Annie Dowson. However, the relatives said Ernest did so, and they are far less likely to get a fact like this wrong than a harassed court reporter is to transpose the first names of two brothers giving evidence in the same case.
8. Marion Plarr, *Cynara*, p 165.
9. MS letter from O'Riordan to Desmond Flower, 14 January 1939. In author's possession.
10. Dowson and Moore, *A Comedy of Masks*, p 233.
11. Dowson, *Letters*, to an unnamed correspondent, draft letter 1895.
12. *Realm*, 21 June 1895; *Athenaeum*, 3 August 1895.
13. Rhys, *Everyman Remembers*, p 106. Rhys 'dates' this event as 'towards the end of the club's second winter' which would put it in the first months of 1893, if we consider the club proper started in 1891. But Dowson's health was not apparently troubling him until mid to late 1893. The end of winter 1893–4 is a more likely time, though the pitiful appearance Dowson presented belongs to a later period – after the death of both his parents, at the end of winter 1894–5.
14. Vincent O'Sullivan, *Aspects of Wilde* (London, 1936), p 74.
15. Sherard, *The Real Oscar Wilde*, pp 77–8.
16. It was alleged in 1890 that the scandal of Lord Somerset and his telegraph messenger boys was hushed up at the instigation of the Prime Minister, Lord Salisbury. Richard Davenport-Hines, *Sex, Death and Punishment* (London, 1990), p 134.
17. *Ibid.*, p 137.
18. Sherard, *The Real Oscar Wilde*, p 78.
19. Robert Harborough Sherard, *The Life of Oscar Wilde* (London, 1906), p 368. The objection to the trial is not only that the law was unjust and should never have been enacted but that even under that law it was not a fair trial. It was utterly prejudiced against the defendant by noxious publicity and the use of tainted witnesses.
20. *Ibid.*, p 369. In fact Wilde's friend, Robbie Ross, was also there, perhaps not in the court room.

21. Robert Harborough Sherard, *Oscar Wilde, The Story of an Unhappy Friendship* (London, 1905), p 192.
22. *National Observer*, 6 April 1895.
23. Harry Quilter, 'The Gospel of Intensity', *Contemporary Review*, 67, June 1895, which incidentally picks out John Davidson for particular criticism.
24. Harris, 'The Swan-Song of Youth'.
25. Sherard, *The Real Oscar Wilde*, p 82.
26. George C. Williamson, 'Ernest Christopher Dowson', *Carmina*, no.11, 1932.
27. Harris, 'The Swan-Song of Youth'.
28. Gray interview.
29. Symons, 'Ernest Dowson, A Memoir', p xv.
30. Robert Harborough Sherard, *Twenty Years in Paris* (London, 1905), p 401.
31. *Ibid.*
32. Plarr, *Dowson: Reminiscences*, p 121. Plarr is vague on the date of this event which I would place between February and September 1895 or shortly after this time, because of the head wound which Sherard's testimony dates to this period, and the location – near Smithers' office. Dowson left the country in October 1895 and Smithers moved his office from Arundel Street in August 1896, before Dowson had returned to London. Plarr next saw him in September 1897 and there was 'no trace' of the wound.
33. Symons, 'Ernest Dowson, A Memoir', p xv.
34. Sherard, *The Real Oscar Wilde*, p 82.
35. William Butler Yeats, 'Modern Poetry: A Broadcast', in *Essays and Introductions* (New York, 1961).
36. Rothenstein, *Men and Memories*, vol 1, p 238.

CHAPTER 10: SAVOY DAYS

1. Dowson, *Letters*, to Samuel Smith, c. 24 March 1896.
2. O'Sullivan, *Aspects of Wilde*, p 110.
3. Oscar Wilde, *Letters* edited by Rupert Hart-Davis (London, 1962), to Reggie Turner, 10 August 1897.
4. Jack Smithers, *The Early Life and Vicissitudes of Jack Smithers* (London, 1939), p 14.
5. Aubrey Beardsley, *Letters* edited by Henry Maas, J.L. Duncan and W.G. Good (London, 1970), to Leonard Smithers, 30 July 1896.
6. O'Sullivan, *Aspects of Wilde*, p 122 and 124.
7. Jepson, *Memories of a Victorian*, p 285.
8. Rothenstein, *Men and Memories*, vol 1, p 245.
9. Malcolm Easton, *Aubrey and the Dying Lady* (London, 1972), p 251.
10. Symons, *The Memoirs of Arthur Symons*, p 170.
11. *Ibid.*, p 183.
12. John Rothenstein, *The Life and Death of Conder* (London, 1938), p 120; and O'Sullivan, *Aspects of Wilde*, p 125.
13. Symons, 'Ernest Dowson, A Memoir', p xvi.
14. Symons, *The Memoirs of Arthur Symons*, p 112–13.
15. O'Riordan, 'Bloomsbury and Beyond'.
16. Longaker, *Ernest Dowson*, p 175.
17. Jepson, 'The Real Ernest Dowson'.
18. Yeats, *Memoirs*, p 94.
19. *Ibid.*, p 93.
20. Symons, 'Ernest Dowson, A Memoir', p xv.
21. Jepson, *Memories of a Victorian*, p 258.
22. Dowson, *Letters*, to Victor Plarr, c. September 1895.

23. Owen Seaman, *The Battle of the Bays* (London, 1896). This was a reprint of verses previously published in the *World*, the *National Observer* and *Punch*. Symons' *London Nights* is probably the specific target of the skit quoted.
24. *Ibid.* No date supplied for quotation from *The Globe*.
25. Yeats, *Memoirs*, p 91.
26. Jepson, *Memories of a Victorian*, p 286.
27. Dowson, *Letters*, to Conal O'Riordan, c. 16 December 1895.
28. O'Sullivan, *Aspects of Wilde*, p 118.
29. Yeats, *Autobiographies*, p 324.
30. Press notices quoted in *The Savoy*, No. 2, April 1896.
31. *Punch*, 1 February 1896.
32. O'Riordan, 'Bloomsbury and Beyond'.
33. *Ibid.*
34. Dowson, *Letters*, to Samuel Smith, c. 4 June 1896.
35. Letter from O'Riordan to Longaker quoted in Longaker, *Ernest Dowson*, p 189.
36. Yeats, *Autobiographies*, p 312.

CHAPTER 11: PARIS NIGHTS

1. Dowson, *Letters*, to Arthur Moore, c. 15 October 1895.
2. Joanna Richardson, *Verlaine* (London, 1971), p 344.
3. *Ibid.*, p 242.
4. Gabriel de Lautrec, *Souvenirs des Jours Sans Souci* (Paris, 1937). Quoted in Dowson, *Letters*, p 312.
5. V.P. Underwood, *Verlaine et L'Angleterre* (Paris, 1936), p 475.
6. Dowson, *Letters*, p 313.
7. Dowson, *Letters*, to Conal O'Riordan, 9 December 1895.
8. *Ibid.*
9. Voltaire, *La Pucelle d'Orléans*, from Canto XXI, translated by Ernest Dowson (London, 1899).
10. 'The Decadent Lover of Fiction', *Punch*, 9 February 1895.
11. 'Dum nos fata sinunt, oculos satiemus Amore' [While the fates allow, let's fill our eyes with love] taken from Propertius, Book II, xv, 23.
12. Dowson, *Letters*, to Arthur Moore, c. 13 December 1895.
13. Dowson, *Letters*, to Conal O'Riordan, early December 1895. It is actually dated 'Heure d'apéritif'.
14. Dowson, *Letters*, to Conal O'Riordan, 22 December 1895.
15. Dowson, *Letters*, to John Gray, c. 27 December 1895.
16. Dowson, *Letters*, to Arthur Moore, c. 20 February 1895.
17. Dowson, *Letters*, to Conal O'Riordan, mid-January 1896.
18. Sherard, *Twenty Years in Paris*, p 409.
19. Dowson, *Letters*, to Conal O'Riordan, 9 December 1895.
20. Dowson, *Letters*, to Conal O'Riordan, mid-January 1896.
21. *Ibid.*
22. Desmond Flower gave me information which led me to this conclusion: he had met a descendant of the Dowson family who also suffered from blackened teeth. Medical reference: *Dorland's Illustrated Medical Dictionary* (Philadelphia, 1988).
23. Dowson, *Letters*, to Leonard Smithers, 30 May 1896.
24. Dowson, *Letters*, to Samuel Smith, c. 20 November 1895. The word rendered here as 'love' in Langdale's letter is 'live' in some printed versions but surely this is an error presumably generated during its transcriptions in the cursive: Langdale to Dowson to Gawsworth, from Smith's copy.

25. Rothenstein, *The Life and Death of Conder*, p 128.
26. Easton, *Aubrey and the Dying Lady*, p 256. John Lewis May, *John Lane and the Nineties* (London, 1936), pp 80–1.
27. Maas, Duncan and Good (eds), *The Letters of Aubrey Beardsley*, to André Raffalovich, 17 November 1896.
28. Beardsley, *Letters*, to Leonard Smithers, c. 22 November 1896.
29. Beardsley, *Letters*, to Leonard Smithers, 23 November 1896.
30. Beardsley, *Letters*, to Leonard Smithers, c. 22 December 1896.
31. Beardsley, *Letters*, to Leonard Smithers, 13 January 1897.
32. O'Sullivan, *Aspects of Wilde*, pp 127–8.
33. *Ibid.*
34. O'Riordan, 'Bloomsbury and Beyond'. He continues that 'under the growing influence of Smithers he was reluctant to leave the house at all unless to go and drink' but this is a false memory: Smithers was never based in Paris, though he would visit for a few days at a time.
35. O'Sullivan, *Aspects of Wilde*, p 130.
36. Dowson, *Letters*, to Henry Davray, c. 15 March 1896.
37. Dowson, *Letters*, to Samuel Smith, c. 24 March 1896.
38. Dowson, *Letters*, to Arthur Moore, June 1896.
39. Dowson, *Letters*, to Leonard Smithers, c. 25 April 1896.
40. Dowson, *Letters*, to Arthur Moore, c. 15 October 1895.

CHAPTER 12: SAVAGE BEAUTY

1. Dowson, *Letters*, to Victor Plarr, 20 February 1868.
2. Dowson, *Letters*, to Arthur Moore, c. 20 February 1896.
3. Dowson, *Letters*, to Victor Plarr, May 1896.
4. Dowson, *Letters*, to Arthur Moore, 22 and 27 December 1895, 22 March and June 1896.
5. Dowson, *Letters*, to Victor Plarr, May 1896.
6. Symons, 'Ernest Dowson, A Memoir', p xxix.
7. The *Times* review quoted in Desmond Flower's notes in *The Poetical Works of Ernest Dowson*, p 235. Other dedications (to persons not known to me and therefore not mentioned in this biography) were to the Countess Sobrieska Von Platt, Leopold Nelkin who was a Pole studying in Paris whom Dowson met between 1895 and 1896, Miss Eugenie Magnus and André Lebey.
8. Marion Plarr, *Cynara: The Story of Ernest and Adelaide*, p 202.
9. *The Bookman*, July 1896.
10. *The Athenaeum*, 13 February 1896.
11. *Daily Courier*, 26 June 1896.
12. Dowson, *Letters*, to Samuel Smith, 25 April 1896 and to John Gray, c. 25 April 1896.
13. Dowson, *Letters*, to Samuel Smith, c. 4 June 1896.
14. Dowson, *Letters*, to Arthur Moore, June 1896.
15. Dowson, *Letters*, to Samuel Smith, c. 4 June 1896.
16. *The Savoy*, August 1896.
17. Jepson, 'The Real Ernest Dowson'.
18. Dowson, *Letters*, to Arthur Symons, 5 July 1896.
19. Jepson, 'The Real Ernest Dowson'.
20. Jepson, *Memories of a Victorian*, p 250.
21. Yeats, *Memoirs*, p 93.
22. Extract from Procès Verbal quoted in Dowson, *Letters*, p 438.
23. Yeats, *Autobiographies*, p 327.
24. Gertrude Atherton, *Adventures of a Novelist* (London, 1932), pp 250–8 and passim.

25. Gertrude Atherton, *The Gorgeous Isle* (London, 1908), p 139.
26. Longaker, *Ernest Dowson*, p 211.
27. Jepson, *Memories of a Victorian*, p 156.
28. Dowson, *Letters*, to Conal O'Riordan, late November 1896.
29. Arthur Symons, *The Savoy*, December 1896. The first two editions cost half a crown (12½p) and the last five two shillings (10p).
30. D. Crackanthorpe, *Hubert Crackanthorpe and English Realism in the 1890s* (Colombia, Missouri, 1977), p 134 and passim.

Chapter 13: The Devil's Dance

1. Jepson, *Memories of a Victorian*, p 220.
2. Marion Plarr, *Cynara: The Story of Ernest and Adelaide*, p 192.
3. Dowson, *Letters*, to Samuel Smith, April 1897. The Latin is from Cicero's oration against Catiline, here just used as a cry of despair.
4. Birkett Marshall, 'A Note on Ernest Dowson'.
5. Sherard, *Twenty Years in Paris*, p 398.
6. Dowson, *Letters*, to Conal O'Riordan, received 21 April 1897.
7. Richard Ellman, *Oscar Wilde* (London, 1988), pp 503–4.
8. Wilde, *Letters*, 3 June 1897.
9. Wilde, *Letters*, to Ernest Dowson, c. 5 June 1897.
10. Dowson, *Letters*, to Conal O'Riordan, c. 10 June 1897.
11. Wilde, *Letters*, to Reginald Turner, 16 July 1897.
12. Dowson, *Letters*, to Conal O'Riordan, postmarked 16 June 1897.
13. Wilde, *Letters*, to Ernest Dowson, 16 June 1897.
14. Christian Krogh, 'Fritz Thaulow and Oscar Wilde at Dieppe', *The New Age*, 10 December 1908.
15. Wilde, *Letters*, to Ernest Dowson, 24 June 1897.
16. Wilde, *Letters*, to Ernest Dowson, postmarked 28 June 1897.
17. Wilde, *Letters*, to Ernest Dowson, c. 30 June 1897.
18. Yeats, *Memoirs*, p 99.
19. Sherard, *Twenty Years in Paris*, p 412.
20. Butler's *Lives of the Saints*, vol iii (London, 1956), p 151. She was also known as Uncumber, Liberata, Regenfledis, Ontkommer and by other names.
21. Yeats, *Autobiographies*, p 311.
22. Wilde, *Letters*, to Ernest Dowson, 9 August 1897.
23. Wilde, *Letters*, to Ernest Dowson, 18 August 1897.
24. Harris, 'The Swan-Song of Youth'.
25. *Ibid.*
26. Plarr, *Dowson: Reminiscences*, p 122.
27. Marion Plarr, *Cynara: The Story of Ernest and Adelaide*, p 219.
28. Plarr, *Dowson: Reminiscences*, p 122.
29. Rosamund Longbridge, 'Ernest Dowson in Ireland', *TP's Weekly*, 30 January 1915. Longbridge does not mention the name of Dowson's friend, MacConnell, presumably out of concern for the sensibilities of his relatives, as he had recently died in the First World War.
30. Dowson, *Letters*, to Leonard Smithers, 14 October 1897.
31. Wilde, *Letters*, to Ernest Dowson, c. 26 October 1897.
32. Dowson, *Letters*, to Leonard Smithers, c. 18 October 1897.
33. Dowson, *Letters*, 7 November 1897 (date uncertain).
34. *The Athenaeum*, 8 May 1897.
35. Notes by Desmond Flower in *The Poetical Works of Ernest Dowson*, p 265.

36. Longaker, notes to *The Stories of Ernest Dowson* (New York 1947), p 160.

CHAPTER 14: THE VALLEY OF HUMILIATION

1. M.P. Shiel, *The Weird O'It* (London, 1902), pp 186–8. This is a curious and uneven book which seems to be moving towards a conventional happy ending but in fact ends with the death of the hero, who has been falsely accused of the murder of his fiancé's father. She has sex with a policeman guarding the mortuary to bribe him into allowing her to be alone with the body, and when she is, she commits suicide by cutting her throat.
2. Guy Thorne (Ranger Gull), 'The Strand Twenty Years Ago', *TP's Weekly*, 11 July 1913. The name and location of this public house are attested by Gull and Thurston Hopkins but I can find no reference to it in the London street directories of the period.
3. Newman Flower, 'Two Interesting Sinners', *The Bookman*, September 1926.
4. Wilde, *Letters*, to Leonard Smithers, 18 February 1898.
5. Rhys, *Everyman Remembers*, p 106.
6. Dowson, *Letters*, to Conal O'Riordan, c. 10 June 1897.
7. Atherton, *Adventures of a Novelist*, p 258.
8. Harris, 'The Swan-Song of Youth'.
9. Longaker, *Ernest Dowson*, p 269.
10. Yeats, *Autobiographies*, p 237.
11. O'Sullivan, *Aspects of Wilde*, p 126.
12. Rothenstein, *The Life and Death of Conder*, p 64–5.
13. Wilfred Niels Arnold, 'Absinthe', *Scientific American*, June 1989.
14. R. Thurston Hopkins, 'A London Phantom', published in Dowson, *Letters*, p 440–3 but undated. Certainly after 1933 as it mentions Robert Colman's film *Cynara* which was made then.
15. Dowson, *Letters*, to Leonard Smithers, June–July 1899.
16. Plarr, *Dowson: Reminiscences*, p 124.
17. Dowson, *Letters*, to Victor Plarr, c. 15 October 1895.
18. Sherard, *The Real Oscar Wilde*, p 82.
19. Sherard, *Twenty Years in Paris*, p 400.
20. Sherard, *The Real Oscar Wilde*, p 83.
21. Sherard, *Twenty Years in Paris*, p 403.
22. Dowson, *Letters*, to Leonard Smithers, c. July 1899.
23. Wilde, *Letters*, to Leonard Smithers, 6 June 1899.
24. G.A. Cevasco, *Three Decadent Poets* (New York, 1990), pp 50–1.
25. *Daily Telegraph*, 17 May 1899.
26. *The Athenaeum*, 21 April 1900.
27. *The Academy*, 21 April 1900.
28. Longaker, *Ernest Dowson*, p 266.
29. Plarr, *Dowson: Reminiscences*, p 22.
30. O'Sullivan, *Aspects of Wilde*, p 134.
31. Harris, 'The Swan-Song of Youth'.
32. Plarr, *Dowson: Reminiscences*, p 126.
33. Thurston Hopkins, 'A London Phantom', p 440.
34. *Ibid.*, p 443. It should be noted, however, that Hopkins became a noted writer of short stories of a similar fanciful type, and that in his book *London Pilgrimages* of 1928 he writes of 'Ernest Dowson's East End' but does not say he knew the poet, rather referring to others who did have direct knowledge of Dowson.
35. Flower, 'Two Interesting Sinners'.

CHAPTER 15: THE DYING OF ERNEST DOWSON

1. Sherard, *Twenty Years in Paris*, p 406 and Robert Harborough Sherard, 'Ernest Dowson', *The Author*, May 1900. The lodging house was soon pulled down to make way for a fire station, opened in 1902, which still stands there.
2. Sherard, *Twenty Years in Paris*, p 405.
3. Dowson, *Letters*, Robert Harborough Sherard to Conal O'Riordan, January 1900.
4. Longaker, *Ernest Dowson*, p 265.
5. Sherard, *The Real Oscar Wilde*, p 83.
6. Longaker, *Ernest Dowson*, p 267.
7. Sherard, 'Ernest Dowson'.
8. Sherard, *Twenty Years in Paris*, p 408.
9. *Ibid.*
10. O'Riordan, 'Bloomsbury and Beyond'.
11. *Ibid.*
12. Longaker, *Ernest Dowson*, p 267.
13. *Ibid.*, p 267.
14. Sherard, 'Ernest Dowson'.
15. *Ibid.*
16. Sherard, *Twenty Years in Paris*, p 410.
17. *Daily Graphic* account quoted in the *Kentish Mercury*, 2 March 1900.
18. Plarr, *Dowson: Reminiscences*, p 128.
19. Longaker, *Ernest Dowson*, p 269.
20. *Daily Telegraph*, 28 February 1900.
21. *Kentish Mercury*, 3 March 1900.
22. *The Athenaeum*, 3 March 1900.
23. Beckson, *Arthur Symons: A Life*, p 201, quoting a letter to Rhoda of 5 March 1900. Sherard does seem to have been a particularly maudlin character, given to what Dowson called 'spleenful outbursts'. After having broken up with his wife, he then omitted her from his published accounts of Dowson's death, referring to her when it was essential to do so as 'a woman who was in attendance'.
24. *Ibid.*, p 191.
25. MS letter in British Library as 674 Symons to Gosse.
26. Beckson, *Arthur Symons: A Life*, p 209.
27. William Butler Yeats, *Letters*, edited by Allan Wade (London, 1954), to Lady Gregory, postmarked 1 March 1900.
28. Sherard, 'Ernest Dowson'.
29. Sherard, *The Real Oscar Wilde*, p 79–80.
30. Wilde, *Letters*, to Leonard Smithers, c. 24 February 1900.

CHAPTER 16: FRIENDS OF ERNEST DOWSON

Some of the ages of death in this chapter may be incorrect by one year: in some cases I had only the basic years from which to calculate, and the individual may have died before the anniversary of their birth.

1. Ellman, *Oscar Wilde*.
2. Lord Alfred Douglas, *The Autobiography of Lord Alfred Douglas* (London, 1931), p 74.
3. Ian Fletcher, introduction to *The Complete Poems of Lionel Johnson* (New York, 1982), p lviii.
4. Rothenstein, *The Life and Death of Conder*, and *Dictionary of National Biography*.
5. Thorne, 'The Strand Twenty Years Ago'.
6. Smithers, *The Early Life and Vicissitudes of Jack Smithers*, p 44.

7. Jepson, *Memories of a Victorian*, p 249. Jepson says it was probably a Jewish shop, to be open on Christmas morning.
8. Sherard, *The Real Oscar Wilde*, p 113.
9. J. Benjamin Townsend, *John Davidson: Poet of Armageddon* (New Haven, Connecticut, 1961), p 190.
10. Symons, The *Memoirs of Arthur Symons*, p 2.
11. Beckson, *Arthur Symons: A Life*, p 320.
12. Private information from Michael Holland's son, David Holland, interviewed on 2 April 1995.
13. Yeats, *Memoirs*, p 134.
14. William Butler Yeats, 'Easter 1916' from 'Michael Robartes and the Dancer', 1921 in *Yeats's Poems* (London, 1989), p 287.
15. Yeats, *Autobiographies*, p 300.
16. Letter, c. 1937 from Sam Smith to Edgar Jepson, from 'John Gawsworth's Dowson file' now in the possession of the author.
17. Jepson, *Memories of a Victorian*, p 267.
18. O'Riordan, 'Bloomsbury and Beyond'.
19. Plarr, *Dowson: Reminiscences*, p 9.
20. K.H.F. O'Brien, in G.A. Cevasco (ed), *The 1890s: An Encyclopaedia of British Literature, Art and Culture* (New York, 1993), p 549.
21. Longaker, *Ernest Dowson*, p 265.
22. Ian Fletcher, 'Poet and Designer: W.B. Yeats and Althea Gyles', in *W.B. Yeats and His Circle* (Brighton, 1987).
23. *News of the World*, 10 January 1904.
24. *Westminster Observer*, 2 January 1904.
25. Longaker, *Ernest Dowson*, p 247.
26. *The Times*, 25 July 1903.
27. *Westminster Mail*, 9 January 1904.
28. *Westminster Observer*, 2 January 1904 and *Westminster Mail*, 9 January 1904.
29. Angus McLaren, 'Illegal Operations: Women, Doctors and Abortion 1886–1939', *Journal of Social History*, vol 26, no 4, 1993. This is a survey from British Columbia, Canada, but there are no obvious differences between the facts reported here and those known from London, and the people involved would largely have been recent immigrants from Britain who took their homespun medical techniques with them.
30. PRO 1226 Crim 4, 21 March 1904.
31. *Westminster Observer*, 2 January 1904.
32. PRO 1226 Crim 4, 6 January 1904.
33. *News of the World*, 10 January 1904; *Westminster Observer*, 2 January 1904.
34. *The Times*, 25 and 26 March 1904.
35. LCC/MIN/1336, 20 June 1904.

CHAPTER 17: THE DOWSON LEGACY

1. Andrew Lang, 'Decadence', *The Critic*, 27 August 1900.
2. Talcott Williams, 'Ernest Dowson', *Book News Monthly* (US), April 1907.
3. Sherard, 'Ernest Dowson'.
4. Rhys, *Everyman Remembers*, p 109.
5. Yeats, *Letters*, to J.B. Yeats, 16 February 1910.
6. Flower, in the introduction to *Poetical Works*, p 15, 20 and 21.
7. B. Ifor Evans, *A Short History of English Literature* (London, 1964), p 64.
8. Chris Snodgrass, 'Ernest Dowson' in G.A. Cevasco (ed), *The 1890s: An Encyclopaedia of British Literature, Art, and Culture*, p 193.

9. T.S. Eliot, quoted in 'Ernest Dowson' in *Missing Persons* (Dictionary of National Biography Supplement) Oxford 1993.

10. T.S. Eliot, Letters, *Times Literary Supplement*, 10 January 1935.

11. David Perkins, *A History of Modern Poetry: From the 1890s to the High Modernist Mode* (Cambridge, Mass.,1976), p 454.

12. Philip Hobsbaum, *Tradition and Experiment in English Poetry* (London, 1979), p 249.

13. R.K.R. Thornton, *The Decadent Dilemma* (London, 1983), pp 71-107.

14. Rupert Brooke, *The Letters of Rupert Brooke* (London, 1969). To Jacques Raverat, April 1909.

15. A. Stringer, *Red Wine of Youth: A Life of Rupert Brooke* (Indianapolis, 1948), pp 38–9.

16. Harry T. Moore (ed), *Collected Letters of D.H. Lawrence, Vol 1* (London, 1936), p 245.

17. Edward Thomas, review of *The Poems of Ernest Dowson*, reprinted in *A Language Not to be Betrayed: Selected Prose of Edward Thomas* (Manchester, 1981), p 61.

18. Christopher Hassall, Preface to *The Prose of Rupert Brooke* (London, 1955), pp xii.

19. I am indebted to Caroline Dowson for this information. Her PhD thesis *Ernest Dowson: The Language of Poetry at the Victorian Fin de Siècle* was completed at Bristol University in 1998.

20. George Dangerfield, *The Strange Death of Liberal England* (London, 1936), p vii.

21. Plarr, *Dowson: Reminiscences*, p 59.

INDEX

Occasional literary references are omitted from this index unless the works or authors had a particular influence on Dowson.